Flex 3 with Java

Develop Rich Internet applications using Adobe Flex 3 and ActionScript 3.0, and integrate them with a Java backend using BlazeDS 3.2

Satish Kore

BIRMINGHAM - MUMBAI

Flex 3 with Java

First published: June 2009

Production Reference: 1220609

Published by Packt Publishing Ltd.
32 Lincoln Road
Olton
Birmingham, B27 6PA, UK.

ISBN 978-1-847195-34-0

www.packtpub.com

Cover Image by Vinayak Chittar (vinayak.chittar@gmail.com)

Credits

Author
Satish Kore

Reviewers
Wim Bervoets
Trevor Burton

Acquisition Editor
James Lumsden

Development Editor
Swapna Verlekar

Technical Editor
Dhiraj Bellani

Copy Editor
Sneha Kulkarni

Indexer
Hemangini Bari

Editorial Team Leader
Abhijeet Deobhakta

Project Team Leader
Lata Basantani

Project Coordinator
Neelkanth Mehta

Proofreaders
Laura Booth
Lynda Sliwoski

Production Coordinator
Aparna Bhagat

Cover Work
Aparna Bhagat

About the Author

Satish Kore is a software engineer, an amateur blogger, and a dreamer based in a beautiful city Bangalore in India. He has worked on a variety of technologies including Adobe Flex, Java, and J2ME over the past eight years. He has always been passionate about Rich Internet application (RIA) technologies and loves working on Adobe Flex. He always enjoyed writing software applications and solving common problems using technology. You can keep up with his work by visiting his blog at `http://blog.satishkore.com`, or by following him on Twitter `http://twitter.com/satishkore`.

I thank my family for being encouraging and supportive and special thanks to my friends for always inviting me on parties even though I constantly refused to join them by giving them the same boring reason that I am busy with writing.

This book means a lot to me since I have spent all my weekends and free time writing this book for the past 6-7 months. However, this book would not have been possible without some individuals who have worked alongside me during the writing, reviewing, and publishing phases.

I would thank James Lumsden for giving me the opportunity to write this book. I would also like to thank Neelkanth Mehta, Swapna Verlekar, Dhiraj Bellani, and all my technical reviewers for proofreading, reviewing, and refining the content of this book; without their efforts, this book wouldn't have been completed.

About the Reviewers

Wim Bervoets is a Senior J2EE/Java software engineer and architect from Belgium, Europe, who helps organizations to implement complex web-based business applications.

Since 2000, Wim Bervoets has specialized in developing and architecting web-based solutions in various companies and industries (for example, banks, pharmacy, and so on) and in various roles (as a lead developer, architect, consultant, designer, and so on).

Since 2008, he has also started working with Adobe Flex RIA Technologies in combination with existing Java applications.

Wim Bervoets is also no stranger to Web2.0, internet marketing and web site launches. He created successful international web sites, such as `http://www.javablog.be`—a blog about Java and Flex, `http://www.dancevibes.be`—a blog about music, and `http://www.wimsbios.com`—a site for PC tech enthusiasts.

To contact Wim Bervoets, please email to **wim@javablog.be** or go to his blog at `http://www.javablog.be`.

Trevor Burton is a software developer based in London, UK. He works primarily in Actionscript and Java. He has been working with Flash since the release of Flash 4 and Flex since the release of version 3 and has a wealth of experience developing Flash games from the banner advergames to multi-million pound online gambling applications.

He currently works for Infrared5, developing a wide range of web applications. In his spare time, he experiments with multi-user interaction and human—computer interaction.

Dedicated to my beautiful wife, Archana.
I remain thankful to her for being supportive and understanding.

Table of Contents

Preface **1**

Chapter 1: Installing and Configuring Adobe Flex **7**

Installing open source Flex 3 SDK **8**
Installation directory structure 8
About configuration files 9
Flex compilers **10**
Using compc—the component compiler 10
Using mxmlc—the application compiler 11
Installing Flex Builder 3 **12**
Creating a Flex project **18**
UI designer and source code editor 22
Flex LiveDocs 23
Summary **24**

Chapter 2: Introduction to Flex 3 Framework **25**

How Flex works **26**
Compiling and running an application **26**
About MXML **28**
Understanding namespaces 29
Using namespaces in your code 30
Containers **31**
Layout manager 31
Layout containers 34
Using Box, HBox, and VBox containers 35
Navigator containers 36
Form containers 38
Constraint-based layout 39
Using events in MXML **41**
Creating custom events **44**

Validating and formatting data **45**
Restricting user entry 50
Formatting 51
Data binding **52**
Using the [Bindable] metadata tag 55
Creating MXML custom components **57**
Understanding Flex itemRenderers **63**
Drop-in itemRenderers 64
Inline itemRenderers 64
External itemRenderers 65
Summary **66**
Chapter 3: Introduction to ActionScript 3.0 **67**
ActionScript 3.0 language features **67**
Strict data typing 68
Runtime exceptions 68
Sealed classes and dynamic classes 68
Method closure 68
XML and E4X 68
New primitive data types 68
Regular expressions 69
Object-oriented programming 69
ActionScript 3.0 fundamentals **69**
Variables 69
Access modifiers 71
Packages 71
Classes and interfaces 72
Classes 72
Interfaces 73
Implementing an interface in a class 73
Inheriting classes 74
Functions and methods 75
Named functions 76
Anonymous functions 76
Function parameters 77
Setter and getter methods 79
Flow control and looping 80
If/else statement 81
switch statement 81
Looping 82
Exceptions and error handling 84
try...catch...finally statements 84
Create your own custom Error class object 86
Reserved words and keywords 87

Using ActionScript 3.0 with MXML 88
Using the <mx:script> tag 88
Using the include directive 90
Working with events 91
Registering event handlers 91
Dispatching an event 93
About the target and currentTarget properties 93
Event propagation 94
Capturing phase 94
Targeting phase 94
Bubbling phase 94
Creating custom events 95
Creating and using ActionScript components 97
The commitProperties() method 98
The createChildren() method 99
The layoutChrome() method 100
The measure() method 101
The updateDisplayList() method 101
Summary 106
Chapter 4: Using External API and LocalConnection 107
Using External API 107
Using the ExternalInterface class 108
Getting information about external container 109
Calling JavaScript code from ActionScript 109
Calling ActionScript code from JavaScript 111
Using LocalConnection 113
Summary 118
Chapter 5: Working with XML 119
XML basics 119
Understanding E4X 120
The XML object 123
The XMLList object 124
Working with XML objects 125
Using XML as dataProvider 126
Loading external XML documents 129
An example: Building a book explorer 131
Summary 140
Chapter 6: Overview of LiveCycle Data Services and BlazeDS 141
LiveCycle Data Services 142
BlazeDS 144
BlazeDS vs LiveCycle Data Services 145

LiveCycle Data Services 145
BlazeDS 146
Understanding AMF 148
Summary **148**

Chapter 7: Flex Data Access Methods **149**

Flex data access components **149**
The HTTPService class 150
Using the HTTPService tag in MXML 150
An example of HTTPService 151
Using the HTTPService class in ActionScript 155
The WebService class 156
Using the WebService tag in MXML 157
An example of WebService 158
WSDL document 160
Using the WebService class in ActionScript 162
Working with SOAP headers 163
The RemoteObject class 164
Using the RemoteObject tag in MXML 165
An example of RemoteObject 166
Working with strongly-typed objects 172
Understanding the Flash Player security sandbox 175
Understanding the cross-domain policy file 176
Creating a proxy service 177
Summary **180**

Chapter 8: Communicating with Server-side Java **181**

The HTTPService class **181**
Working with XML data 182
Working with JSON data 186
Summary **189**

Chapter 9: Debugging Techniques **191**

Flash Debug Player **191**
Using client-side logging 192
Flex Builder Debugger 194
The Debug view 196
The Variables view 197
The Breakpoints view 198
The Expressions view 198
Network monitoring 199
ServiceCapture 199
Charles Web Debugging Proxy 200
Summary **200**

Chapter 10: Styling your Application 201

Using inline styles 202

Using external CSS files 204

Creating and designing Cascading Style Sheets 207

Loading stylesheets at runtime 210

Summary 215

Chapter 11: Packaging and Deployment 217

Packaging your application 217

Using Flex Ant Tasks 220

Deploying your application 224

Flex deployment options 228

Using a single SWF file deployment 228

Using web-tier compilation 230

Summary 231

Chapter 12: Internationalization and Localization 233

Internationalization (i18n) and localization (l10n) 233

Language 234

Assets 234

Culture 234

Time zones 234

Localization of Flex applications 235

Creating a resource file 235

Creating resource modules 242

Summary 246

Chapter 13: Creating an E-commerce Application 247

The general anatomy of the application 247

Let's start coding 250

The Flex code 251

The Java code 272

Directories and files 276

Summary 278

Index 279

Preface

Rich Internet applications (RIAs) are a new breed of web applications that are capable of doing things such as loading and handling heavy data ten times faster than HTTP, designing great-looking and sophisticated user interfaces that resemble desktop-based applications, and having the possibility of utilizing existing server technology such as Java, that would have never been possible with typical web technologies, such as HTML. Flex 3 is a leading technology for developing RIAs for the Web, as well as for the desktop. This book gives you an insight into, and provides a hands-on experience in, programming in Flex 3 by utilizing your existing knowledge of Java programming.

This book includes comprehensive information on various concepts of Flex 3 and ActionScript 3.0, such as developing simple applications and handling events to creating custom components and events, using RPC services, integration with Java and BlazeDS, styling and formatting, and how to package and deploy Flex applications. Finally, this book provides a step-by-step tutorial for developing e-commerce applications using Flex 3, ActionScript 3.0, BlazeDS, and Java.

You will start with downloading, installing, and configuring Flex 3 SDK and Flex Builder 3 and learn basic concepts, such as what is Macromedia Flex Markup Language (MXML) and ActionScript, understanding UI components, controls and compilers, and so on. Furthermore, you will start developing simple applications and slowly go into more depth where you will learn advanced concepts, such as creating custom components, debugging, integrating with Java, using RPC services, styling, internationalizing, and deploying Flex applications, and much more.

What this book covers

Chapter 1: Installing and Configuring Adobe Flex—In this chapter, you will learn the basics of Flex programming, that is, downloading, installing, and configuring Flex SDK and Flex Builder 3.

Chapter 2: Introduction to Flex 3 Framework—This chapter will introduce you to the MXML scripting for laying out User Interfaces (UI) in the Flex world. This chapter also provides hands-on examples required to get you started with MXML programming.

Chapter 3: Introduction to ActionScript 3.0—This chapter will introduce you to the ActionScript 3.0 programming language along with detailed code samples.

Chapter 4: Using External API and LocalConnection - In this chapter, you will learn how to communicate with JavaScript from a Flex application and vice versa.

Chapter 5: Working with XML—In this chapter, you will learn how to work with XML data using Flex's E4X approach.

Chapter 6: Overview of LiveCycle Data Services and BlazeDS—This chapter will provide an overview of BlazeDS and LiveCycle Data Services.

Chapter 7: Flex Data Access Methods—This chapter provides you with in-depth information about various data access methods available in Flex with detailed and step-by-step code samples along with Flash Player security model. It also gives you a detailed insight into how to use RemoteObject to communicate with Java code.

Chapter 8: Communicating with Server-side Java—This chapter provides step-by-step code examples to get started with Flex and Java communication along with clear and simple code examples..

Chapter 9: Debugging Techniques—In this chapter, you will learn how to debug your Flex application using Flex Builder 3 and some third-party tools.

Chapter 10: Packaging and Deployment—You will learn how to build and package a Flex application using available tools, such as Apache Ant, and learn about various deployment options that you can use.

Chapter 11: Styling Your Application—This chapter will give an overview of using Cascading Style Sheet (CSS) for changing the look and feel of your Flex application and components with brief code examples and tools for designing CSS files.

Chapter 12: Internationalization and Localization—This chapter will give you an overview of internationalizing your application.

Chapter 13: Creating an E-commerce Application—This chapter will provide a step-by-step guide for creating an end-to-end e-commerce application using Flex 3, ActionScript 3.0, BlazeDS, and Java.

What you need for this book

First and foremost, you need to have a need for learning Flex 3 technology; yes, I say that because most of us learn a new technology either by accident or because of some need, such as client/project demand or for doing things that are not possible with current technology or maybe you just want to upgrade your skill sets. Whatever is your reason behind learning Flex 3, I assure you that this book will serve as a simple and clear handbook for any developers to get started with Adobe Flex 3 programming.

Although this book is very easy to read and understand for any novice programmer, having some basic knowledge of Java programming in general, including Java Server Pages (JSP), would help you to pick up quickly. Apart from this, I assume that you have already heard about terms such as Rich Internet applications (RIAs) and understand theory behind it; if not, then please visit `http://en.wikipedia.org/wiki/Rich_Internet_application`.

Conventions

In this book, you will find a number of styles of text that distinguish between different kinds of information. Here are some examples of these styles, and an explanation of their meaning.

Code words in text are shown as follows: " The `ExternalInterface.available` property can be used to determine if the container application that is hosting your Flash Player instance supports an external interface."

A block of code is set as follows:

```
<mx:Style>
   Label
   {
      color: #ffff00;
      fontSize: 20;
      fontWeight: bold;
   }
</mx:Style>
```

When we wish to draw your attention to a particular part of a code block, the relevant lines or items are set in bold:

```
<mx:Style>
Label
{
    color: #ffff00;
    fontSize: 20;
    fontWeight: bold;
}
Label.helloStyle
{
    color: red;
    fontSize: 20;
    fontStyle: italic;
}
Label.bonjourStyle
{
    color: blue;
    fontFamily: Arial;
    fontSize: 20;
}
</mx:Style>
```

Any command-line input or output is written as follows:

```
mxmlc -library-path+=..../MyLibraries/bin/Main.mxml
```

New terms and **important words** are shown in bold. Words that you see on the screen, in menus or dialog boxes for example, appear in the text like this: "clicking the **Next** button moves you to the next screen".

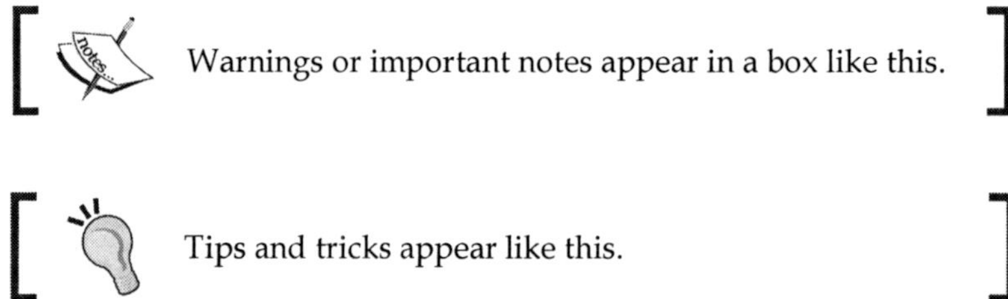

notes
Warnings or important notes appear in a box like this.
Tips and tricks appear like this.

Reader feedback

Feedback from our readers is always welcome. Let us know what you think about this book—what you liked or may have disliked. Reader feedback is important for us to develop titles that you really get the most out of.

To send us general feedback, simply send an email to `feedback@packtpub.com`, and mention the book title via the subject of your message.

If there is a book that you need and would like to see us publish, please send us a note in the **SUGGEST A TITLE** form on `www.packtpub.com` or email `suggest@packtpub.com`.

If there is a topic that you have expertise in and you are interested in either writing or contributing to a book on, see our author guide on `www.packtpub.com/authors`.

Customer support

Now that you are the proud owner of a Packt book, we have a number of things to help you to get the most from your purchase.

Downloading the example code for the book

Visit `http://www.packtpub.com/files/code/5340_Code.zip` to directly download the example code.

The downloadable files contain instructions on how to use them.

Errata

Although we have taken every care to ensure the accuracy of our content, mistakes do happen. If you find a mistake in one of our books—maybe a mistake in the text or the code—we would be grateful if you would report this to us. By doing so, you can save other readers from frustration, and help us to improve subsequent versions of this book. If you find any errata, please report them by visiting `http://www.packtpub.com/support`, selecting your book, clicking on the **let us know** link, and entering the details of your errata. Once your errata are verified, your submission will be accepted and the errata added to any list of existing errata. Any existing errata can be viewed by selecting your title from `http://www.packtpub.com/support`.

Piracy

Piracy of copyright material on the Internet is an ongoing problem across all media. At Packt, we take the protection of our copyright and licenses very seriously. If you come across any illegal copies of our works, in any form, on the Internet, please provide us with the location address or website name immediately so that we can pursue a remedy.

Please contact us at `copyright@packtpub.com` with a link to the suspected pirated material.

We appreciate your help in protecting our authors, and our ability to bring you valuable content.

Questions

You can contact us at `questions@packtpub.com` if you are having a problem with any aspect of the book, and we will do our best to address it.

1

Installing and Configuring Adobe Flex

In this chapter, you will learn how to install and configure Basic Flex 3.0 **SDK** (**Software Development Kit**) and Flex Builder 3. The Adobe Flex SDK contains everything you need to build and deploy Flex Rich Internet applications (RIAs). You can write Flex programs typically using any freely available text editing tools, such as Notepad, TextPad, or any **Integrated Development Environment** (**IDE**) of your choice. Adobe provides a specialized IDE for developing and designing Flex applications known as Flex Builder. Flex Builder is built on top of Eclipse platform. So if you are familiar with the Eclipse development paradigm, it will be very easy for you to use Flex Builder.

Although you do not need Flex Builder to write and compile Flex applications, Flex Builder does facilitate development with powerful tools, such as debugger, profiler, and visual designer apart from what the Eclipse platform offers you.

I prefer using Flex Builder 3, since I use Eclipse a lot for my Java development and I have installed Flex Builder 3 as a plugin to my Eclipse IDE.

I am assuming that you have prior knowledge of installing and configuring software packages on the Windows platform. In this chapter, I will explain how to install Flex Builder 3 on Windows. Mac and Linux users should visit Adobe's web site at `http://www.adobe.com/support/documentation/en/flex/3/releasenotes_flex3_fb.html` for installation instructions.

Installing open source Flex 3 SDK

Flex SDK comes in different types such as licensed Free Adobe Flex SDK (with a mixture of open source and closed open source components) and open source Flex SDK. The latter package contains entirely open source components under the Mozilla Public License version 1.1 (MPL) agreement, which includes its binaries. To know more about the available types of SDKs, visit `http://opensource.adobe.com/wiki/display/flexsdk/Downloads`. In this chapter, I will cover open source Flex SDK as an example.

In order to install Flex 3 SDK, download the latest open source SDK from Adobe's web site at `http://opensource.adobe.com/flex/`. Adobe is continuously working on improving and fixing bugs in Flex SDK and they release nightly builds on a regular basis. You can download them from `http://opensource.adobe.com/wiki/display/flexsdk/Download+Flex+3` and install them in order to stay updated with the latest feature and bug fixes in Flex 3 SDK.

> At the time of writing this book, Adobe was actively working on Flex 4, code named **Gumbo**. For more information, you can visit `http://opensource.adobe.com/wiki/display/flexsdk/Gumbo`.

Installation directory structure

Once you have downloaded the latest SDK in a ZIP format, extract it at your desired location, for example, `C:\Flex3.1_SDK`. That's it; you are done with the Flex SDK's installation. Now before you jump into coding, let's first understand the Flex SDK's installation directory structure.

When you install Flex SDK, the installer creates the following directory structure under the installation directory:

Directory	**Description**
`/ant`	Contains the Flex Ant tasks, which provide a convenient way to build your Flex projects
`/asdoc`	Contains ASDoc, a command-line tool that you can use to create API language reference documentation as HTML pages from the classes in your Flex application
`/bin`	Contains the executable files, such as the `mxmlc` and `compc` compilers
`/frameworks`	Contains configuration files, such as `flex-config.xml` and `default.css`

Directory	Description
/frameworks/libs	Contains the library (SWC files); you use the files to compile your application
/frameworks/locale	Contains the localization resource files.
/frameworks/projects	Contains the Flex framework source code
/frameworks/rsls	Contains the Runtime Shared Libraries (RSLs) for the Flex framework
/frameworks/themes	Contains the theme files that define the basic look and feel of all Flex components
/lib	Contains JAR files
/runtimes	Contains the standard and debugger versions of Adobe ® Flash® Player and the Adobe® AIR™ components
/samples	Contains sample applications
/templates	Contains template HTML wrapper files

In order to compile your Flex application, you need to set your `bin` folder in the Windows `PATH` environment variable under your System settings, so that you can use `mxmlc` and `compc` compilers from your project root folder.

About configuration files

There are a couple of important configuration files that you need to be aware of before you start using SDK. They are as follows.

The `flex-config.xml` file defines the default compiler options for the `compc` and `mxmlc` command-line compilers. You can set and tweak many compiler- and application-related configuration parameters in the `flex-config.xml` file located under the `sdk_install_directory/frameworks/` folder such as namespaces, library path, accessibility, and locale for application internationalization.

All of the Flex component names are defined in the `mxml-manifest.xml` file. This manifest file maps Flex component namespaces to class names with complete package names. This is similar concept as XML namespaces. The `mxml-manifest.xml` file is used to avoid element name conflicts and it also helps in organizing your source files. Don't worry about these files right now. You will learn more about them and their usage in a better manner further in the book.

Example:

```
<?xml version="1.0"?>
<componentPackage>
    <component id="HelloLabel" class="usa.hello.HelloLabel"/>
    <component id="NamasteLabel" class="ind.namaste.NamasteLabel"/>
</componentPackage>
```

In a manifest file, the `id` property of each `<component>` tag must be unique. That id is the name you use for the tag in your Flex applications, for example:

```
<local:HelloLabel label="Hello!"/>
```

You will learn more about how to use namespaces in Chapter 2 of this book.

The Flex compiler requires Java Runtime Environment (JRE) to compile Flex source code; configuring Java Virtual Machine (JVM) parameters can actually result in much faster and optimized compilation in some cases. Without JRE you cannot use Flex compilers, such as `mxmlc` and `compc`.

You can configure JVM settings in the `jvm.config` file, which is typically located under the `sdk_install_dir/bin` folder. The most common JVM configuration you may ever need is the JVM heap size. The Java heap is the amount of memory reserved for a particular JVM instance for faster performance; for example:

```
java.args=-Xms256m -Xmx512m
```

Flex compilers

Flex SDK is bundled with two command-line compiler tools—one for compiling component library SWC files and the other for compiling executable Shockwave Flash (SWF) files.

The SWC files are Flex component archive files that include compiled binaries and embedded assets of a component. The SWC files can be referenced by Flex application as the external library of component definition. You can think of SWC files as JAR files in Java. To read more about the SWC format, visit `http://livedocs.adobe.com/flex/3/html/help.html?content=building_overview_5.html`.

The SWF files are complied binaries of Flex application. Think of these files as executables of the Flex applications which are executed by Flash Player either inside the Internet browsers or standalone Flash Player. To read more about the SWF file, visit `http://www.adobe.com/devnet/swf/`.

Using compc—the component compiler

You use the component compiler to generate SWC files from component source files and other asset files, such as images and stylesheets. The SWC files are more like the `.jar` files in Java. They are typically used as library files in a Flex project.

This is the general compc syntax:

```
compc -namespace http://www.mynamespace.com manifest.xml
 -source-path .
 -include-namespaces http://www.mynamespace.com
 -include-classes com.mycomponents.Component1 com.mycomponents.Component2
 -include-file icon.png mx/containers/icon.png
 -output=bin/MyComponents.swc
```

Type the preceding command on a single line. It appears here on multiple lines for the sake of clarity.

You can use the -namespace and -include-namespaces options to include any number of components. This can keep the command line from being untidy.

The source-path option includes the current directory in the source path. This is how compc finds the various classes that are listed in the include-classes option.

The output option specifies the output location of the SWC file. In this case, compc writes the MyComponents.swc file to a folder named bin.

The include-classes option specifies the classes that you want to include in the SWC file. The compc component compiler is typically used in Flex for creating an external components library that can be referenced into Flex application or for creating Runtime Share Libraries, and so on. This is different from the mxmlc application compiler, which generates a Flex application executable.

Using mxmlc—the application compiler

You use the mxmlc application compiler to compile your Flex application source into an SWF binary file. The SWF files are executables of the Flex application that are executed into Flash Player. You can use the SWC files generated by component compiler, that is compc, when compiling MXML files. You typically use the library-path option to specify which SWC files the application uses.

This is the general mxml syntax:

```
mxmlc -library-path+=..../MyLibraries/bin/Main.mxml
```

The `-library-path` option includes the SWC files from the `MyLibraries/bin` folder for referencing any component referenced inside `Main.mxml`. For example, if `Main.mxml` is referencing any component which is part of the `MyComponents.swc` file, then you will need to include `MyComponents.swc` into the `-library-path` option. This is similar to what you do by including JAR files in `-classpath` while compiling the Java source.

Installing Flex Builder 3

Flex Builder is the official IDE for creating Flex applications, and as I mentioned earlier, it is built on the Eclipse platform. Flex Builder provides very powerful coding tools, such as MXML, ActionScript, and CSS editors with syntax coloring and hinting, statement completion, code collapse, interactive step-through debugging, code profiling; and very importantly, a rich visual-designing user interface layout, and more.

Later in this book, I will be using this Flex Builder IDE for demonstrating Flex code examples.

Also, make a note that if you are installing Flex Builder 3, then you need not install Flex SDK separately because Flex Builder 3 installs Flex SDK automatically as a part of its installation. You will learn more about the directory structure that the installer creates when you install Flex Builder in Flex Builder installation directory structure section.

Unlike the open source Flex SDK, Flex Builder is a licensed product from Adobe which you need to buy. But you can download a 60-day evaluation copy from Adobe's web site at `http://www.adobe.com/go/flex_trial`. Flex Builder 3 is available on Windows, Mac OS, and Linux operating systems.

Flex Builder comes with two different installation options. They are:

- **Flex Builder as a standalone IDE**: This option installs Flex Builder as a standalone IDE with **only** the Flex perspective. So if you need to work on a Java project, go for Flex Builder plugin installation on top of Eclipse or install JDT (Java Development Tools) in Flex Builder to support Java development. You can download JDT from `http://www.eclipse.org/jdt/`.
- **Flex Builder as an Eclipse plugin**: This option installs Flex Builder as an Eclipse plugin on an existing Eclipse IDE. Before installing it, you must first install Eclipse 3.2, or higher. So make sure you have done that.

> An Eclipse perspective is a collection of windows/views and a mechanism of providing task-oriented interactions in the IDE that are associated with a particular programming language.

Flex Builder 3 installation consists of the following main components:

- Flex SDK
- The Eclipse-based IDE (Integrated Development Environment)
- Flash Player 9 or higher versions

Now, assuming that you have downloaded Flex Builder 3 and are ready for installation, follow these steps. Please note that depending on which operating system you use, these steps will change. So please refer to the Adobe installation documentation at `http://www.adobe.com/support/documentation/en/flex/3/releasenotes_flex3_fb.html#installation` for installing it on Mac OS or Linux. There is only a one-step difference between installing Flex Builder as an Eclipse plugin and a standalone. I have combined installation steps for both into the following tutorial.

Start the installation by double-clicking on the downloaded file. A program, `InstallAnywhere`, should start. It may take a few minutes before the first screen appears. It is a good idea to close any running Windows applications (especially browser applications) because Flex Builder will install Flash Player 9 or higher.

The first screen will prompt you to choose a language. Choose the appropriate language from the drop-down list and click on the **OK** button to proceed.

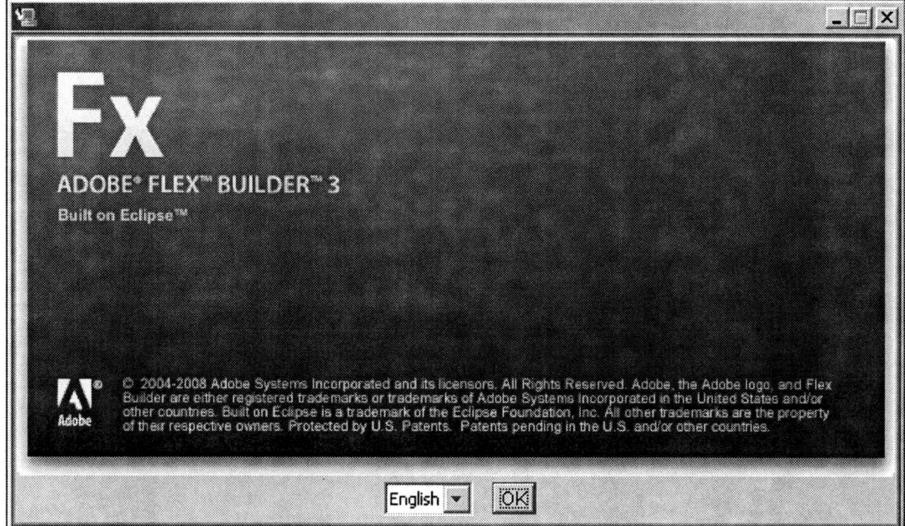

The introduction screen will be displayed. Click on **Next**.

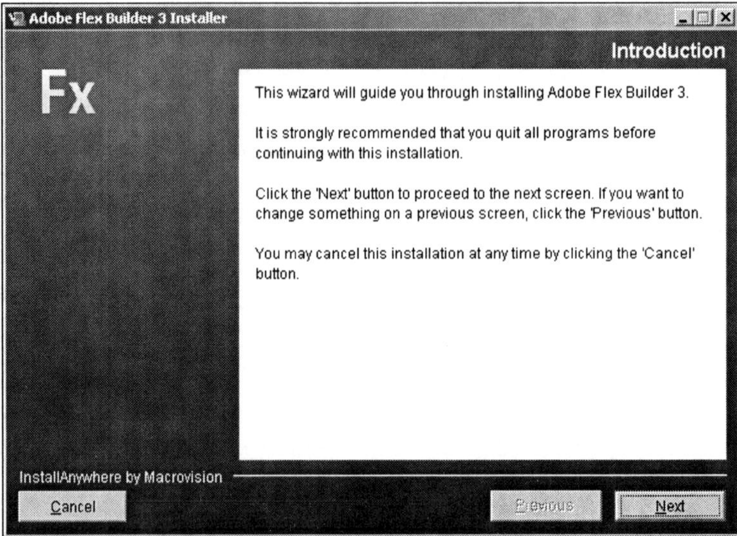

The next screenshot is the license agreement screen. Read the agreement, select the **I accept the terms of the License Agreement option**, and click on the **Next** button, as shown in the following screenshot:

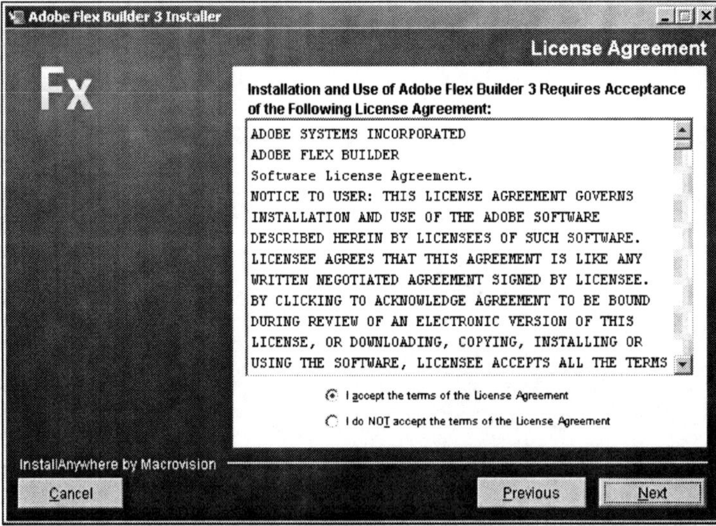

Now you need to choose the installation folder. Click the **Choose** button to choose anything other than the default location. Now click on **Next** to proceed, as shown in the following screenshot:

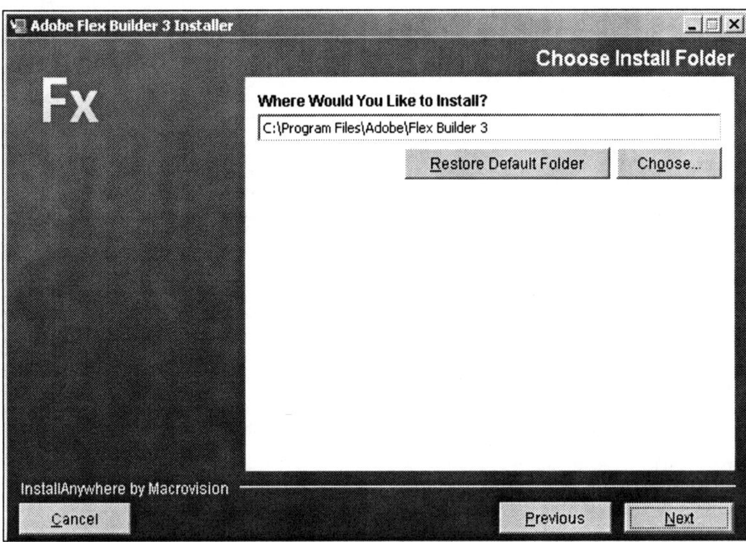

The next screen will appear **only** if you are installing Flex Builder as an Eclipse plugin. In this step, you need to choose the existing Eclipse installation root folder so that the installation wizard can configure the Flex Builder plugin. This works only with Eclipse 3.2 or higher versions. Please skip this step if you are installing Flex Builder as a standalone version.

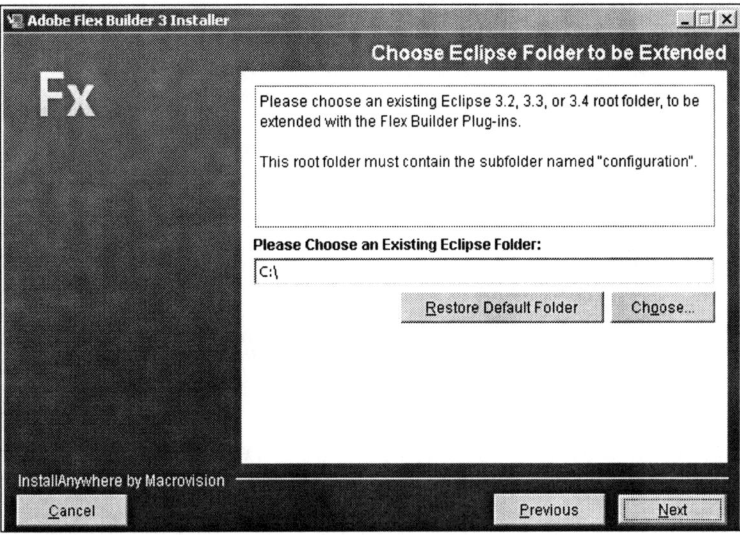

The next screen is an optional installation, but it is a quite important step because it prompts you to install the debug version Flash Player in each of your installed browsers on your computer. Installing the debug version of Flash Player is very important in order to use Flex Builder's debugger to debug Flex applications. So, for now, we will continue with the default selection and allow the install wizard to install the debug version of Flash Player. We will skip other optional components in this tutorial, so click on **Next** to proceed.

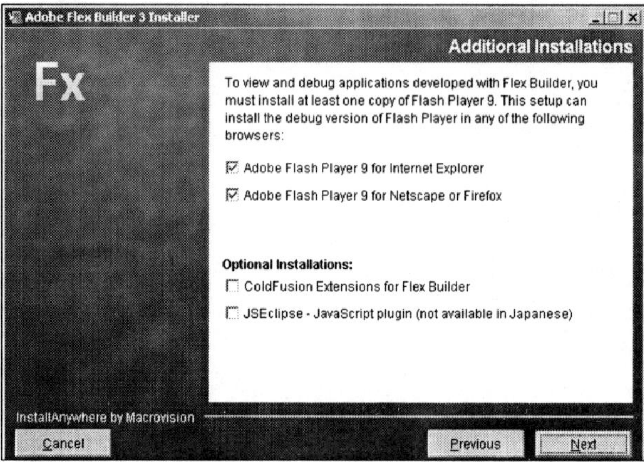

The following screen details the pre-installation summary of your selections throughout this install wizard. Just confirm that the details are correct and click on the **Install** button to begin the installation process.

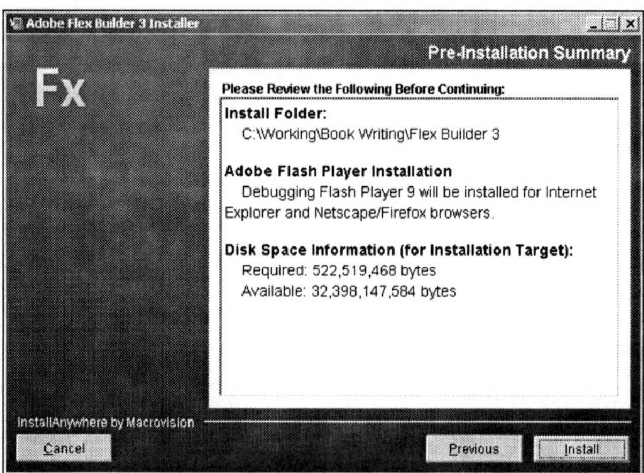

The next screen shown notifies the user of the installation's progress. The install wizard will install all necessary files on your system, including Java Runtime Environment. This may take a while, so please be patient.

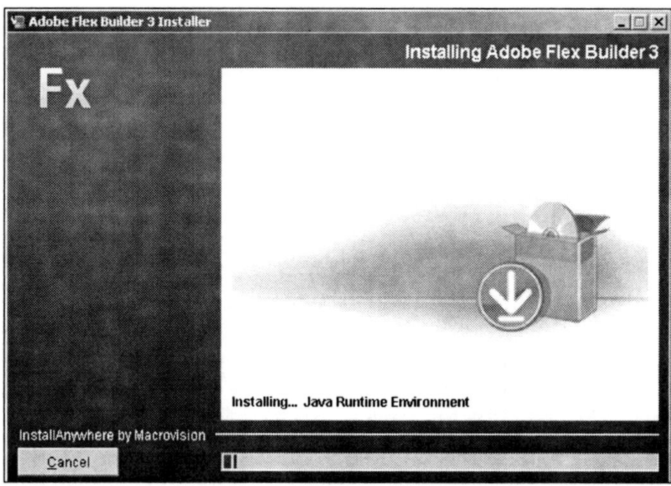

Once the installation is finished, you can launch Flex Builder 3 from **Windows | Program Files | Adobe | Flex Builder 3**.

Adobe has a unique program called **Free Flex Builder Pro for Education**, where students and faculties can get a free licensed copy of Flex Builder 3 Professional. In order to register for this program, please visit `http://www.adobe.com/products/flex/faq/#section-4`.

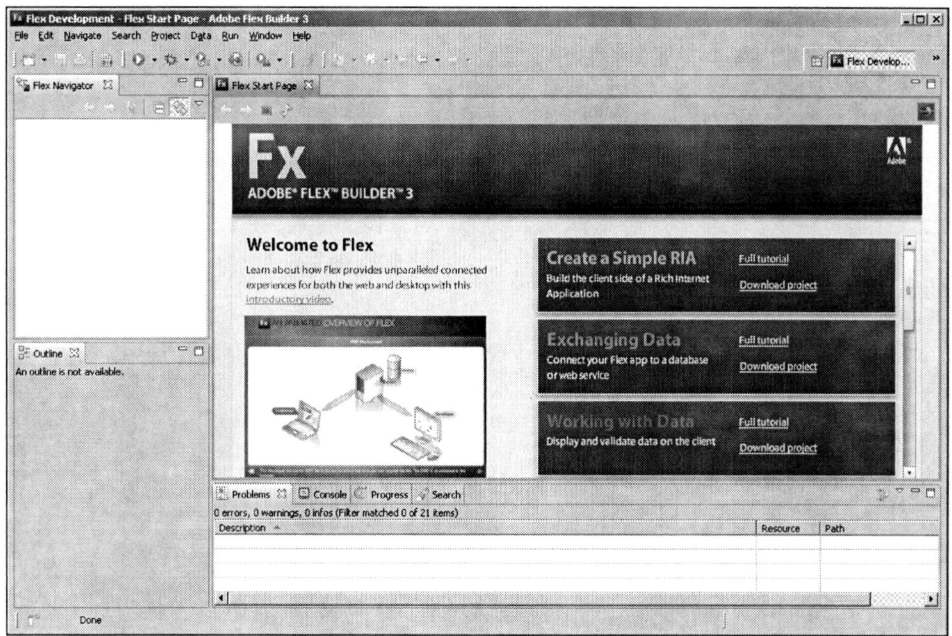

Before we start using Flex Builder 3, let's have a quick look at its directory structure. The installer creates the following directory structure:

Directory	Description
`Flex Builder 3`	The top-level directory for Flex Builder
`/configuration`	A standard Eclipse folder that contains the `config.ini` file and error logs
`/features`	A standard Eclipse folder that contains the plugins corresponding to the features of Flex Builder
`/jre`	Contains Java Runtime Environment installed with Flex Builder, used by default when you run the standalone version of Flex Builder
`/Player`	Contains the different versions of Flash Player—the standard version and the debugger version
`/plugins`	Contains the Eclipse plugins used by Flex Builder
`/sdks`	Contains the different Flex SDKs for a directory description

Creating a Flex project

If you are already using Eclipse IDE, then you are aware of a project definition. In Flex Builder 3, the same process is followed for creating a new Flex project. Let's start by creating one.

Select **File** | **New** to bring up options as shown in the following screenshot:

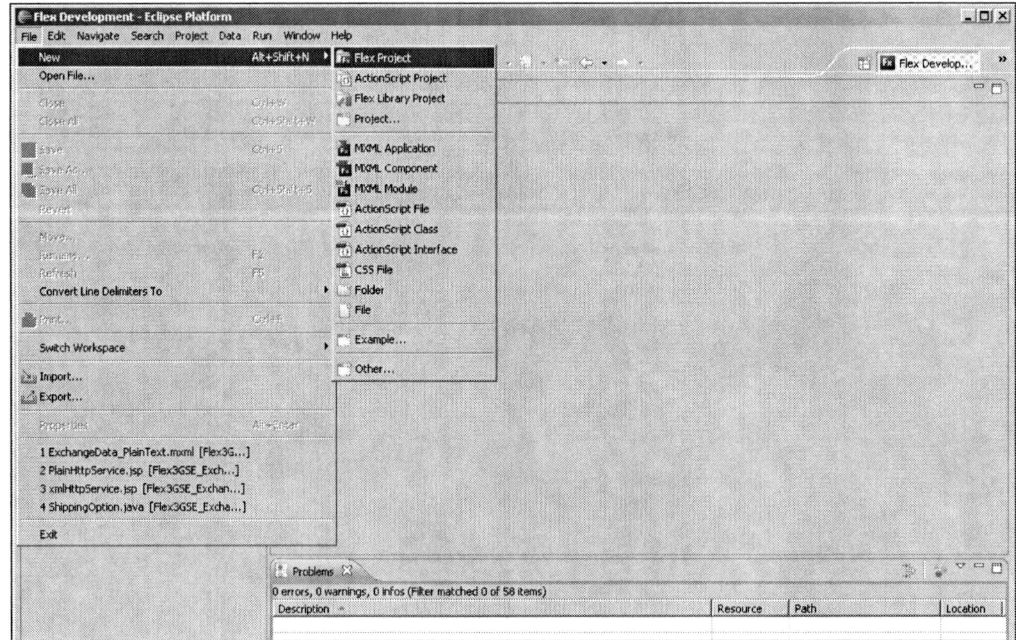

Select **Flex Project**, which will display the dialog box shown here:

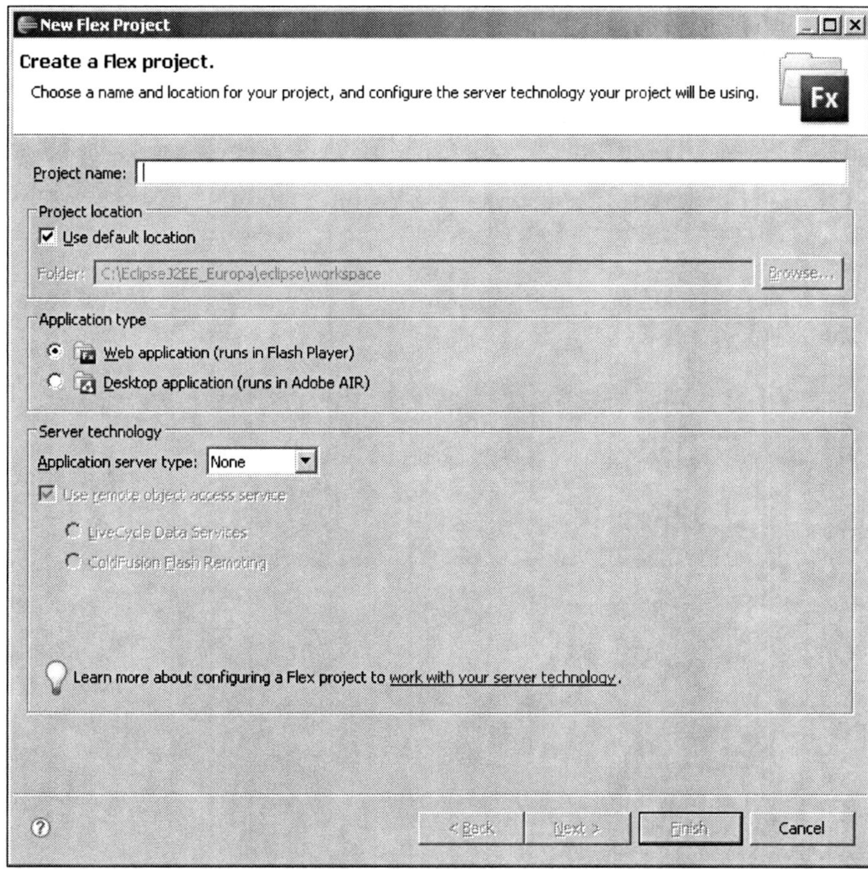

In the **Project name** field, enter the name of your project. To change the location of your project (other than default), uncheck **Use default location** and choose a new location. Using Flex Builder, you can create desktop applications (that run in Adobe AIR) and web applications. In this book, we will be focusing on web applications, so leave the **Application type** as **Web application (runs in Flash Player)**.

The **Server technology** section lets you select the **Application server type**. For example, if you are planning to use Java on the server side, then you can select **J2EE** as the application server type. This lets you create combined Java and Flex projects with output deployment configured on the server. Leave the application server type set to **None** for now.

For more information on different server types and configuration, visit `http://livedocs.adobe.com/flex/3/html/index.html?content=Part1_Using_FB_1.html`.

The following screen lets you specify the **Output folder** for the compiled Flex application. Click on **Next**.

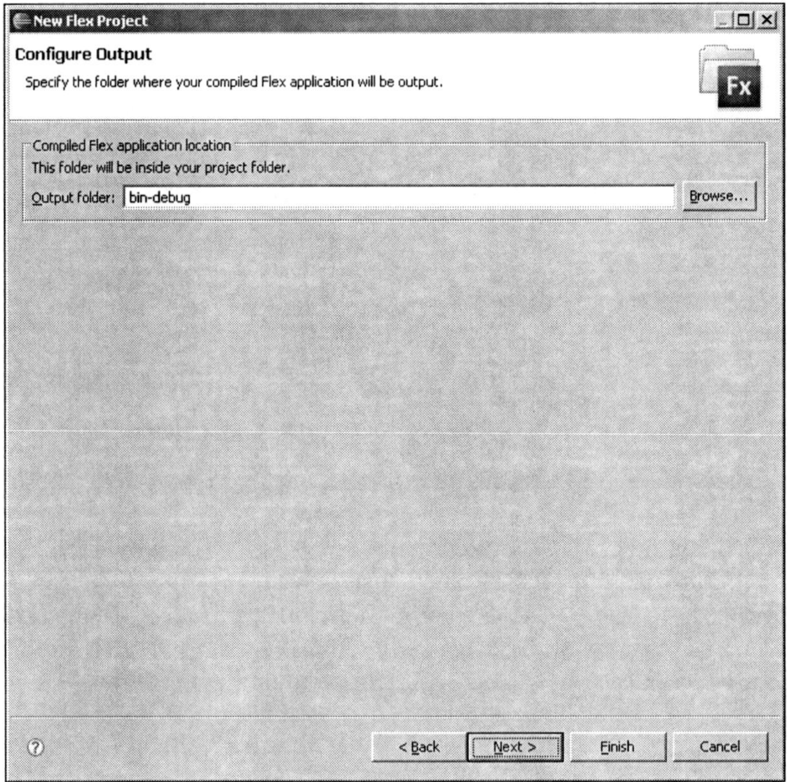

The next screen lets you select your source folder and sets a main application filename. By default, Flex Builder gives the application MXML file the same name as the project. You can change this if you want. Usually, a Flex project consists of one MXML file called the `application` file and several other components files. Don't worry too much about this now; just think of this as a Java file having a `main()` method, which is equivalent to the main entry point of the application. Click on **Finish** to create the project with these default settings.

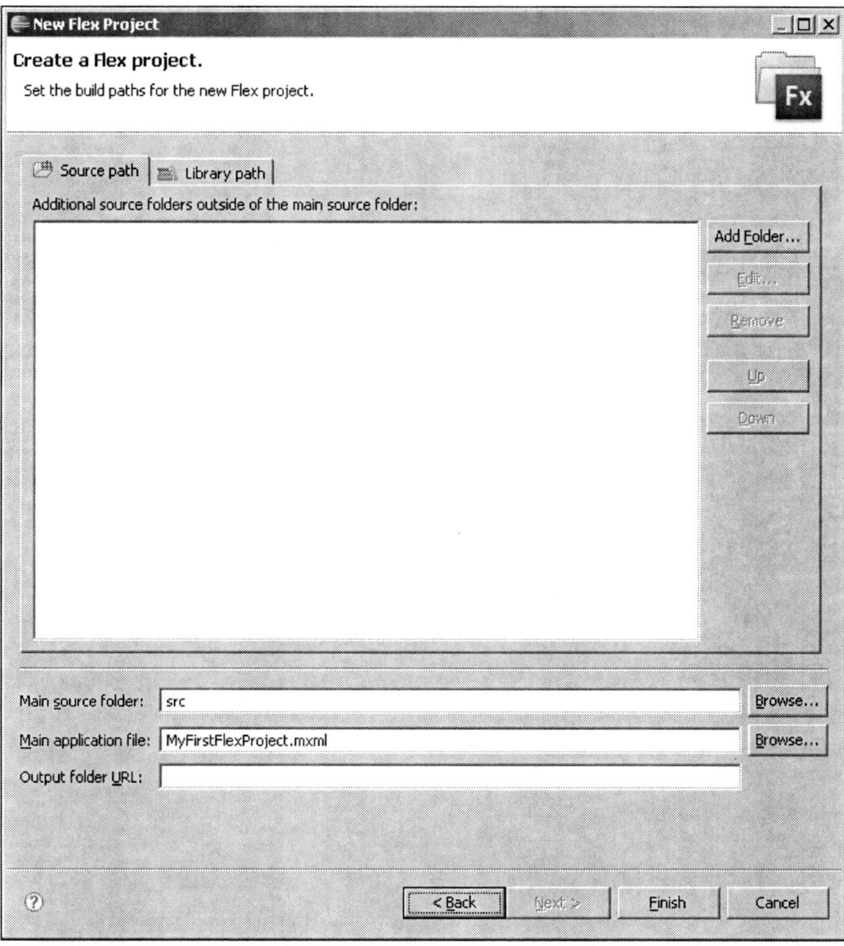

Flex Builder will open a project as shown in the following screenshot:

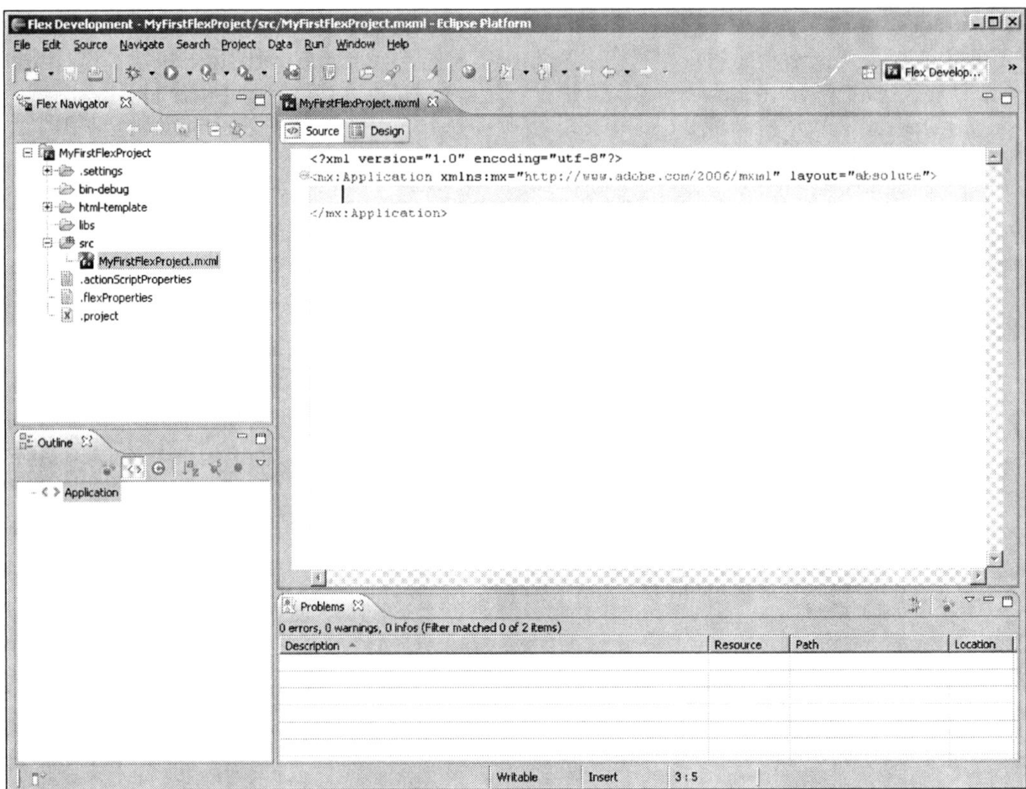

Notice how the **Flex Navigator** view now contains all the necessary project files and folders. The **Outline** view shows the structure of the application, and you will see how this helps you while writing code later in this book. The right-side area, where code is displayed, is called the Editor view. Here you can write your MXML or ActionScript code.

UI designer and source code editor

Notice that the Editor view has two tabs in the top left corner of the window—**Source** and **Design**. The **Source** tab is obviously used to edit the source code and the **Design** tab will put you into a design perspective where you can design and layout your UI components by using drag-and-drop. You can switch between these two tabs while writing code and designing UI layout.

Click on the **Design** tab to bring up the design perspective as shown in the following screenshot:

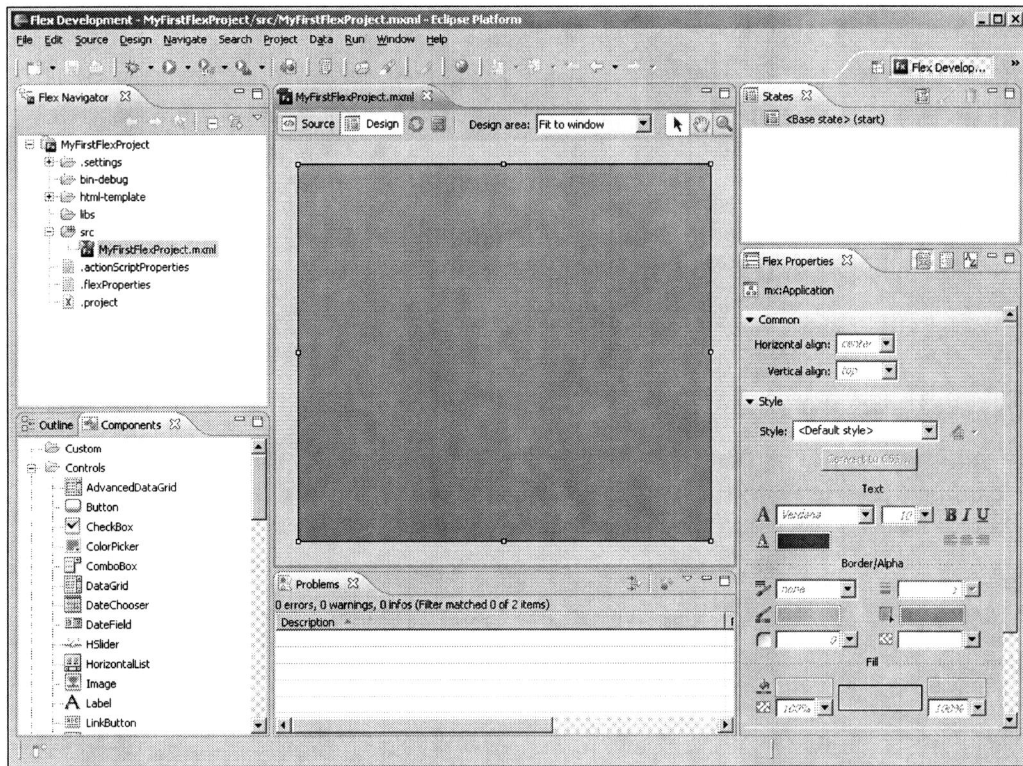

Notice that in the design perspective, you see some views that you didn't see in the source perspective. For example, you see the **Components** view, **States** view, and **Flex Properties** view.

In the design perspective, we can create our application visually in much the same way as Microsoft's popular Visual Basic or Adobe's Dreamweaver.

Flex LiveDocs

Flex LiveDocs can be accessed from `http://livedocs.adobe.com/flex/3/langref/index.html`, or it can be downloaded from `http://livedocs.adobe.com/flex/3/flex3_documentation.zip` for offline use.

When you install Flex Builder, it also installs all documentation and language reference along with it for offline use and contextual help purpose. To access language reference from Flex Builder, press the *Shift+F2* key combination. This will launch offline LiveDocs.

This documentation contains ActionScript and MXML language references in the HTML and PDF format. The language reference format is similar to JavaDoc, so it will be familiar to Java developers. LiveDocs covers very brief API information for MXML and ActionScript along with good examples wherever it is applicable.

I suggest you read this documentation for in-depth API-level information. You can also find many other related tutorials and documentations at `http://livedocs.adobe.com/flex/3/`.

Summary

In this chapter, you learned how to install and configure Flex 3 SDK and Flex Builder 3 on the Windows platform. You also learned about creating a Flex project and the various views available in the Flex perspective.

In the next chapter, you will learn about general Flex application architecture and MXML language. You will also start writing your first Flex program.

2
Introduction to Flex 3 Framework

Traditionally, web pages come with a number of restrictions such as slow and synchronous request and response models, different cross-browser rendering, and reloading the entire page for each action. They also lack what you find with the features of desktop applications such as sophisticated user interfaces and great design, view states, the ability to handle large amounts of data, reusability, and fast communications.

When it comes to designing great-looking and performing desktop-like applications, we need more than just HTML pages. Flex gives you just what you need for transforming a traditional web user interface into a great user experience. Typically, these applications are known as RIAs—a term that was originally introduced by Macromedia (now merged into Adobe) and which stands for **Rich Internet applications**.

Flex is a set of technologies for building and deploying RIAs on a Flash platform. Flex uses a mixture of MXML scripting and ActionScript. MXML is simple XML-based scripting used for laying out user interfaces and adding interactions to Flex applications. ActionScript is an object-oriented language based on ECMAScript. Java developers will find it familiar due to its close resemblance to Java programming structure. You will learn more about ActionScript in Chapter 3.

In this chapter, you will learn about the Flex application architecture and how to write them using the MXML language. You will also learn about the MXML language features and custom events and component creation.

How Flex works

Flex is an MXML- and ActionScript-based framework that is compiled into Flash applications with a `.swf` file extension. It is also commonly known as SWF files, which render on Flash Player embedded in browser.

Typically, `.swf files` are hosted in HTML wrappers using the `<embed>` tag. Flex Builder will automatically generate HTML wrapper file using the HTML template provided with the Flex SDK whenever you build or compile the Flex project.

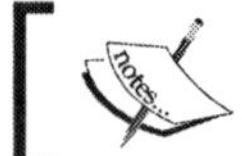

The `<embed>` tag defines embedded content, such as a plugin. In this case, it refers to a Flash Player plugin.

This HTML wrapper file along with the SWF can be hosted on any web server environment and can be accessed through any web browser.

The following illustration will give you an idea about this process:

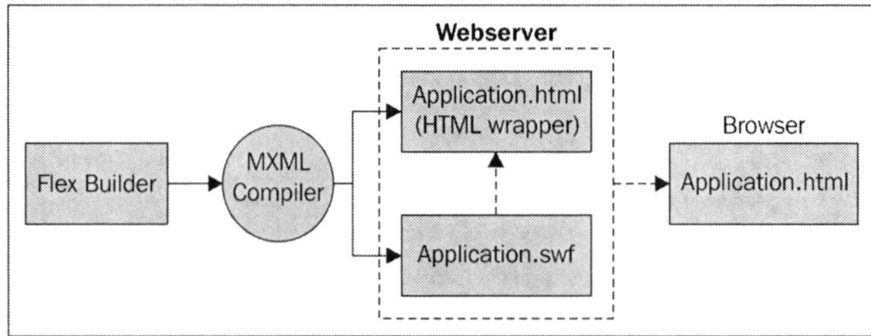

Flex applications are generally built on client-server architectures with server technologies such as Java. In this case, Flex applications require an extra server-side layer to be deployed on web server so that it can communicate with server-side data. This server layer is called BlazeDS or LiveCycle Data Services. You will learn more about this server layer later in the book.

Compiling and running an application

Going forward, we will be using many small examples to explain Flex concepts, so it is important that you understand how to compile and execute Flex applications in Flex Builder. The compiling process generates common `.swf` file or binary file from your source files including MXML, ActionScript, SWC files (Flex component library files), and assets and resources. The Flash Player uses the binary (`.swf`) file to execute the application. This process is similar to the way Java files are compiled into `.class` files known as **bytecode**.

To understand how the .swf files are executed, let's look at the following diagram:

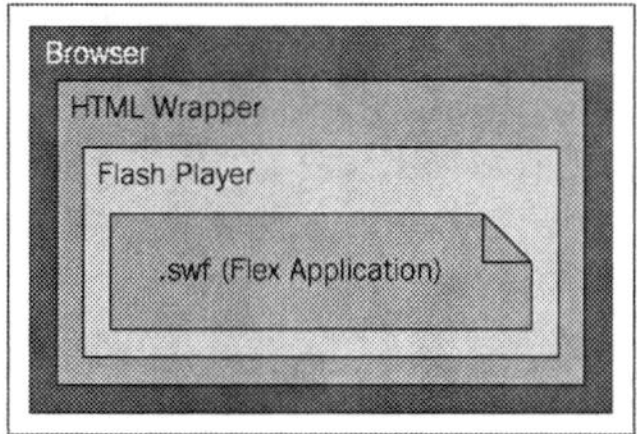

The two Flex compilers—**mxmlc** and **compc**—can be configured and launched from either Flex Builder or the command line. By default, Flex Builder will compile your application whenever you change and save any Flex source code files. To disable this default behavior, you can click on the **Project** menu and deselect the **Build Automatically** menu item.

If the **Build Automatically** option is deselected, then you can compile your project by right-clicking on your project from the **Flex Navigator** view and selecting the **Build Project** option from the menu, or from the **Project | Build Project** menu.

Flex Builder lets you set compiler options to enable accessibility, enable debug information in the output, set library paths, and set other options from your project properties. To open project properties, right-click on your project from the **Flex Navigator** view and select **Properties** from the menu, as shown in the following screenshot:

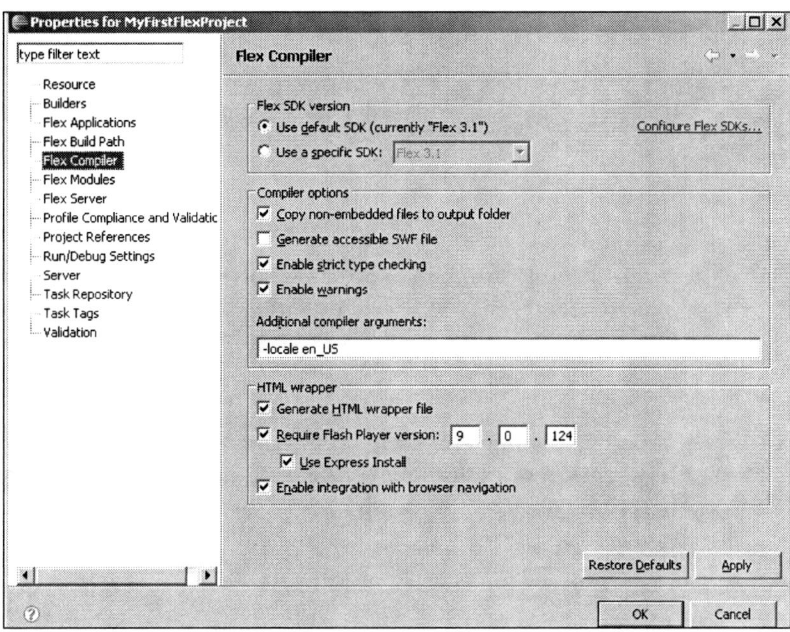

The **Problems** view (usually located at the bottom of the **Editor** view) is used to see warnings and errors found by the compiler.

You can launch and execute your Flex application MXML in a browser window by selecting **Run | Run As | Flex Application** from the menu bar, or by clicking on the **Run** icon from the toolbar and selecting **Run As | Flex Application**.

About MXML

MXML is a declarative XML-based language which is used to lay out user interfaces in Flex. MXML is mainly used to declaratively lay out the user interfaces of Flex applications, but it can also be used to create complex business logic and behaviors. As I mentioned earlier, MXML is based on XML standards which makes it easy to understand and learn. The MXML acronym does not have any official meaning, but some believe that it stands for **Multimedia eXtensible Markup Language**.

Let's take a look at the anatomy of a general MXML file. All MXML documents begin with an XML declaration. This declaration is used by the XML standard to specify the type of document and a small amount of information about versioning (for the parsers) and encoding of the document. You don't need to have an XML declaration, but you should have it as a good practice.

The following is an XML declaration:

```
<?xml version="1.0" encoding="utf-8"?>
```

The next line is where you declare your `Application` tag as a main application, or any other Flex container tag, as a component root:

```
<mx:Application xmlns:mx="http://www.adobe.com/2006/mxml"
layout="absolute">

</mx:Application>
```

Please note that only the main application files should start with the `<Application>` tag. Any one Flex project should only have a single main application file. As I mentioned earlier, consider this file as a Java file having a `main()` method as an entry point to your application.

There is a property called `layout` in the `<Application>` tag, which decides on the orientation of your application or container. By default, it is set to `absolute` and it can take values such as `horizontal` and `vertical`.

When you are building an application, you must deal with two different types of components—**container** and **controls**. Containers are the components which can hold other child controls. Think of this as an HTML table containing form elements. Flex containers provide many built-in features, such as a constraint-based layout which ensures that all child controls are resized and arranged accordingly when a container is resized. You will learn more about constraint-based layouts in a later section in this chapter entitled *Constraint-based layout*.

Example of containers:

```
<?xml version="1.0" encoding="utf-8"?>
<mx:Application xmlns:mx="http://www.adobe.com/2006/mxml"
layout="absolute">
   <mx:Panel>
      <mx:Label text="This is a label"/>
   </mx:Panel>
</mx:Application>
```

In the example above, the `<mx:Application>` tag contains a container called `<mx:Panel>`, which is holding one child component called `<mx:Label>`.

When a component has children, you must have a corresponding closing tag after the last child, which must include `mx:` namespace; notice `</mx:Panel>` in the example above. Notice that `<mx:Application>` is also a container which serves as the **root container** for your entire application.

Controls are usually used to represent data or user interactions in your application depending and are type-dependent. Controls are placed in the container that defines their layout; controls do not have their own layout information.

Every MXML tag represents a corresponding ActionScript class. For example, `<mx:Label>` has a corresponding ActionScript class called `Label.as`. When you use this tag in MXML, you suffix it with `mx`. This is called the `Default Namespace`. Let's explore this in greater detail in our next section.

Understanding namespaces

MXML inherits its `namespace` concept from XML. XML namespaces are a way of naming your elements to avoid naming conflicts with other elements. For example, you can define an XML element `<title>` to represent a book title, whereas someone else may define it as a job title.

If you observe the `<mx:Application>` tag, it has a property called `xmlns` which stands for XML namespace. This namespace is declared as `xmlns:mx="http://www.adobe.com/2006/mxml"`. What it essentially means is that all components which are mapped with the URI (Universal Resource Identifier) `http://www.adobe.com/2006/mxml` are substituted under the short name `mx`. So, any component defined as a part of the above URI mapping can be accessed as `<mx:componentName>`, for example, `<mx:Application>` or `<mx:Label>`, and so on.

When you install the Flex SDK, all of the Flex component ActionScript classes get installed. These ActionScript classes will be mapped with Flex component names with their respective packages in the `mxml-manifest.xml` file. You saw how to configure the component manifest in Chapter 1, in the *About configuration files* section.

This Flex component manifest file will be mapped with a namespace in the `flex-config.xml` file using a unique URI as follows:

```
<namespaces>
  <namespace>
     <uri>http://www.adobe.com/2006/mxml</uri>
     <manifest>mxml-manifest.xml</manifest>
  </namespace>
</namespaces>
```

In this way, the compiler finds the Flex SDK components included in the MXML file using the `mx` namespace. You will be using this concept while creating custom components later in this chapter. The `<mx:Application>` tag uses a default namespace called `mx` as a substitute for the Flex SDK components path. If that namespace is not defined as shown in the `<mx:Application>` tag, your Flex application will not work. So I strongly recommend not changing it.

The **Universal Resource Identifier** (URI) listed in the `<mx:Application xmlns:mx="http://www.adobe.com/2006/mxml">` tag does not represent an actual web site. It is just a way to create a unique string to differentiate all namespaces from each other.

Using namespaces in your code

To use the Flex SDK components, reference them using the `mx` prefix. For example, you can use a text area component in the following way:

```
<mx:TextArea id="textArea"/>
```

When creating your own custom component, it is best practice to place them in a separate namespace. This assures that your component will not conflict with any of the standard Flex components.

Containers

Now that you have understood the general Flex application anatomy and the MXML syntax, let's understand the core of Flex's user interface design—**containers**.

Containers are Flex components in which other UI elements can be placed. These containers have a special property to control how child elements are laid out inside them. In other words, you can use containers to control the sizing and positioning of all its children UI elements.

Containers have predefined layouts and navigational rules, which makes the laying out of user interfaces easier. All containers except `Canvas` support automatic layouts. The canvas container uses absolute positioning (using `x` and `y` coordinates) to lay out child UI elements. You will learn more about automatic layouts later.

In this section, we will focus on the following types of containers:

- Layout containers
- Navigation containers

It is very important to understand these containers to start designing Flex application user interfaces. So make sure you take some time to thoroughly comprehend them.

Layout manager

Every container, except `Canvas`, has a built-in support for the layout manager. The layout manager decides how the content of any container is positioned when the container is resized. This includes the resizing of all child components and rearranging their positions relatively (based on the container area). The following are three types of layouts supported by layout containers:

- `absolute`: With `absolute` layout, you must specify the x and y coordinates of the child components to place them on screen
- `vertical`: With `vertical` layout, all child components will be placed vertically and centered in the container
- `horizontal`: With `horizontal` layout, all child components are arranged horizontally from left to right

As I mentioned earlier, the `<mx:Application>` tag is also a container, commonly known as **root container**, which holds your entire application and its controls. If you look at the `<mx:Application>` tag, you will see that the `layout` property is set to `absolute`. This is set by default by Flex Builder when you create an MXML application file. If you do not specify any layout, then `vertical` will be used as default.

Now, we will jump into Flex Builder to understand how you can set the `layout` properties in the design perspective. Open the Flex project, which we created in Chapter 1, or create a new Flex project and follow these steps:

1. Select the **Design** button in the **Editor** view to open the design perspective.
2. Click anywhere inside the design area to activate the **Flex Properties** view.
3. In the **Flex Properties** view, go to the **Layout** section. If it is not visible, then scroll down. This is shown in the following screenshot:

   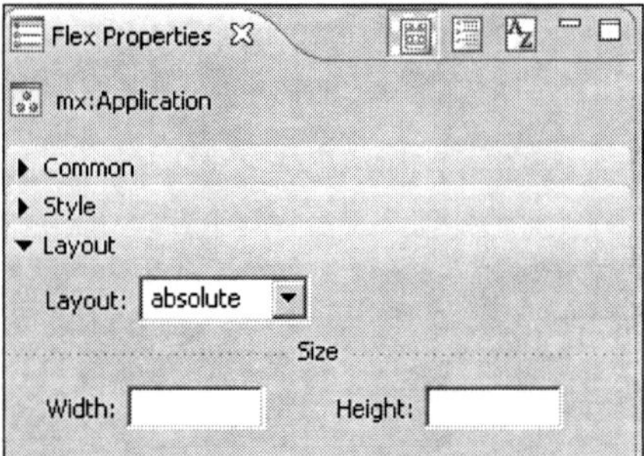

   You will notice that `absolute` is selected. Change the layout by selecting `vertical`, `horizontal`, or `absolute` from the drop-down. This will automatically make changes to the `<mx:Application>` tag in the source code.

4. From the **Components** view, drag a few **Button** controls on stage. Their position and text does not matter. What we want to confirm is that when an `absolute` layout is used, the x and y coordinates need to be specified.
5. If you do not see the **Components** view, then click on **Window menu | Show View | Components** in Flex Builder.

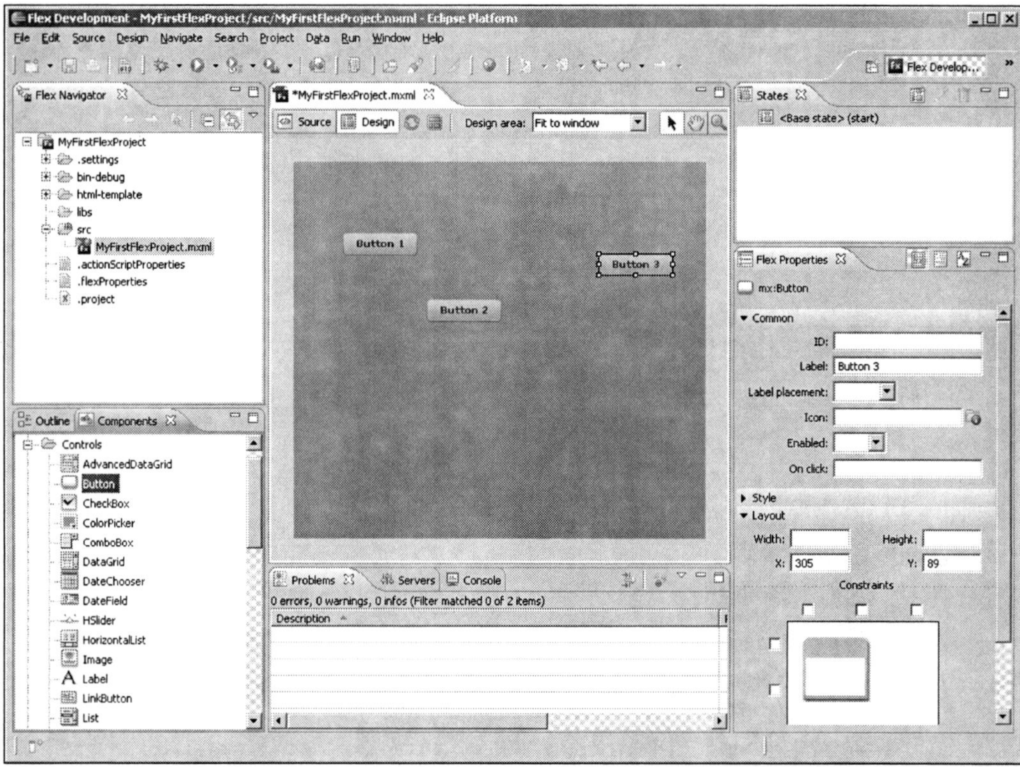

6. Now switchback to the source view by clicking on the **Source** button from the **Editor** view. Notice how the code was automatically added when you dragged and dropped the **Button** controls in the **Design** view.

```
<?xml version="1.0" encoding="utf-8"?>
<mx:Application xmlns:mx="http://www.adobe.com/2006/mxml"
layout="absolute">
  <mx:Button x="49" y="69" label="Button 1"/>
  <mx:Button x="133" y="134" label="Button 2"/>
  <mx:Button x="305" y="89" label="Button 3"/>
</mx:Application>
```

You will notice that the x and y coordinates are added for three button controls. Without the x and y coordinates, everything is defaulted at the (0, 0) coordinate. So, if you remove the x and y coordinates from all buttons, then all three buttons will appear as overlapped when you run the application. Let's take a look at the other two layouts.

7. Switch back to the **Design** view and select the application container by clicking on the empty area. Go to the **Layout** section in the **Properties** view as described in step 3.
8. Select `vertical` from the **Layout** drop-down and you will notice that the **Design** view reflects the new layout and arranges buttons vertically, as shown in the following screenshot:

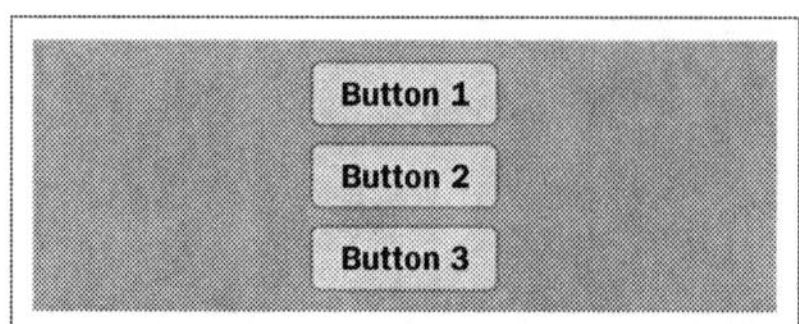

9. Similarly, select `horizontal` from the **Layout** drop-down and notice that the buttons are now automatically arranged horizontally.

You can also change the layout property from the source code by modifying the application tag's `layout` property value.

Now, as you have understood the basics of the layout manager, let's take a look at the different types of containers.

Layout containers

Flex provides many different layout containers. You can explore them from the **Layout** section of the **Components** view in Flex Builder, as shown in the following screenshot:

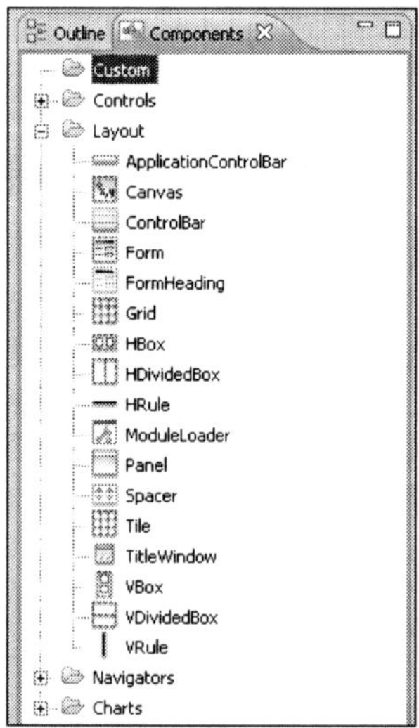

Please note that you need to be in the **Design** view in order to view the **Components** view. If you do not see the **Components** view section, then select **Windows menu | Show View | Components** in Flex Builder.

Also note that some of the layout containers have graphical elements. The `TitleWindow` and `Panel` containers have title bars and borders around them.

While laying out a user interface, you will need to use the `HBox` and `VBox` layout containers more often than any other container. These are non-graphical layout containers. Let's understand how they can be used.

Using Box, HBox, and VBox containers

The `Box` layout container lays out its children in single vertical columns and single horizontal rows. You use its `direction` property to determine either vertical (default) or horizontal layout. The `HBox` and `VBox` containers are inherited from the `Box` container with a predefined `direction` property value.

The following example shows the usage of the `HBox` and `VBox` combination for laying out complex user interfaces:

As you can see, the screen above is pretty complex and it would have taken a lot of code to adjust the user interface. I have used the `backgroundColor` properties for these containers to set the background color of each container to differentiate them. Here is the code behind this layout:

```
<?xml version="1.0" encoding="utf-8"?>
<mx:Application xmlns:mx="http://www.adobe.com/2006/mxml"
 layout="vertical">
   <mx:HBox width="100%" height="303" backgroundColor="#FFFFFF">
     <mx:VBox height="100%" width="133" backgroundColor="#5F638F">
     </mx:VBox>
     <mx:VBox height="100%" backgroundColor="#8C8C8E" width="216">
       <mx:HBox width="100%" height="148" backgroundColor="#3A478D">
```

```
            </mx:HBox>
            <mx:HBox width="100%" height="146" backgroundColor="#4E84B9">
            </mx:HBox>
        </mx:VBox>
    </mx:HBox>
</mx:Application>
```

To understand the hierarchical relationship of containers starting from root container, go to the **Outline** view that's usually located at the left side of your **Design** view. See the following screenshot:

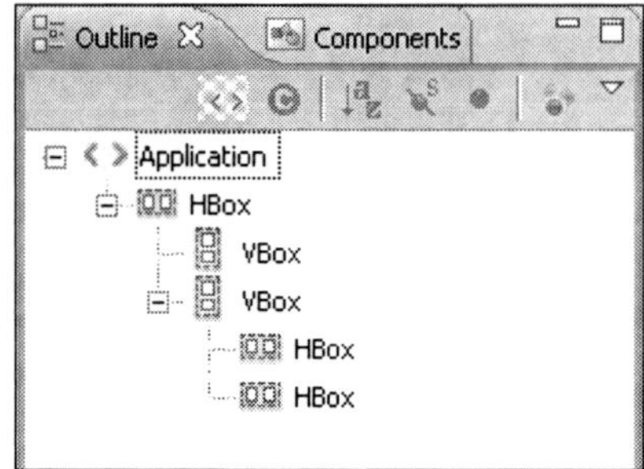

The above layout formation is commonly called **nested layout**.

For more information on these containers, please have a look at the Flex API documentation.

> **Warning**: Using too many nested layout containers may result in poor application performance because, at runtime, Flash Player needs to determine each container and each of its child controls, position and size.

Navigator containers

Navigator containers control user movement, or navigation, among multiple child containers. The individual child containers (not the navigator container) control the layout and positioning of their children. In simple words, navigator containers are special kind of containers that provide extra navigational capabilities to their content. For example, `Accordion` or `TabNavigator` lets you build multiple form-based user interfaces.

Flex is usually a single SWF file embedded into a single HTML file, and Navigator containers are typically used to build multipage applications.

To create a `TabNavigator` control, switchback to the **Design** mode and follow these steps:

1. Drag and drop a `TabNavigator` container from the **Navigators** section in the **Components** view, in the design area.
2. Notice that `TabNavigator` will be created with one default tab—**Tab 1**. It can be seen in the following screenshot:

3. You can add another tab to this container by clicking on the **+** (the plus sign) that is displayed above the container. Similarly, use the **-** (the minus sign) to delete a tab.
4. Adding a tab will prompt you to enter a new tab label and the type of container you want to use. Remember the definition of navigator containers: *Navigator container controls user movement, or navigation, among multiple child containers*. These tabs are actual containers, which will be added as children of the `TabNavigator` container. For now, I am leaving selection to default `Canvas`.
5. Once you click on **OK**, a new tab will be added to `TabNavigator`.

You can explore these containers from the **Navigators** section of the **Components** view, as shown in the following screenshot:

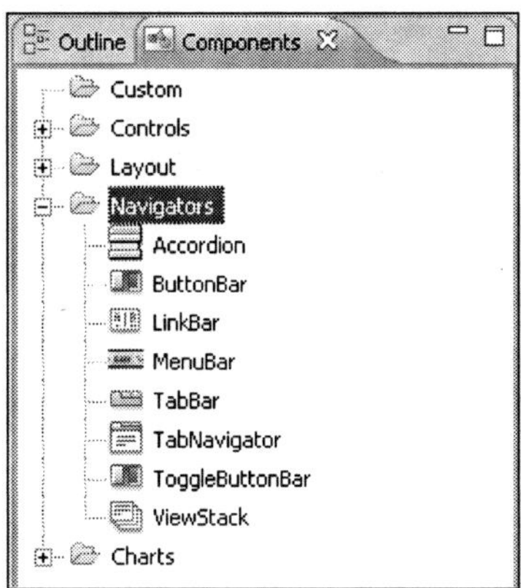

Form containers

Forms are commonly used containers in the web world. Forms are typically used to collect user information, such as registration, purchases, billing, and so on. Flex provides a form-based container with various built-in advantages, such as form validation, required field indicator, auto-alignment, auto-layout, and so on.

Forms are constructed using the following three types of components:

- `Form` container - Represents the main Form container
- `FormHeading` - Represents Form heading
- `FormItem` - Represents individual control on the Form container, such as text field, button, and so on

Example of creating a form control:

```
<?xml version="1.0" encoding="utf-8"?>
<mx:Application xmlns:mx="http://www.adobe.com/2006/mxml"
layout="vertical">
    <mx:Form>
        <mx:FormHeading label="Registration Information"/>
        <mx:FormItem label="First Name:" required="true">
            <mx:TextInput id="fname"/>
        </mx:FormItem>
        <mx:FormItem label="Last Name:" required="true">
            <mx:TextInput id="lname"/>
        </mx:FormItem>
        <mx:FormItem label="Email:" required="true">
            <mx:TextInput id="email"/>
        </mx:FormItem>
        <mx:FormItem label="Phone Number:">
            <mx:TextInput id="phone"/>
        </mx:FormItem>
        <mx:FormItem>
            <mx:Button label="Button"/>
        </mx:FormItem>
    </mx:Form>
</mx:Application>
```

You can also create forms in the Design view by dragging and dropping `Form`, `FormHeading` located in the **Layout** section of the **Components** view, or individual controls such as `TextInput`, `Button` in the Design view. Flex Builder will automatically add the `FormItem` tag around the individual control.

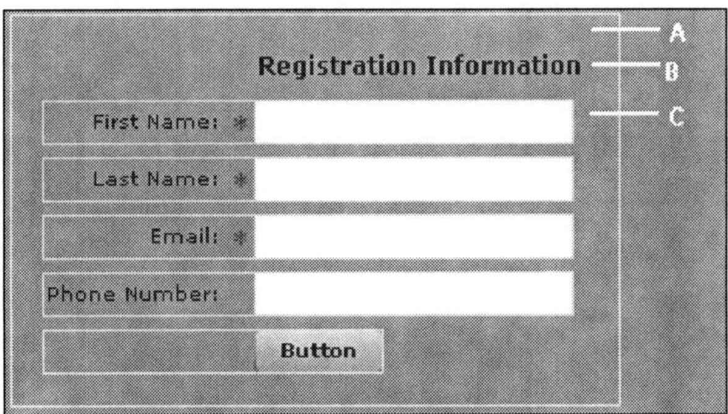

In the previous image, **A** indicates the main `Form` container; **B** indicates `FormHeader`; and **C** indicates `FormItem`. You will also notice the red asterisk (*) symbol that indicates a mandatory field. You can set a mandatory field by adding the `required="true"` property to your `FormItem` tag.

Constraint-based layout

Flex supports adding a **constraint-based** layout to relatively arrange components inside a container. This layout can only be used when the `layout` property is set to `absolute`. I will use the previous form example to demonstrate a constraint-based layout:

1. Switch to the **Design** view.
2. Click on the Application area and change the `layout` property of the `Application` tag to `absolute` from the **Flex Properties** view, or you can change it manually from code by switching back to code view.
3. Select the `Form` container by clicking on its border or selecting the Form node from the **Outline** view.

4. Now in the **Flex Properties** view, scroll down to the **Layout** section. You will notice that you now see a **Constraints** preview window with a couple of checkboxes, as shown in the following screenshot:

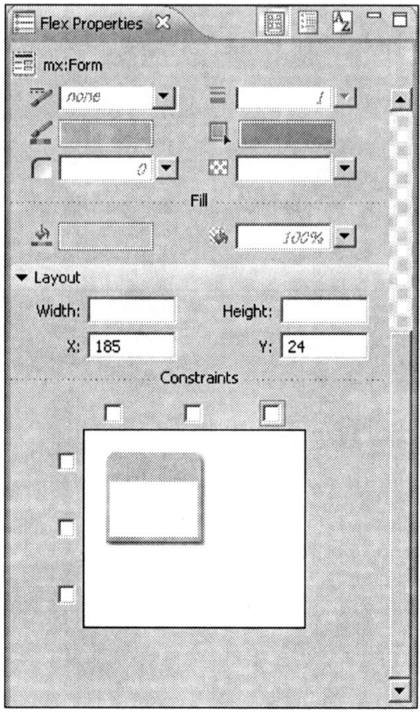

5. You can select checkboxes to set constraints. I have selected `top` and `right` constraints, as shown in the following screenshot:

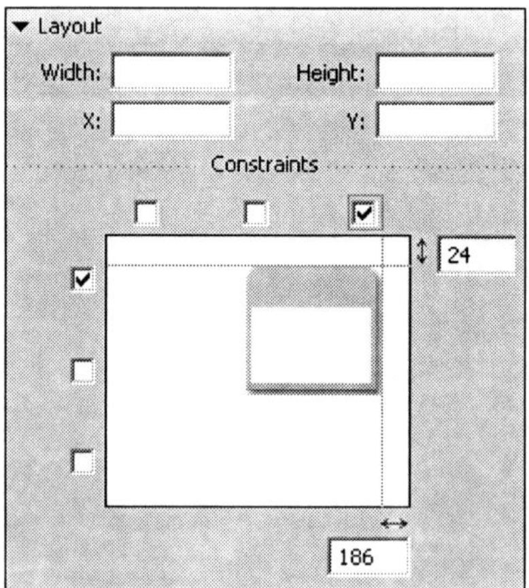

6. Now, the Form container will stay in the top right corner even if you resize your Flex application window.

Now that you have understood Flex containers and their usage, it's time to dive into the MXML event model.

Using events in MXML

Events let a developer know when something happens within an application. Events can be triggered by either user interactions (such as keyboard or mouse clicks), or they can be system-generated to notify the user that something happened internally (for example, the application finishes loading, the application closes, and so on). The event model in Flex provides an excellent way to design loosely-coupled applications that can consume or dispatch events. This simply means that you can design components that can perform tasks and notify the outside world by broadcasting one or more custom events. The event model is broadly based on a well-known design pattern known as the **observer pattern**. The observer pattern allows one object, known as the observer, to watch another object, known as the subject, by registering a listener(s) for a specific event(s), and then the subject broadcasting event(s) to all subscribed observers.

For example, you might have two list components where one shows the list of countries and the other shows the list of states pertaining to the selected country. In this case, the states list component will listen for any change in the country list selection and reload itself to show a list of states of the selected country. So, in this case, the state list component is an observer and the country list component is a subject.

Events are used to add behavior and actions to your user interface. You can handle these events in your code by adding **event handlers**. **Event handlers** are basically functions or methods that you write to handle and respond to specific events. They are also called **event listeners**.

For listening to specific events from a component, you need to register your event listener(s) with that component. For example, to listen when an application has loaded, you can employ a `creationComplete` event of the `Application` container. `creationComplete` is dispatched by the `Application` container when it finishes creating all its children components. You can use this event to initialize variables, for example.

Example of the `creationComplete` event:

```
<?xml version="1.0" encoding="utf-8"?>
<mx:Application xmlns:mx="http://www.adobe.com/2006/mxml"
creationComplete="initApp(event);" layout="absolute">
   <mx:Script>
      <![CDATA[
         import mx.controls.Alert;
         private function initApp(event:Event):void {
            Alert.show("Application is initialized.");
         }
      ]]>
   </mx:Script>
</mx:Application>
```

In the code above, you must have noticed a new `<mx:script>` block. This block is used in MXML to write ActionScript code. For the time being, ignore the details as we are going to learn ActionScript and how to use it with MXML in our next chapter.

The important thing to note is that you are using **event handler** mechanisms to handle the application's `creationComplete` to display an alert dialog box. Check the following example to see how to handle a `click` event of a `Button` control:

```
<mx:Button label="Click me" click="Alert.show('Button Clicked');"/>
```

This time, I have not specified an event handler function on the `click` event. Instead, I have written ActionScript code inside the `click` event block. This is another way to write event handlers.

The following example will show you how to handle keyboard events:

Example: Keyboard event:

```
<?xml version="1.0" encoding="utf-8"?>
<mx:Application xmlns:mx="http://www.adobe.com/2006/mxml"
layout="absolute">
   <mx:Script>
      <![CDATA[
         import mx.controls.Alert;
         private function handleKeyUpEvent(event:KeyboardEvent):void {
            Alert.show("Text: "+txtArea.text);
         }
      ]]>
   </mx:Script>
   <mx:TextArea id="txtArea" x="252" y="133" width="172" height="126"
    keyUp="handleKeyUpEvent(event);"/>
</mx:Application>
```

In this example, I added a `TextArea` control to the application and added an event handler for the `keyUp` event. Notice that I am passing the `event` argument to the `handleKeyUpEvent` method. This is known as passing the event reference to the event handler.

Next, we will see how to handle mouse events in MXML.

An example of mouse events:

```
<?xml version="1.0" encoding="utf-8"?>
<mx:Application xmlns:mx="http://www.adobe.com/2006/mxml">
   <mx:Script>
      <![CDATA[
         import mx.controls.Alert;
         private function handleMouseOver():void {
            txtArea.text += "Mouse is over text area\n";
         }
         private function handleMouseOut():void {
            txtArea.text += "Mouse is out of text area\n";
         }
      ]]>
   </mx:Script>
   <mx:TextArea id="txtArea" mouseOver="handleMouseOver();" mouseOut="
handleMouseOut();" width="238" height="217"/>
</mx:Application>
```

In the example above, I registered two mouse events, namely `mouseOver` and `mouseOut`, for the `TextArea` component. These mouse events will be triggered when the user moves the mouse over and out of the `TextArea` control. Try it.

Some of the commonly used mouse and keyboard events are as follows:

Mouse events:

Event	Description
`mouseUp`	Dispatches when the user releases the mouse button.
`mouseDown`	Dispatches when the user clicks on the mouse button.
`mouseMove`	Dispatches when the user moves the mouse.
`mouseOver`	Dispatches when the user moves the mouse over a specific component area.
`mouseOut`	Dispatches when the user moves the mouse out of a specific component area.
`mouseWheel`	Dispatches when the user scrolls the mouse wheel.
`click`	Dispatches when the user clicks the mouse button.
`doubleClick`	Dispatches when the user double-clicks the mouse button.

Keyboard events:

Event	Description
keyUp	Dispatches when the user releases a key on the keyboard.
keyDown	Dispatches when the user presses a key on the keyboard.

You will learn more about events in Chapter 3. To find more information about various events, visit `http://livedocs.adobe.com/flex/3/html/help.html?content=events_02.html`.

Creating custom events

Along with the built-in Flex events, you can also define your own custom events. To define custom events in MXML, the `[Event]` metadata tag is used. Metadata tags provide information to the Flex compiler that describes how your components are used in a Flex application.

The following is the syntax for the `[Event]` metadata tag:

```
<mx:Metadata>
    [Event(name="eventName", type="package.eventType")]
</mx:Metadata>
```

The `eventName` argument specifies the name of the event. The `eventType` argument specifies the class that defines the event, including the package. Once you define a custom event using the `[Event]` metadata tag, this metadata tag makes the custom event known to the compiler so that it can be referenced into the MXML component declaration. In simple words, the Flex compiler inserts the necessary code for enabling your component to register event listeners while compiling your application. Once you define event metadata, it's your responsibility to dispatch the event from your component. Flex will not dispatch custom events automatically. To dispatch any custom event, use the `dispatchEvent()` method provided by Flex in the following manner:

```
dispatchEvent(new Event("eventName"));
```

You can add event listeners or handlers to custom events in the same way you did previously:

```
<myComp:FooCustomComponent fooEvent="handleFooEvent()"/>
```

In the previous example, `<myComp:FooCustomComponent>` is a custom component that defines a custom event called `fooEvent`. The process of adding event listeners for custom events is similar to adding listeners to Flex events.

Example:

```
<mx:Button click="handleClick()"/>
```

You will learn more about how to use custom events in custom components later in the chapter.

By now, you should have a basic understanding of how to lay out your application, and how to create and handle events in your application. Now, let's understand how data validation and formatting is done in Flex.

Validating and formatting data

When you are building forms for collecting user information, it's often necessary to validate the data entered by the user **on the client** to avoid unnecessary traffic to the server.

You saw how to add the required field indicators (*) in forms using the `required` field property of the `FormItem` control. However, this does not perform any validating; this just adds a red asterisk symbol before the field. To perform validation, you need to implement Flex framework validators.

The Flex framework provides common validators for validating common strings and number-based data, such as phone number, email address, and so on. The following list shows the available validators in Flex for common data entry needs:

Validators	Description
`<mx:CreditCardValidator>`	For validating credit card information
`<mx:CurrencyValidator>`	For currency
`<mx:DateValidator>`	For validating dates
`<mx:EmailValidator>`	For validating email addresses
`<mx:NumberValidator>`	For validating numbers
`<mx:PhoneNumberValidator>`	For validating phone numbers
`<mx:RegExpValidator>`	For validating using Regular Expressions
`<mx:SocialSecurityValidator>`	For validating social security numbers
`<mx:StringValidator>`	For validating basic strings
`<mx:ZipCodeValidator>`	For validating ZIP codes

Let's understand the validator syntax:

```
<mx:EmailValidator id="emailValidator"
   source="{email}"
   property="text"/>
<mx:TextInput id="email"/>
```

Validation tag must be the immediate child of MXML file's root tag. Cannot be defined as the child of any other component inside the root container.

Generally, one validator is created for one field. All validators have the following properties:

- `id`—an instance name for the validator
- `source`—binding to the ID of the field to be validated
- `property`—the name of the field's property to validate
- `required`—specifies that a missing or empty value causes a validation error. It is set to `true` by default

In the previous example, I added a `TextInput` control for demonstrating the validator syntax. Notice that the instance name of email `TextInput` control is `email`. I have used the instance name of `TextInput` for binding with the `property` field of `EmailValidator`, for example `property="{email}"`. This binding ensures that the validator is set for validating the email text field. Also notice that the `source` property of `EmailValidator` is set to `text`, for example `source="text"`. This ensures that the validator will validate the `text` property of the email `TextInput`. It is as good as saying validate the `text` property of the email text box. So whatever text you enter in the email text box will be validated to check if it is a valid email address.

Now that you have understood the general syntax to write validators, it's time to try one example. I will create a Form control for collecting a user's billing details and implement email, phone, and number validators. Let's get started.

1. Open the existing Flex project or create a new one.
2. Create the `Form` control by adding following `TextInput` fields inside the `FormItem` tag:
   - First name
   - Last name
   - Email
   - Phone number

    - Billing address
    - City
    - State
    - ZIP
    - Social security number

3. Make sure that the first name, last name, email, phone number, ZIP, and social security number fields have the `required` property set to `true`.
4. Now, let's start adding validators for each required field immediately after the `<mx:Application>` tag.
5. Remember to add specific validators for specific fields. For example, use `<mx:EmailValidator>` for the **Email** field.
6. And that's it. Now run the application and click on every field to focus and move out of it (to trigger validation).

The code is as follows:

```
<?xml version="1.0" encoding="utf-8"?>
<mx:Application xmlns:mx="http://www.adobe.com/2006/mxml"
layout="vertical">

<!-- validator declaration start -->
   <mx:StringValidator id="fnameValidator"
      source="{fname}"
      property="text"/>
   <mx:StringValidator id="lnameValidator"
      source="{lname}"
      property="text"/>
   <mx:EmailValidator id="emailValidator"
      source="{email}"
      property="text"/>
   <mx:PhoneNumberValidator id="phoneValidator"
      source="{phone}"
      property="text"/>
   <mx:ZipCodeValidator id="zipValidator"
      source="{zip}"
      property="text"/>
   <mx:SocialSecurityValidator id="ssnValidator"
      source="{ssn}"
      property="text"/>
<!-- validator declaration end -->

<!-- form declaration start -->
   <mx:Form>
```

```
        <mx:FormHeading label="Billing Information"/>
        <mx:FormItem label="First Name:" required="true">
           <mx:TextInput id="fname"/>
        </mx:FormItem>
        <mx:FormItem label="Last Name:" required="true">
           <mx:TextInput id="lname"/>
        </mx:FormItem>
        <mx:FormItem label="Email:" required="true">
           <mx:TextInput id="email"/>
        </mx:FormItem>
        <mx:FormItem label="Phone Number:" required="true">
           <mx:TextInput id="phone"/>
        </mx:FormItem>
        <mx:FormItem label="Billing Address:">
           <mx:TextArea id="address"/>
        </mx:FormItem>
        <mx:FormItem label="City:">
           <mx:TextInput id="city"/>
        </mx:FormItem>
        <mx:FormItem label="State:">
           <mx:ComboBox id="state">
              <mx:Array>
                 <mx:String>ALABAMA</mx:String>
                 <mx:String>ALASKA</mx:String>
              </mx:Array>
           </mx:ComboBox>
        </mx:FormItem>
        <mx:FormItem label="ZIP:" required="true">
           <mx:TextInput id="zip"/>
        </mx:FormItem>
        <mx:FormItem label="Social Security Number:" required="true">
           <mx:TextInput id="ssn"/>
        </mx:FormItem>
        <mx:FormItem>
           <mx:Button id="mySubmit" label="Submit"/>
        </mx:FormItem>
    </mx:Form>
<!-- form declaration end -->
</mx:Application>
```

Notice that when you set the focus on any field and move out without typing anything, it displays a red border around that field:

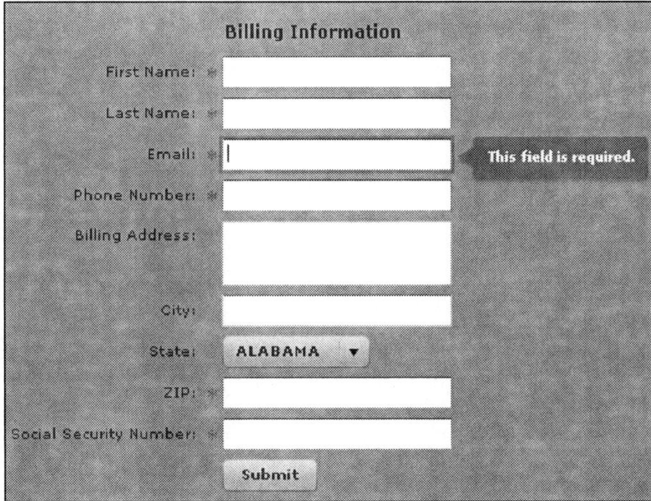

When you move your mouse over the field, it displays an error message. These are the default error messages set for every validator. These default error messages can also be customized by setting the specific validator's error message properties.

In `<mx:EmailValidator>`, to change the default error message (**This field is required**), set the `requiredFieldError` property of `<mx:EmailValidator>` (for example, `requiredFieldError="Enter email address"`). The `requiredFieldError` property is derived from the `Validator` class. Similarly, you can also set a `missingAtSignError` property to your own message to change the error message when users do not enter the @ symbol in the email address. This is shown in the following screenshot:

The code is as follows:

```
<mx:EmailValidator id="emailValidator"
   source="{email}"
   property="text"
   requiredFieldError="Enter email address."
   missingAtSignError="Please enter an at sign(@)in email address."/>
```

By default, Flex uses the `valueCommit` event to trigger validations, that is, usually when components lose their focus. You can change this default behavior by using the `trigger` and `triggerEvent` properties of validator to trigger the validation on a specific event of a specific object. The `trigger` property specifies the component name that is generating the event that triggers the validation. By specifying the event name in the `triggerEvent` property, you can instruct the validator as to when to trigger the validation.

Let's quickly look at how this is done.

You need to add two more properties to the validator. They are:

- `trigger`—binding to the ID of the object instance that will trigger the validation
- `triggerEvent`—The name of the event on the trigger object that will trigger the validation

Example:

```
<mx:EmailValidator id="emailValidator"
   source="{email}"
   property="text"
   trigger="{mySubmit}"
   triggerEvent="click"/>
```

In the previous example, the email validator will be triggered when the user clicks on the **Submit** button.

Please go through Flex API documentation for more information on validator-specific error message properties.

[Flex Builder shortcut to open Flex API documentation: Select a component syntax on which you need help and then press *Shift+F2* to open the Flex API documentation.]

Restricting user entry

Sometimes while designing user entry forms, you need to restrict the user from entering certain type of data into the field. For example, you might want to allow the user to enter only numbers or letters, or a combination of both, and want to restrict special character entries. This is achieved using the `restrict` property of the `TextInput` field.

The following is an example of restricting the user to enter only numbers and alphabets, and no special characters:

```
<mx:FormItem label="First Name:" required="true">
   <mx:TextInput id="fname" restrict="[A-Za-z0-9]"/>
</mx:FormItem>
```

You can use regular expressions to restrict the user entry in the field. However, this property only restricts user interaction; the user can put any text into a text field using ActionScript. To know more about the `restrict` property and its expression, see the Flex language reference documentation for the `TextInput` control.

Formatting

Sometimes the client needs to perform some formatting of raw data in order to display proper data on screen (such as dates). In Flex, you use formatter classes to format data into strings.

The Flex framework provides the following different types of formatter classes:

Formatters	Description
`<mx:CurrencyFormatter/>`	Used to format currencies
`<mx:DateFormatter/>`	Used to format dates
`<mx:NumberFormatter/>`	Used to format numbers
`<mx:PhoneFormatter/>`	Used to format phone numbesr
`<mx:ZipCodeFormatter/>`	Used to format ZIP codes

In the following example, I will use `<mx:DateFormatter>` to format raw date information into a formatted date string. When using `DateFormatter`, you have to specify the `formatString` property. It specifies the appropriate formatting for the `DateFormatter` class. For example, `MMMM D, YYYY` will format the date as **September 18, 2008**. To see more pattern strings, go through the language reference for `DateFormatter`.

Example of date formatting:

```
<?xml version="1.0" encoding="utf-8"?>
<mx:Application xmlns:mx="http://www.adobe.com/2006/mxml"
layout="vertical">
   <mx:Script>
      <![CDATA[
         [Bindable]
         public var currentDate:Date = new Date();
      ]]>
```

```
    </mx:Script>
    <mx:DateFormatter id="dateFormatter" formatString="MMMM D, YYYY"/>
    <mx:Label text="Before Formatting:"/>
    <mx:Label text="{currentDate}"/>
    <mx:Label text="After Formatting:"/>
    <mx:Label text="{dateFormatter.format(currentDate)}"/>
</mx:Application>
```

The previous example looks like this when you run it:

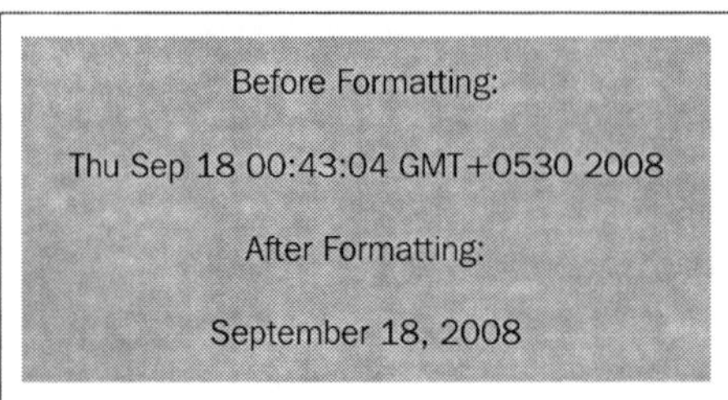

Similarly, you can also create other formatters, for example, `CurrencyFormatter` or `PhoneFormatter`, and so on.

> Notice the `[Bindable]` and `{}` curly brackets in the text property. This is called a Bindable metadata tag and data binding. You will learn about binding mechanisms in our next section.

Data binding

Data binding is the process of tying the data of one object to another object. This is a very convenient way to tie data sources with the Flex component without worrying about how to update components if data source changes dynamically. When you use data binding, the destination object gets updated automatically if the source object changes. It may sound very confusing at this point, but let me give you a simple example.

In the following example, I will use the `TextInput` and `Label` controls, and bind the `TextInput` control's `text` property with the `Label` control's `text` property. So whenever you change text in the `TextInput` control, it will automatically reflect in the `Label` control's `text` property.

Example of data binding:

```
<?xml version="1.0" encoding="utf-8"?>
<mx:Application xmlns:mx="http://www.adobe.com/2006/mxml">
    <mx:TextInput id="myTextBox"/>
    <mx:Label id="myLabel" text="{myTextBox.text}»/>
</mx:Application>
```

And that's it. You have successfully implemented the data binding concept. If you run the above example and type some text in the text box, then you will notice that the same text is automatically copied into the label.

Flex provides three ways to specify data binding—the curly braces ({}) syntax in MXML, the `<mx:Binding>` tag in MXML, and the `BindingUtils` methods in ActionScript. All three do the same thing of dynamically tying data sources with destinations. In the previous example, I have used curly braces ({ }) to show data binding.

The property name inside the curly braces is the source property of the binding expression. When the value of the source property changes, Flex copies the current value of the source property, that is `myTextBox.text`, to the destination property—the `Label` control `text` property.

You can also use data binding to bind data from complex data types, such as arrays. In order to do that, you will need to know the available properties or data in an object. In the following example, I will show you how to bind an array of objects with `ComboBox` control's `dataProvider`, and how to bind ComboBox's selected element's properties with other controls. The following example is a bit complex, but it is very important to understand the data binding concept, so take your time to digest this example.

The `dataProvider` property defines the external data variable that will be used to populate the control.

Example of using complex data structures like Array in data binding:

```
<?xml version="1.0" encoding="utf-8"?>
<mx:Application xmlns:mx="http://www.adobe.com/2006/mxml" creationComp
lete="init();">
    <mx:Script>
        <![CDATA[
            [Bindable]
            private var contactDetails:Array = new Array();

            private function init():void {
```

```
                contactDetails.push({name:"John", phone:"+442768574629",
                                     email:"john@email.com"});
                contactDetails.push({name:"Joe", phone:"+445632564367",
                                     email:"joe@email.com"});
                contactDetails.push({name:"Steve", phone:"+445632564367",
                                     email:"steve@email.com"});
            }
        ]]>
    </mx:Script>
    <mx:Form>
        <mx:FormItem label="Select Contact">
            <mx:ComboBox id="contacts" dataProvider="{contactDetails}"
                         labelField="name"/>
        </mx:FormItem>
        <mx:FormItem label="Name:">
            <mx:TextInput id="firstName" text="{contacts.selectedItem.
                                               name}"/>
        </mx:FormItem>
        <mx:FormItem label="Phone Number:">
            <mx:TextInput id="phoneNumber" text="{contacts.selectedItem.
                                                 phone}"/>
        </mx:FormItem>
        <mx:FormItem label="Email Address:">
            <mx:TextInput id="emailAddress" text="{contacts.selectedItem.
                                                  email}"/>
        </mx:FormItem>
    </mx:Form>
</mx:Application>
```

The `labelField` property inside the `<mx:ComboBox>` contact is used to choose a specific field from `dataProvider` to display as a label of a control. In the above example, the `ComboBox` control is using `name` as its `labelField`. Note that the `dataProvider` `contactDtails` array contains objects which have a property called `name`. Thus, `ComboBox` will be filled in with all the name property values for all objects in the array.

Note that I did not add any event listeners or handlers in order to create automatic data update functionality. Flex creates broadcaster/listener methods automatically and listens for the changes in the bound value, and immediately reflects it everywhere that the value is bound.

In the previous example, you will notice a couple of new things, such as the [Bindable] metadata tag. This tag tells the Flex compiler that this variable will be used for data binding so that the compiler can add broadcaster and listener methods to detect a value change.

You can use the <mx:Binding> tag as an alternative to the curly braces syntax. When you use the <mx:Binding> tag, you provide a source property in the <mx:Binding> tag's source property, and a destination property in its destination property. The following example uses the <mx:Binding> tag to define data binding from a TextInput control to a Label control:

```
<?xml version="1.0" encoding="utf-8"?>
<mx:Application xmlns:mx="http://www.adobe.com/2006/mxml">
    <mx:TextInput id="myTextBox"/>
    <mx:Label id="myLabel"/>
    <mx:Binding source="myTextBox.text" destination="myLabel.text"/>
</mx:Application>
```

In contrast to the curly braces syntax, you can use the <mx:Binding> tag to completely separate the view (user interface) from the model. And it also lets you bind multiple source properties to the same destination property because you can specify multiple <mx:Binding> tags with the same destination.

Using the [Bindable] metadata tag

By using the [bindable] metadata tag, you instruct the Flex compiler to add code in your application or component to detect any changes in the source property. If change is detected, Flex copies the source property value into the destination property. The [Bindable] tag is used to signal Flex to perform this copy action. When [Bindable] is used, the Flex compiler automatically generates PropertyChangeEvent and PropertyWatcher code to detect any changes.

You can use the [Bindable] metadata tag in the following different ways:

```
[Bindable]

[Bindable(event="event_name")]
```

The only difference between both syntaxes is that if you do not specify an event name, then Flex automatically creates propertyChangeEvent for you.

You can use the [Bindable] metadata tag inside MXML to make all public variables the source of data binding by including the [Bindable] metadata tag in the <mx:Metadata> block. This is shown in the following code snippets:

```
<mx:Metadata>
   [Bindable]
</mx:MetaData>
```

Or

```
<mx:Metadata>
   [Bindable(event="event_name")]
</mx:MetaData>
```

You can also use the [Bindable] metadata tag inside the <mx:Script> block of MXML to make individual properties the source of data-binding expression, as shown in the following code snippet:

```
<mx:Script>
   [Bindable]
   public var fooProperty:String = "fooValue";
</mx:Script>
<mx:TextInput text={fooProperty}/>
```

However, by default, you can use any property as a source of data-binding expression. Flex performs data binding when the application starts, but it will not be able to detect any change in that property until it is defined as bindable using metadata tag. You cannot declare constant properties as bindable for the very obvious reason that they are constants and cannot be changed.

When you declare any object or property as bindable, Flex not only monitors it for changes but its children properties as well. For example, you may have a bindable object that contains another two properties. So you can use the source object's child as the source of the data-binding expression, as shown in the following snippet:

```
<mx:TextInput text={book.author}/>
```

Or

```
<mx:TextInput text={book.author.firstName}/>
```

This is known as bindable property chains and you can have fairly long property chains.

You can use the `[Bindable]` metadata tag ActionScript (about which you will learn in detail in the next chapter) in the following places:

- Before the public class definition to make the entire class and its public properties bindable

  For example:

  ```
  [Bindable]
  Public class FooClass extends FooBase {}
  ```

- Before a public, protected, or private variable of class, to make that specific variable support binding

  For example:

  ```
  [Bindable]
  Public var foo:String;
  ```

- Before a public, protected, or private variable's setter and getter method

In ActionScript, you can use setter and getter methods to hide your property from public access. You can use the `[Bindable]` metadata tag before a setter or getter method.

Example:

```
[Bindable]
public function set firstName(val:Boolean):void {}
public function get firstName():Boolean {}
```

The getter and setter methods in ActionScript are equivalent of `getFirstName` and `setFirstName` in Java. If you just define the setter method, you create a write-only property that you cannot use as the source of any data-binding expression. If you just define the getter method, you create a read-only property that you can use as the source of a data-binding expression without using the `[Bindable]` metadata tag. You will learn more about setter and getter methods in Chapter 3.

Creating MXML custom components

So far, you have used only default components available in Flex. Though Flex provides a vast variety of simple and complex components as part of its SDK, sometimes you need to create your own. For example, you might want to add some functionality to the existing component, or you might want to build a reusable component.

For example, if you are creating registration and billing information forms, then you might want to show the `ComboBox` component for selecting the country in the home address section, as well as in the billing address section. Creating two different `ComboBox` components and adding the country list to it in two places is not a good way forward. Instead, we will create an MXML component that can be reused in the billing address and home address sections.

To create a custom MXML component in Flex Builder, follow these steps:

1. Open the existing Flex project or create a new one.
2. Click and select **File | New | MXML Component** from the menu bar. It will open a **New MXML Component** dialog box, as shown in the following screenshot:

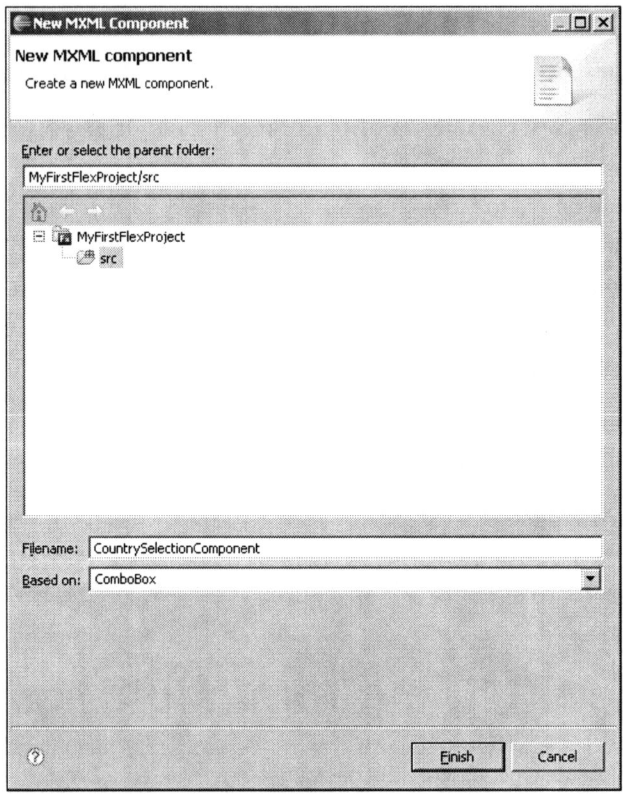

3. Enter a **Filename** and select the base component for your component. The base component could be any Flex component on which you want to design your component. I have given a Filename of **CountrySelectionComponent** and selected `ComboBox` in the **Based on** field. Click on the **Finish** button to create your MXML file. Notice that the MXML file is created with root tag `<mx:ComboBox>` and with the Flex default namespace `xmlns:mx="http://www.adobe.com/2006/mxml"`. The default namespace must be specified in root tag of your MXML file:

```
<?xml version="1.0" encoding="utf-8"?>
<mx:ComboBox xmlns:mx="http://www.adobe.com/2006/mxml">

</mx:ComboBox>
```

4. Now, we will add the country list to this `ComboBox` using the `dataProvider` property. This is shown in the following code:

```
<?xml version="1.0" encoding="utf-8"?>
<mx:ComboBox xmlns:mx="http://www.adobe.com/2006/mxml">
   <mx:dataProvider>
      <mx:String>India</mx:String>
      <mx:String>United Kingdom</mx:String>
      <mx:String>United States</mx:String>
      <!-- Add other country list -->
   </mx:dataProvider>
</mx:ComboBox>
```

5. You can now reference and use the **CountrySelectionComponent** from your main application as shown here:

```
<?xml version="1.0" encoding="utf-8"?>
<mx:Application xmlns:mx="http://www.adobe.com/2006/mxml" xmlns:
myComp="*">
   <myComp:CountrySelectionComponent/>
</mx:Application>
```

In the example above, the main application file includes a new namespace definition of `xmlns:myComp="*"` as a part of the `<mx:Application>` tag. This namespace definition specifies the location of the MXML component. In this case, it specifies that the component is in the same directory as the main application file.

As best practice, store all your custom components in a subdirectory under your source folder. You will learn more about development directory structure in Chapter 6, *Packaging and Deployment*.

Now let's create a little more advanced MXML component. This MXML component will be used for displaying book information. It will contain a book image, title, author, price, and description fields, and will display book information dynamically based on selected books from `ComboBox`. This component will dispatch a custom event when the user clicks on the **add to cart** button.

1. Let's start by creating a custom component MXML file and naming it `BookDetails.mxml`. This custom component is based on `HBox` and it is saved in the `src` directory.

```
<?xml version="1.0" encoding="utf-8"?>
<mx:HBox xmlns:mx="http://www.adobe.com/2006/mxml" width="440"
height="154" borderThickness="4" borderStyle="solid"
borderColor="#404AAF" cornerRadius="8">
    <mx:Metadata>
        [Event(name="addToCart", type="flash.events.Event")]
    </mx:Metadata>
    <mx:Script>
        <![CDATA[
            import mx.controls.Alert;
             [Bindable]
            public var bookInfo:Object;
             [Bindable]
             [Embed(source="../assets/images/cart.gif")]
            public var cartImage:Class;
            private function addToCardEventDispatcher():void {
                dispatchEvent(new Event("addToCart"));
            }
        ]]>
    </mx:Script>
    <mx:Image id="bookImage" source="{bookInfo.image}"
height="100%" width="106" maintainAspectRatio="false"/>
    <mx:VBox height="100%" width="100%">
        <mx:HBox width="100%">
            <mx:Label id="bookTitle" text="{bookInfo.title}"/>
            <mx:Spacer width="100%"/>
            <mx:Button icon="{cartImage}" width="18" height="18" clic
k="addToCardEventDispatcher();"/>
            </mx:HBox>
        <mx:Label id="bookAuthor" text="By {bookInfo.author}"/>
        <mx:Label id="coverPrice" text="{bookInfo.price}"/>
        <mx:TextArea id="bookDetails" width="100%" text="{bookInfo.
description}" height="100%"
editable="false" cornerRadius="8"/>
    </mx:VBox>
</mx:HBox>
```

The `BookDetails.mxml` custom component defines its own properties and a custom event called `addToCart` using the `[Event]` metadata. And notice that I'm dispatching the `addToCart` event on the button's `click` event.

> Also note that I have used a new metadata tag `[Embed]` to add a custom icon for the button control. The `[Embed]` tag is used to embed external assets into a Flex application—such as a sound, image, or font—that are included in a SWF file at compile time. Embedding an asset instead of loading it dynamically ensures that it will be available at runtime, but at the cost of increased SWF file size.

2. Now create an MXML application file to use this custom component and handle the `addToCart` custom event:

```
<?xml version="1.0" encoding="utf-8"?>
<mx:Application xmlns:mx="http://www.adobe.com/2006/mxml" xmlns:
myComp="*" creationComplete="init();">
   <mx:Script>
      <![CDATA[
         import mx.controls.Alert;
         public var booksArray:Array = new Array();

         private function init():void {
            //Populating Array with default book data
            booksArray.push({
               title:"Linux Thin Client",
               author:"David Richards",
               price:"Rs.1200",
               image:"../assets/images/1847192041.jpg",
               description:"A quick guide for System
                            Administrators"
            });
            booksArray.push({
               title:"CUPS Administrative Guide",
               author:"Ankur Shah",
               price:"Rs.800",
               image:"../assets/images/1847192580.jpg",
               description:"A practical tutorial to installing,
                            managing, and securing this powerful
                            printing system"
            });
            //Assign booksArray to the dataProvider property of
              ComboBox
            booksCombo.dataProvider = booksArray;
         }
```

```
            private function addToCardHandler():void {
                Alert.show("Book successfully added to shopping
                            cart.");
            }
        ]]>
    </mx:Script>
    <mx:ComboBox prompt="Select a book to preview" id="booksCombo"
                 labelField="title"
        change="bookPreview.bookInfo = booksCombo.selectedItem"/>
    <myComp:BookDetails id="bookPreview"
                        addToCart="addToCardHandler();"/>
</mx:Application>
```

3. Compile and run the application using Flex Builder and select a book from `ComboBox`. It will populate a selected book's details into the custom component, as shown in the following screenshot:

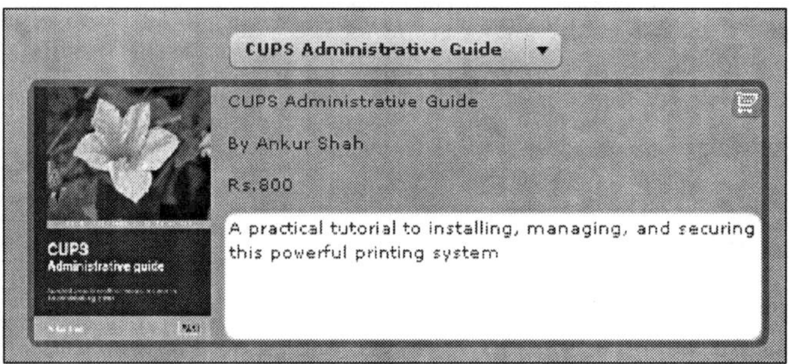

4. Now click on the green button in the top right corner. This will dispatch the `addToCart` custom event. Notice that now you are able to see an alert dialog box appearing on screen from the event handler method `addToCardHandler`, as shown in the following screenshot:

So far, in this section, you have learned to create simple and advanced custom MXML components. Creating custom components is a vast subject itself, so I have covered only major aspects of it. To know more about custom component creation, I suggest you read the Flex documentation at `http://livedocs.adobe.com/flex/3/html/help.html?content=Part1_intro_1.html`.

Understanding Flex itemRenderers

Flex provides a number of components to display and handle large amounts of data in a variety of ways, for example data grid with rows and columns. Apart from providing these rich components, Flex provides a very useful way to customize how these components display their content using `itemRenderers` by giving you complete control over each row or cell. There are `List`, `DataGrid`, and `Tree` controls. By default, these list controls display the data they are given as simple text.

Example of default behavior of List box control:

```
<?xml version="1.0" encoding="utf-8"?>
<mx:Application xmlns:mx="http://www.adobe.com/2006/mxml" applicationC
omplete="init();">

    <mx:Script>
        <![CDATA[
            [Bindable]
            private var contactDetails:Array = new Array();

            private function init():void {
                contactDetails.push({name:"John", phone:"+442768574629",
email:"john@email.com"});
                contactDetails.push({name:"Joe", phone:"+445632564367",
email:"joe@email.com"});
                contactDetails.push({name:"Steve", phone:"+445632564367",
email:"steve@email.com"});

                theList.dataProvider = contactDetails;
            }
        ]]>
    </mx:Script>

    <mx:List id="theList" labelField="name" width="286" height="190"/>
</mx:Application>
```

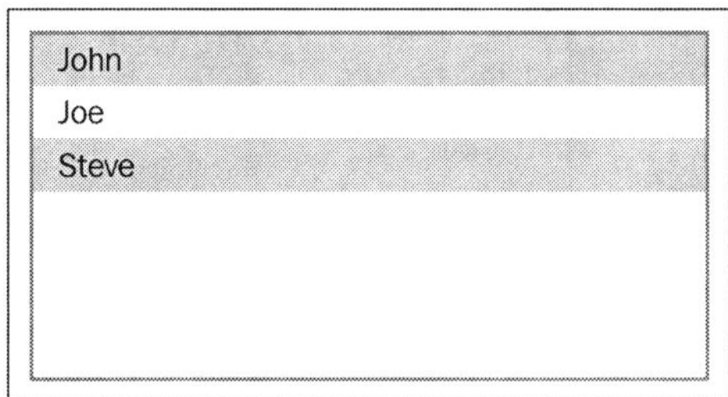

The list-based controls have a default item renderer that controls how it displays the data. By default, content is rendered as simple text. In many scenarios, simple text rendering isn't sufficient to display the content. In these cases, you can use custom item renderers to customize the default display behavior of the component.

Let's examine one such scenario where we need to display three different property values in a single item from the data provider object and highlight it with different colors. This would not be possible with default List control's default display behavior. But by using `itemRenderers`, you can customize the way List box displays its content.

You can use `itemRenderers` in three different ways:

- Drop-in `itemRenderers`: Many of the Flex's built-in controls can be used as item renderers. In short, you can specify Flex's built-in control as the `itemRenderer` value.
- Inline `itemRenderers`: Inline `itemRenderers` are those that are written directly inside the MXML code as a part of a component declaration.
- Component `itemRenderers`: External `itemRenders` are separate custom components used as the `itemRenderer` of the component.

Drop-in itemRenderers

Refer the following example:

```
<mx:List id="theList" itemRenderer="mx.controls.TextInput" width="286"
height="190">
```

The code above uses Flex's TextInput control as item renderer of List control, which basically renders a text box as a list item.

Inline itemRenderers

Here is an example to change the font to red:

```
<mx:List id="theList" width="286" height="190">
   <mx:itemRenderer>
      <mx:Component>
         <mx:HBox>
            <mx:Label text="{data.name}" color="green"/>
            <mx:Label text="{data.email}" color="blue"/>
            <mx:Label text="{data.phone}" color="red"/>
         </mx:HBox>
      </mx:Component>
   </mx:itemRenderer>
</mx:List>
```

This `itemRenderer` is very simple and basic, but it is good enough to give you a sense of what itemRenderers can do. To define an inline `itemRenderer` for a component, use a `<mx:itemRenderer>` tag inside the `<mx:List>` component. Now, define the desired itemRenderer component you want to use. You can typically use any Flex component as an itemRenderer. In this case, I am using `<mx:Hbox>` with three `<mx:Label>`, with its text field set to a data-binding expression: `data.name` and `data.email`. **This is very important.** The List control sets each `itemRenderer` instance's `data` property with a record from `dataProvider`. So, in the example above, it means that for any given row of the list, the inline `itemRenderer` instance will have its `data` property set to a single contact object from the `contactDetails` array.

In other words, the `itemRenderer` instance of row 1 has its `data.name` set to John's contact details, row 2 is set to Joe's contact details, and so on. Flex does not create `itemRenderer` instances for every row in List, instead it creates instances only for visible rows. For example, if your list box has got 100 rows and only 10 are visible, then Flex creates only 10 instances of `itemRenderer` and reuses it every time you scroll through it.

External itemRenderers

The following are the steps used to create an external `itemRenderer`:

1. Create custom `itemRenderer` MXML component and name it `CustomItemRenderer.mxml`.

```
<?xml version="1.0" encoding="utf-8"?>
<mx:HBox xmlns:mx="http://www.adobe.com/2006/mxml">
   <mx:Label text="{data.name}" color="green"/>
   <mx:Label text="{data.email}" color="blue"/>
   <mx:Label text="{data.phone}" color="red"/>
</mx:HBox>
```

2. Save custom component MXML file in the same folder where your application MXML is stored.
3. Change your application MXML code and add the following List control declaration in it:

```
<mx:List id="theList" itemRenderer="CustomItemRenderer"
width="286" height="190"/>
```

Note that the `itemRenderer` property of `<mx:List>` is set to `CustomItemRenderer`. Please make sure that you set this property with the complete package name of your custom component if you have used that package in your custom component.

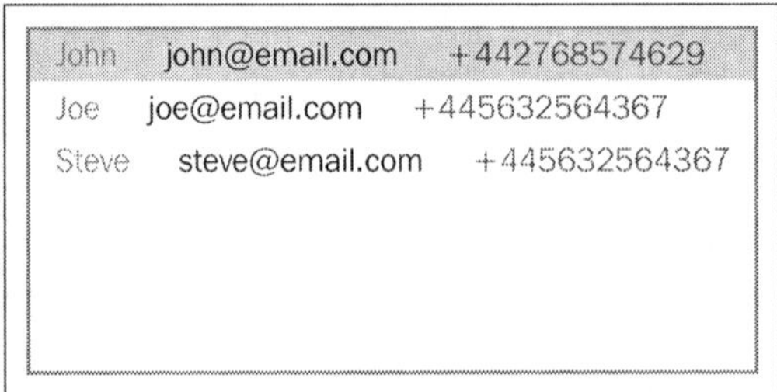

Summary

In this chapter, you learned how Flex works and how to layout applications. You also learned about MXML, MXML components and containers, handling and creating custom events, and using `itemRenderers`. In the next chapter, you will learn about ActionScript 3.0 language and its features, and how to use ActionScript with MXML.

3

Introduction to ActionScript 3.0

ActionScript 3.0 is a powerful, object-oriented programming language. It is one of the core languages used for building Flex applications. As a robust programming language, Actionscript 3.0 enables developers to build very efficient, seamless, and data-rich interactive applications in Flex. ActionScript 3.0 integrates well with Macromedia Flex Markup Language (MXML) scripting to give developers an extra edge to develop **Rich Internet applications** (RIAs).

ActionScript 3.0 is based on ECMAScript—the international standardized programming language for scripting. ActionScript 3.0 is compliant with the ECMAScript Language Specification (`http://www.ecma-international.org/publications/standards/Ecma-262.htm`).

ActionScript 3.0 is usually used to add interactivity and behavior in Flex applications alongside MXML. However, you can also build only ActionScript 3.0 based applications using Flex Builder. The ActionScript 3.0 programming model will be familiar to developers with a basic knowledge of object-oriented programming.

If you are a Java developer, then you will instantly notice many similarities between ActionScript 3.0 and Java, such as syntaxes, object-oriented concepts like implementing interfaces and extending classes, and so on. Syntaxes in ActionScript 3.0 are more or less the same as in Java with few differences which might take a little time for you to get used to, but I am sure you will enjoy programming in ActionScript 3.0.

Let's go through the important language features of ActionScript 3.0.

ActionScript 3.0 language features

The ActionScript 3.0 language has been architecturally and conceptually improved in many ways since its previous 1.0 and 2.0 versions. ActionScript 3.0 not only delivers on object-oriented concepts, but it also makes it possible to write highly scalable and performing applications. In this section, we will discuss some of the important features of ActionScript 3.0 language that speed up the development.

Strict data typing

ActionScript 3.0 requires strict data typing of variables, arguments, function returns, and so on. Data typing was introduced in ActionScript 2.0, but it was optional. Now, ActionScript 3.0 enforces strict data typing. This enforcement improves error reporting and checking while you are coding. This also helps to reduce memory usage, since the type of information represents variables in the native machine's representation.

Runtime exceptions

ActionScript 3.0 introduces many improved and new runtime exceptions for common error conditions. These runtime exceptions display the stack trace, making it easier to find the root cause of the error, improving the debugging experience. This allows applications to handle errors robustly.

Sealed classes and dynamic classes

In Java, if you create a particular class instance, then you cannot change its properties and methods at runtime. In ActionScript 3.0, such classes are called **sealed classes**. In ActionScript 3.0, all classes are sealed at runtime unless you define them as dynamic classes, which allows you to programmatically add public properties and methods.

Method closure

In ActionScript 3.0, methods are now bound to their respective class instances and they automatically remember their original object instance—the method will execute in `this` object scope. This allows efficient event handling by eliminating the need for delegates.

XML and E4X

In ActionScript 3.0, XML is a native data type and it handles XML using the E4X standard. E4X is an XPath- and XQuery-like language for manipulating XML documents based on ECMA standards.

New primitive data types

ActionScript 3.0 adds new `int` type—a 32-bit signed integer that lets ActionScript code take advantage of the fast integer math capabilities of the CPU. Another new type is `uint`—an unsigned 32-bit integer type similar to `int`.

Regular expressions

ActionScript 3.0 includes native support for regular expressions so you can quickly search for and manipulate strings. ActionScript 3.0 implements the regular expressions defined in the ECMAScript Language Specification.

Object-oriented programming

This is the last but not the least feature; if you are coming from an ActionScript 2.0 background, then unlike ActionScript 2.0, you will find that ActionScript 3.0 is fully compliant with object-oriented programming concepts and its features, such as interfaces, classes, inheritance, and so on.

Now, after understanding language features, let's take a look at ActionScript 3.0 core concepts one by one.

ActionScript 3.0 fundamentals

Originally, ActionScript was developed as a way for Flash developers to program interactivity in Flash applications. Since then, it has evolved from being a minor programming language to its current form as a sophisticated object-oriented programming language. However, before you start writing code, you need to understand some fundamental concepts of ActionScript 3.0.

As you progress through this book, you will see these concepts in action. However, having knowledge about OO programming would be an added benefit. If you have done any programming in Java or any other OOP language, then you will quickly pick up speed.

Variables

Variables are used to store temporary values during the execution of your application. To declare a variable in ActionScript 3.0, you must use the `var` keyword followed by the variable name. You can declare a variable with or without a value. Variables are declared and set with a statement, as shown here:

```
<variable_scope> var <variable_name> : <data_type> = <value>;
```

For example:

```
public var color:String = "Blue";
```

The string value `Blue` is assigned to the `color` variable. The semicolon at the end of the line alerts ActionScript that this is the end of the statement.

The technique is to assign a value to a variable at the time it is declared; it is commonly used for assigning a primitive value to a variable. A similar technique can be used to declare arrays, as shown here:

```
var numArray:Array = ["zero", "one", "two"];
```

You can also declare a variable without assigning any value, as shown below:

```
public var color:String;
```

The above declaration assigns a default value to the variable. A default value is the value that a variable contains before you set its value. If you declare a variable without setting its value, then it remains uninitialized. The value of an uninitialized variable depends on its data type. The following table describes the default values of variables, organized by data type:

Data Type	Default Value
`Boolean`	`false`
`int`	`0`
`Number`	`NaN` (Not a Number)
`Object`	`null`
`String`	`null`
`uint`	`0`
Not declared (equivalent to type annotation *)	`undefined`
All other classes, including user-defined classes.	`null`

If you declare a variable, but do not declare its data type, the default data type * will apply, which actually means that the variable is untyped. Also, if you do not initialize an untyped variable with a value, its default value is `undefined`.

Any variable without scope will be scoped to the default namespace, that is, `internal`, and it will not be visible outside of this package.

Variable names cannot contain spaces, but underscores are often used instead to split up words in a variable name. Variables cannot be the same as reserved words, which are ActionScript keywords, such as `for`, `while`, and `if`.

[**Caution**: ActionScript is a case-sensitive language, so `color` is different from `Color`.]

Access modifiers

Access modifiers are used to specify access control restrictions on both functions and variables. The modifiers will state who has access to something, and who does not have access to it.

There are four special access modifiers in ActionScript 3.0: `public`, `private`, `protected`, and `internal`.

The following table lists a set of access modifiers and special attributes that can be used to control access of functions and variables:

Attribute	Definition
`internal` (default)	Visible to references inside the same package
`public`	Visible to references everywhere
`private`	Visible to references in the same class
`protected`	Visible to references in the same class and derived classes

For example, the following code defines access modifiers to the variable and function:

```
public var color:String = "red";
```

Or

```
public function getColor():void {…}
```

Packages

In ActionScript 3.0, packages are used for logically grouping sets of classes and interfaces. Packages are also useful for organizing code and avoiding name conflicts. A package represents a physical directory structure where you create and maintain your source files. In ActionScript 3.0, you can declare a package using `package` statement and define a class inside it by enclosing it in { } curly braces. Packages can be defined delimited by the `.` (dot) character (for example, `vehicle.car`) and each delimited package name represents an independent physical region. You need to keep your ActionScript files under the same folder names as it is defined in the package declaration. In this case, you will need to create two nested folders **vehicle | car** and place your ActionScript files there.

Let's take a look at its syntax:

```
package packageName {
   public class ClassName {
      ...
   }
}
```

All package definitions start with the `package` keyword and are followed by the package name. By convention, package names start with lowercase and classes start with uppercase. Curly braces ({ and }) are used to mark the beginning and end of package content. Hence, to add a class to a package, you insert the class declaration between these curly braces. And because the class is inside the package, the compiler automatically qualifies the class name at compile time into its fully qualified name: `packageName.ClassName`.

ActionScript 3.0 allows you to write multiple classes inside one source file, but only one class can be defined under `package` declaration to make it visible outside package; any additional classes needs to be defined outside of package declaration and these classes will not be visible outside package.

Classes and interfaces

Every object-oriented language is based on classes, interfaces, and objects, and ActionScript 3.0 is no different; you can define classes, interfaces, and create object instances much as you do in Java or the C# world.

Classes

In ActionScript 3.0, all public classes must be defined under the packages declaration and, as best practice, you should scope your classes. If you do not scope your class, then compiler will autoscope your classes to the `internal` scope. You will learn more about scoping further in this chapter.

Let's take a look at a class in ActionScript 3.0:

```
package cars
{
    public class BMW
    {
        public function BMW()
        {
        }
    }
}
```

The class definition starts with the `class` keyword followed by the class name and curly braces to mark its beginning and end, as shown in the previous example. Classes may also contain properties and methods as part of its declaration. In the previous example, the `BMW` class is defined under the `cars` package.

Interfaces

In ActionScript 3.0, declaration of interfaces is similar to the Java interface declaration. Let's look at the following interface declaration example:

```
package cars
{
   public interface IBaseVehicle
   {
      function start():void;
      function stop():void;
      function reverse():void;
   }
}
```

Interfaces start with the `interface` keyword followed by the interface name. By convention, and for good coding practice in ActionScript 3.0, interfaces start with a capital I letter and an interface can only be declared as `public` or `internal`. In ActionScript 3.0, interface members cannot be declared as `public`, `private`, `protected`, or `internal`. Unlike Java, ActionScript 3.0 interfaces cannot have variables or constant declarations. However, you can have setter and getter methods.

Implementing an interface in a class

Use the `implements` keyword in your class definition to implement one or more interfaces (use `,` (comma) to separate interfaces if you are implementing more than one interface).

```
package cars
{
   public class BMW implements IBaseVehicle
   {
      private var color:String;
      public function BMW()
      {
      }
      public function start():void {}
      public function stop():void {}
      public function reverse():void {}
   }
}
```

In the above example, the `BMW` class implements the `IBaseVehicle` interface for its three methods.

Inheriting classes

Like Java, in ActionScript 3.0, you can use the `extend` keyword in a class declaration for inheriting classes. For example:

```
public class BMW extends FourWheeler {}
```

Though there are no fundamental differences between Java and ActionScript 3.0 inheritance concepts, there are some syntactical differences that a developer needs to be aware of, such as for overriding a method in ActionScript 3.0, you have to use the `override` keyword before the overridden method declaration, as shown in the following example snippet:

```
public class Animal
{
    public function Speak():String
    {
        return "No Language";
    }
}
```

The above class is a base class which defines a method called `Speak` that returns a string. Next, we will declare two classes by inheriting them from the `Animal` class.

```
public class Dog extends Animal
{
    override public function Speak():String
    {
        return "Bark!";
    }
}
```

And

```
public class Cat extends Animal
{
    override public function Speak():String
    {
        return "Meow!";
    }
}
```

Above, both `Dog` and `Cat` classes are inherited from the `Animal` base class using the `extends` keyword, and both the classes use the `override` the keyword to override `Speak` method, as highlighted in the above code blocks. A call to `Dog`'s `Speak` method will result into `Bark` and a call to `Cat`'s `Speak` method will result into `Meow`.

Functions and methods

Functions in ActionScript 3.0 can be defined as either **named** or **anonymous**. A function can take zero (0) or more parameters and they return an optional single value.

Methods are simply another name for the functions when they are part of a class. However, the difference between both is that methods are tightly linked with their associated class objects, so unlike functions, methods cannot be used apart from the instance to which they are attached.

Methods and functions are defined using the `function` keyword and they return either nothing (`void`) or a single value. A function's return type is specified after colon (`:`).

There are two ways in ActionScript 3.0 to define functions—using **function statements** and using **function expressions**.

The function statement is more of a static way of defining functions using the `function` keyword followed by function name and then return type, as shown in the following example:

```
private function fooFunction(param1:String, param2:int):void
{
   //Function body
}
```

The function expression is more of a dynamic way of defining functions using the `var` keyword followed by:

- Variable/function name
- The colon operator (`:`) and variable type as `Function` class
- The assignment operator (=)
- The `function` keyword and optional comma delimited parameter list enclosed inside parentheses
- The colon operator (`:`) and the return type of the function
- Then followed by function body enclosed in curly braces

The function expressions are also known as anonymous functions or function literals. Function expression example:

```
public var fooFunction:Function = function (param1:String, param2:
int):void
{
   //Function body
}
```

In most cases, you would want to use a function statement instead of function expressions for the following reasons:

- It is more concise and easy to read
- It allows you to use the `override` and `final` keywords
- They are strongly linked with their original class instance

Named functions

A named function is just what it sounds like; you are defining a function by giving it a name. By convention, function names start with lowercase and functions follow similar rules to naming variables, such as:

- Function names should be descriptive enough to indicate their purpose
- Function names should start with alphabet characters, and should not contain spaces and special characters, such as @, #, %, $, *, !, and so on
- Functions cannot be named using ActionScript reserved words

Example: Named function

```
public function calculateStringLength(str:String):Number {
    return str.length();
}
```

Anonymous functions

Unlike a **named** function, an **anonymous** function is a function defined and called without using a name. Anonymous functions are often used in a place where you never have to call them. For example, tasks such as event handling, running timer tasks, or any other place where you don't need a named function.

Example: The following example is using Flex's built-in function `setInterval()` to run a specified task every 100 milliseconds.

```
setInterval(function(){
    //execute some task
}, 100);
```

Or, the following example uses an unnamed function for event handling. You will learn more about event handling in the later part of this chapter.

```
public var validator:StringValidator = new StringValidator();
val.addEventListener(ValidationResultEvent.VALID, function(){
    Alert.show("Validated");
});
```

In ActionScript 3.0, every function is represented by an instance of the `Function` class. As such, a function can be assigned to a variable, passed to a function, or returned from a function just like any other value, as shown below:

```
var fun:Function = function(x:int):Number {
    return x+10;
}
var foo:Function = fun;
```

Once a function has been assigned to a variable, it can be invoked normally using function name followed by `()`. For example:

```
foo(10);
```

You can use an `arguments` object inside an anonymous function to achieve function recursion. `arguments` gives a method called `callee` which references to the current instance of the anonymous function, as shown in the below example.

```
public var fun:Function = function(x:int):void {
    if(x<=1)
    return;
    x-=1
    trace(x);
    arguments.callee(x);
}
```

`trace()` is a global method. You can use the debugger version of Flash Player to capture output from the global `trace()` method and write that output to the client log file. You can use `trace()` statements in any ActionScript or MXML file in your application. Because it is a global function, you are not required to import any ActionScript classes, packages to use the `trace()` method. For example:

```
trace(param1, param2, ...n)
```

The anonymous functions work like named functions, but they are defined differently.

Function parameters

In ActionScript 3.0, function parameters are more or less the same as Java accept few additional features that may be new to you in ActionScript.

The default parameter values

ActionScript 3.0 introduces a new way of defining functions with default parameter values, which means that you can declare function parameters with default values set and if the function caller caller omits the parameter with default value then the default value will be used. That means the parameter that you declare with default value becomes optional while calling the function. All parameters with default values must be placed at the end of the parameter list.

The following example shows you how to declare default valued parameters:

```
public function fooFunction(str:String, x:int = 5, y:int = 10):void
{
    trace(str, x, y);
}
```

You can call this function by just passing the first string parameter, since the other two `int` parameters are set to default value as shown in the following snippet:

```
fooFunction("fooString"); //Output: fooString 5 10
```

The ...(rest) parameter

ActionScript 3.0 introduces a new parameter declaration called the ...`(rest)` parameter. This specifies that the function will accept any number of comma-delimited arguments. The list of arguments will become an array that will be available in the function body.

For example:

```
public function theRestFunction(x:int, y:String, ...args):void{
    trace(x, y);
    for (var i:uint = 0; i < args.length; i++)
    {
        trace(args[i]);
    }
}
theRestFunction(10, 'second', 1, 'two', 3, 4);
```

Output:

```
10 second
1
two
3
4
```

The `x` and `y` parameters are not part of the ...`(rest)` parameter, so they must be accessed separately.

There are some general rules that need to be followed in order to use the ...`(rest)` parameter. They are as follows:

- The parameter cannot have a reserved word as its name
- This parameter declaration must be the last parameter specified in the argument list

Note that use of the ...`(rest)` parameter makes the `arguments` object unavailable, so make sure that you don't need `arguments.callee` before using it.

Setter and getter methods

In ActionScript 3.0, you can define the properties of your components by using setter and getter methods. The advantage of setter and getter methods is that they isolate the underlying variable from direct public access so that you can control user interaction with your component. By having setter and getter methods, you can perform data manipulation, validation, and control the read and write access of a property.

To define setter and getter methods, just precede the method name with the `get` or `set` keyword followed by a space and property name.

The following example shows the declaration of a public property named `carColor` using getter and setter to get and set the value to the property.

First, you need to define the internal private variable:

```
private var _carColor:String;
```

Then, use the `set` and `get` keywords to define the public getter and setter for the above private variable that will be used as a property of our class.

```
public function set carColor(value:String):void {
   _carColor = value;
}
public function get carColor():String {
   return _carColor;
}
```

It is recommended that the variable that stores the property value should be declared as `private` or `protected`, and it cannot have the same name as of the setter or getter method. By convention, precede the variable name with the (_) underscore character as it is used in the above example.

User of the above class can use this property as:

```
myCar.carColor = "red" //Setting value
```

Or

```
trace(myCar.carColor); //Getting value
```

Or, you can use this in MXML as the following:

```
<mx:Application xmlns:mx="http://www.adobe.com/2006/mxml"
xmlns:MyComp=»myControls.*» >
    <MyComp:BMW carColor=»red»/>
</mx:Application>
```

You can also create read-only or write-only properties using setter and getter methods. Let's look at the following examples for creating read-only and write-only properties.

Example: Read-only property

```
private var _carColor:String;
public function get carColor():String {
   return _carColor;
}
```

Notice that in the above example, I have defined only the getter method. If you do not define setter for the property, then it becomes read-only. Hence, it cannot be set.

Example: Write-only property

```
private var _carColor:String;
public function set carColor(value:String):void {
   _carColor = value;
}
```

Notice that in the above example, I have defined only the setter method. If you do not define getter for the property, then it becomes write-only. Hence, it cannot be used for getting its value.

Flow control and looping

Flow control and looping are one of the major features of any language. ActionScript 3.0 provides you with all the flow control and looping statements, and they are similar to the ones available in Java.

Let's go through their syntaxes.

If/else statement

if/else statements are probably one of the most used features of any language. In ActionScript 3.0, the syntax for an if/else statement is as shown below:

```
if (expression) {
   //If expression evaluation is true
} else {
//If expression evaluation is false
}
```

Or

```
if (expression1) {
} else if (expression2) {
} else {
}
```

The if/else statement is also known as a nested if/else block, which checks for multiple expressions.

switch statement

switch statements are alternatives for nested if/else conditional statements. A switch statement evaluates the expression and based on the result it determines which code block to execute. A switch statement begins with the `switch` keyword followed by the expression enclosed within parenthesis, and then different code blocks for possible results followed by the `break` statement. A switch statement can also have default code block that will get executed if none of the cases matched. While you can do this with nested if/else statements, a switch statement executes faster. Unlike Java, ActionScript 3.0 switch statements can evaluate many types of expressions, such as strings, integer, and objects. The following example shows you a simple switch statement that evaluates the days of a week string and prints different output:

```
switch (week_day) {
   case "Monday":
      trace("yawn, Monday blues!");
      break;
   case "Tuesday":
      trace("not another status meeting");
      break;
   case "Wednesday":
      trace("halfway there");
      break;
   case "Friday":
      trace("TGIF");
```

```
        break;
    case "Saturday":
    case "Sunday":
        trace("Hurray! Its weekend!");
        break;
    default:
        return("oops!");
}
```

You can also use a switch statement for evaluating objects as shown in the following example:

```
switch(obj) {
    case aDog:
        trace("It's a DOG");
        break;
    case aCat:
        trace("It's a CAT");
        break;
    default:
        trace("Don't Know");
}
```

In the above example, `aDog` and `aCat` are instance objects of the `Dog` and `Cat` classes which we created in the *inheriting classes* section earlier in this chapter. The above `switch` statement determines the type of the object.

Looping

Unlike if/else and switch flow control statements, looping is used when executing a task continuously until a specified condition is satisfied.

ActionScript supports two types of looping:

- while
- for

While looping

A While loop executes a block of code until its while condition is false. Its syntax is:

```
while(expression) {
    //execute this block of code
}
```

do..while looping

A do..while loop is the same as a while loop except that do..while guarantees that the code block executes at least once. The difference between while and do..while is that in a do...while loop the condition block is checked after executing code block, and that is the reason it is placed at the end of the statement. Its syntax is:

```
do {
   //execute this block of code
} while(expression);
```

for looping

A for loop is constituted by three parts that are separated by a semicolon—initializiation, stop condition, and then the iterate statement. A for loop iterates over a range of values that you specify in its parameters. Its syntax is:

```
for(var i:int=0 ; i<=10; i++) {
   //execute this block of code
}
```

for..in looping

A for..in loop iterates through the properties of the given object and elements of the array. The following example shows you how to use this loop. This loop is very similar to a for loop.

```
var array:Array = ["one", "two", "three"];
for(var i:String in array) {
   trace(array[i]); //Output: one, two, three
}
```

for each..in looping

Unlike a for..in loop, this loop iterates through items of the collection starting from XML nodes, XMLList, object properties, and array elements. The following example shows you how to use this loop:

```
var array:Array = ["one", "two", "three"];
for each(var i:String in array) {
   trace(i); //Output: one, two, three
}
```

Exceptions and error handling

As long as your application doesn't encounter any problematic situations, it should run successfully. However, if you do not handle possible erroneous situations in your code, then the chances are high that your application may fail and crash.

Handling errors means that you build logic into your code in such a way that it will respond to erroneous situations and possibly fix it. However, error handling is a broad subject that includes responding to many kinds of errors that are thrown during compilation or at run-time.

Compile-time errors are often easy to identify and you must fix them in order to compile and run your application. Unlike compile-time errors, runtime errors are hard to identify and fix. You must write your code very carefully and test it for handling unknown cases. Most importantly, your program should handle these cases in a graceful manner and show a friendly message to the user explaining what went wrong.

This section focuses on common strategies in ActionScript 3.0 for error handling.

There are different ways to handle and respond to an error. However, the most commonly used approaches are as following:

- Use try...catch...finally statements. These will catch synchronous errors as they occur. You can use nested catch statements to handle multiple types of errors.
- Create your own custom error objects. You can use the `Error` class to create your own custom error class for the errors, which are not covered by built-in error types. And you can use `try...catch...finally` statements to handle and display appropriate messages to the user.

Apart from the above strategies, it is good practice to write event listeners to respond to various asynchronous error events. In this way, you can create global error handlers that let you handle similar events without duplicating a lot of code in `try...catch...finally` blocks.

try...catch...finally statements

The try...catch...finally statements work in a similar way as in Java. When an error occurs, Flash Player suspends normal execution and creates a special object of type `Error`, and this error object is thrown to the first available `catch` block.

The following code demonstrates the syntax for `try...catch...finally` statements:

```
try
{
 //some code that could throw an error
}
catch (err:Error)
{
 //code to react to the error
}
finally
{
 //Code that runs whether or not an error was thrown. This code can
clean
 //up after the error or take steps to keep the application running.
}
```

If your code is prone to throwing multiple types of errors, then you can use nested catch statements to catch hierarchical errors. For example, take a look at the following code snippet:

```
try
{
throw new ArgumentError("I am an ArgumentError");
}
catch (err:Error)
{
   trace("<Error> "+err.message);
}
catch(err:ArgumentError)
{
   trace("<ArgumentError> "+err.message);
}
finally
{
}
```

Each catch statement identifies a specific type of error. When an error occurs, each catch statement will be checked in order, and only the first catch statement that matches the type of error will execute.

The above code displays the following output:

```
<Error> I am an ArgumentError
```

This output is not what was intended because our code is throwing an `ArgumentError` type error, and it should be caught at the second catch statement. Let's understand why.

Remember that all error classes in ActionScript 3.0 are inherited from the `Error` class, so in the above code, even though it is throwing specific `ArgumentError`, it will get caught at first catch statement. Because inherently `ArgumentError` is of type `Error` and the first catch statement matches with it. What that means is that the `Error` class is the parent class of `ArgumentError` class, so its type is equivalent to the `Error` class.

So in order to correctly catch the errors, you need to arrange them in the most specific way first and then the generic way. So in order to catch correct errors, we need to rearrange the catch statements as following:

```
try
{
throw new ArgumentError("I am an ArgumentError");
}
catch(err:ArgumentError)
{
    trace("<ArgumentError> "+err.message);
}
catch (err:Error)
{
    trace("<Error> "+err.message);
}
finally
{
}
```

Create your own custom Error class object

In ActionScript 3.0, you must extend the standard `Error` class to create your own custom `Error` classes. Here is an example of a custom `Error` class:

```
package cars.errors
{
   public class BreakFailureError extends Error
   {
      public function BreakFailureError(message:String="", id:int=0)
      {
         super(message, id);
      }
   }
}
```

The following example shows how to use a custom `Error` class in your application:

```
try
{
    throw new BreakFailureError("Breaks failure!!", 29);
}
catch (error:BreakFailureError)
{
    trace(error.errorID + ": " + error.message)
}
```

Reserved words and keywords

Reserved words are words that you cannot use as identifiers in your code because the words are reserved for use by ActionScript. Reserved words include lexical keywords which are removed from the program namespace by the compiler. The compiler will report an error if you use a lexical keyword as an identifier. The following table lists ActionScript 3.0 lexical keywords:

as	break	case	catch
class	const	continue	default
delete	do	else	extends
false	finally	for	function
If	implements	import	in
instanceof	interface	internal	is
native	new	null	package
private	protected	public	return
super	switch	this	throw
to	true	try	typeof
use	var	void	while
with			

There is a small set of keywords called **syntactic keywords** which can be used as identifiers, but which have special meaning in certain contexts. The following table lists ActionScript 3.0 syntactic keywords:

each	get	set	namespace
include	dynamic	final	native
override	static		

There are also several identifiers that are sometimes referred to as future reserved words. These identifiers are not reserved by ActionScript 3.0, though some of them may be treated as keywords by software that incorporates ActionScript 3.0. You might be able to use many of these identifiers in your code, but Adobe recommends that you do not use them because they may appear as keywords in a subsequent version of the language.

abstract	boolean	byte	cast
char	debugger	double	enum
export	float	goto	intrinsic
long	prototype	short	synchronized
throws	to	transient	type
virtual	volatile		

Using ActionScript 3.0 with MXML

To build a Flex application, you need to use a combination of MXML and ActionScript 3.0 languages. For example, you may use MXML to layout and design your user interfaces and write business logic in ActionScript. This is a common practice followed by Flex developers. In this section, we will see how to mix ActionScript and MXML to build Flex applications.

There are two ways to include an ActionScript file in your Flex application:

- With the help of the `<mx:script>` tag
- With the help of the `include` statement

Using the <mx:script> tag

In the Flex development environment, you can add ActionScript code in MXML file by using the `<mx:script>` tag. See the following example:

```
<?xml version="1.0" encoding="utf-8"?>
<mx:Application xmlns:mx="http://www.adobe.com/2006/mxml"
layout="vertical">
    <mx:Script>
        <![CDATA[
            private var color:String = "red";
            private function calculateSum(x:Number, y:Number):Number {
                return x+y;
            }
        ]]>
```

```
    </mx:Script>
    <mx:TextInput id="num1"/>
    <mx:TextInput id="num2"/>
    <mx:Label id="output"/>
    <mx:Button label="Sum" click="output.text =
     String(calculateSum(Number(num1.text), Number(num2.text)))"/>
</mx:Application>
```

Notice that the above MXML code is using a `<mx:script>` tag to write ActionScript code to declare a variable and a function. You cannot use one script tag to specify a source attribute and include code within its body. The `<mx:script>` tag should be under `Application` or any other top-level component tag.

The term CDATA is used to represent the text data (in this case, it's ActionScript code) that should not be parsed by the XML parser.

This works well if your application requires less ActionScript code. But if your application uses many MXML files and involves significant ActionScript code, then the best way is to separate your ActionScript code from MXML files and store it in external ActionScript file(s) with the `.as` extension.

The `<mx:script>` tag lets you specify the `source` attribute that identifies the external ActionScript file to be included at that point in the application. The `source` attribute supports both absolute and relative paths. For example, the following `script` tag will load an external ActionScript file named `Util.as`:

```
<?xml version="1.0" encoding="utf-8"?>
<mx:Application xmlns:mx="http://www.adobe.com/2006/mxml"
layout="vertical">
    <mx:Script source="/cars/Util.as" />

    <mx:TextInput id="num1"/>
    <mx:TextInput id="num2"/>
    <mx:Label id="output"/>
    <mx:Button label="Sum" click="output.text =
     String(calculateSum(Number(num1.text), Number(num2.text)))"/>
</mx:Application>
```

`Util.as`:

```
// ActionScript file
private var color:String = «red»;

private function calculateSum(x:Number, y:Number):Number {
    return x+y;
}
```

The approaches above have no difference except that the second approach improves code maintainability and readability. At the end of the day, the compiler copies the entire content of the external ActionScript file into the MXML application.

Using the include directive

The `include` directive is an ActionScript directive that copies the content of an external ActionScript file into your MXML application. The `include` directive can only be used inside the `<mx:script>` tag and you can specify only a single ActionScript file for each `include` directive.

Syntax:

```
include "file_name"
```

The following example includes `Util.as`:

```
<?xml version="1.0" encoding="utf-8"?>
<mx:Application xmlns:mx="http://www.adobe.com/2006/mxml"
layout="vertical">
    <mx:Script>
        <![CDATA[
            include "/cars/Util.as";
        ]]>
    </mx:Script>
    <mx:TextInput id="num1"/>
    <mx:TextInput id="num2"/>
    <mx:Label id="output"/>
    <mx:Button label="Sum" click="output.text = String(calculateSum(Num
ber(num1.text), Number(num2.text)))"/>
</mx:Application>
```

To create an ActionScript file to be included in Flex Builder, click on **File | New | ActionScript File.** This will create a blank file with an `.as` extension. You can start writing your ActionScript code in this file.

The ActionScript file is a normal file with `.as` as its extension, but this file will have no package or class declaration. The following are some of the general guidelines for writing an ActionScript file for including.

- ActionScript statements can only be inside functions, which means that you cannot define statements like `if/else` or `for` loop directly in the ActionScript file; you must put these statements under the function body.
- Included files can also declare constants and namespaces, include other ActionScript files, import declarations, and use namespaces.

- You cannot define classes in included files.
- Variables and functions defined in an included ActionScript file are available to any component in the MXML file.
- Included ActionScript files do not need to be in the same directory as the MXML file. However, organizing ActionScript files in a logical directory structure is best practice.

At the end of the day, when you compile your Flex application, everything boils down to ActionScript code. So including files is just a way to separate your ActionScript code from MXML.

Working with events

In a previous chapter, you saw how to work with events in MXML. Now, in this section, you will learn how to work with events in ActionScript. The event model in ActionScript 3.0 is based on the Document Object Model (DOM) Level 3 event specification (`http://www.w3.org/TR/DOM-Level-3-Events/events.html`). This model provides a very powerful, yet intuitive, event handling tool for Flex developers.

Registering event handlers

Flash Player dispatches event objects whenever an event occurs. Every component has different events associated with it and in order to handle these events you need to register the event handler or event listener with specific events using the `addEventListener()` method. This is the syntax of `addEventListener()`:

```
displayObj.addEventListener(type:String,listener:Function,useCapture:
Boolean=false,priority:int=0,useWeakReference:Boolean=false):void
```

For example:

```
myButton.addEventListener(MouseEvent.CLICK, clickHandler);
```

The `addEventListener()` method takes five parameters but only the first two are required to register any event; the remaining parameters are optional. If you do not pass optional parameters, they will be initialized with their default values.

- `type`: The type of an event. The event type is a string and it can also be set from constant variables, for example, Flex's built-in events use constants to define event type, such as `MouseEvent.CLICK`, `MouseEvent.DOUBLE_CLICK`, and so on.

- `listener`: The instance name of the listener function that processes the event. It should accept an event as only a parameter and should not return anything.
- `useCapture`: This determines whether the listener works in the capture phase (when `useCapture` is `true`) or the target and bubbling phases (when `useCapture` is `false`). To listen for the event in all three phases, call `addEventListener` twice, once with `useCapture` set to `true`, then again with `useCapture` set to `false`. The default value is set to `false`. You will learn about all of the different phases of an event in event propagation later in this chapter.
- `priority`: Sets the priority level of the event listener. It takes the `int` value, where the higher the number, the higher the priority. You can only set the priority at the time of registering the event, and once it is set, it cannot be changed using subsequent calls for `addEventListener()`. All listeners with priority *n* are processed before listeners of priority *n-1*. If two or more listeners share the same priority, they are processed in the order in which they were added. The default priority is `0`.
- `useWeakReference`: This determines whether the reference to the listener is strong or weak. A strong reference (the default) prevents your listener from being garbage-collected, which a weak reference does not prevent. By default, it is set to `true`. That means all event listeners that you add have a strong reference. You should carefully set this parameter based on which event listeners you need and which you do not. For example, if there's some UI component you do not expect to be displayed on the screen after some time, then any event listeners of this component can easily set `useWeakReference` to `false`.

It is always a good idea to use weak references while registering events if you do not need them throughout your application lifecycle, or else memory problems could result.

You can also remove a registered event listener and stop listening for that event by using the `removeEventListener()` method. This is the syntax for removing the event listener:

```
displayObj.removeEventListener(type:String, listener:Function,
useWeakReference:Boolean=false):void
```

For example:

```
myButton.removeEventListener(MouseEvent.CLICK, clickHandler);
```

The `useCapture:Boolean (default = false)` parameter specifies whether the listener was registered for the capture phase or the target and bubbling phases. If the listener was registered for both the capture phase and the target and bubbling phases, two calls to `removeEventListener` are required to remove both, one call with `useCapture` set to `true`, and another call with `useCapture` set to `false`.

Dispatching an event

Flex components dispatch various events. In this case, Flex takes care of dispatching events, but when you write your own event-driven component, it is often required by developers to dispatch events manually. You can manually dispatch events using a component instance's `dispatchEvent()` method. All components that extend `UIComponent` have this method. The method is inherited from the `EventDispatcher` class, which `UIComponent` extends. The following is the syntax for dispatching the event.

```
objectInstance.dispatchEvent(event:Event):Boolean
```

When dispatching an event, you must create a new `Event` object. The syntax for the `Event` object constructor is as follows:

```
Event(event_type:String, bubbles:Boolean, cancelable:Boolean)
```

The `event_type` parameter is the type of the event. The `bubbles` and `cancelable` parameters are optional and both default to `false`. For information on bubbling and capturing, see the *Event propagation* section later in this chapter.

About the target and currentTarget properties

Every event object has the `target` and `currentTarget` properties. These properties indicate which object has dispatched the event originally, and which is listening to it. The `target` property refers to the dispatcher of the event, and the `currentTarget` property refers to the current node that is being examined for an event listener block. These properties are dynamically changed in various event phases during the propagation process.

When an event is dispatched, it travels through the display list to reach its event target. This is known as **event flow**. In other words, the event flow describes how an event object travels through the display list. The display list is a hierarchy of display objects or controls on stage that can be described as a tree. At the top of the display list hierarchy is `Stage`, which is a special display object container that serves as the root of the display list. `Stage` is represented by the `flash.display.Stage` class and can only be accessed through a display object. Every display object has a property named `stage` that refers to the `Stage` object for that application.

It is important to understand how event travels when it occurs. Whenever an event occurs, it travels from the target node to the stage. The display object in which the event occurs is known as the target node.

Event propagation

When events are triggered, they travel through the following three phases:

- Capturing
- Targeting
- Bubbling

Capturing phase

In the capturing phase, Flex searches for event listeners in a top-to-bottom manner that is, from root display object to the event target. For example, given the following hierarchy of components, if the event is in the capturing phase, then it travels in the following order:

-Application (1)

 |_Panel (2)

  |_TitleWindow (3)

   |_Button (4) (The event target)

Targeting phase

In the targeting phase, Flex invokes the event listener. In this process, no other nodes are examined.

Bubbling phase

This phase is the reverse of the capturing phase. In this phase, Flex searches for event listeners from bottom to top, that is, from the event target to root display object.

For example, if you have the following hierarchy of controls:

-Application (4)

 |_Panel (3)

  |_TitleWindow (2)

   |_Button (1)

And if you have a listener for the click event of the Button control, then the following steps occur during the bubbling phase:

1. Check the TitleWindow for the click event listener.
2. Check the Panel for the click event listener.
3. Check the Application for the click event listener.

As you can see, the bubbling phase is the exact reverse of the capturing phase.

An event only bubbles if its `bubbles` property is set to `true` while dispatching the event. An event only bubbles up the parent's chain of ancestors in the display list. Siblings, such as two Button controls inside the same container, do not intercept each other's events.

During the bubbling phase, an event's `currentTarget` will be changed to its current node whose listener is being called; the `target` property holds the original reference of the display object which originally dispatched the event. For example, in the above component list, if you have the event listener defined at Panel level, then an event's `currentTarget` property will be set to Panel instance and its `target` property will be set to Button instance. So you should generally use the `currentTarget` property instead of the `target` property when referring to the current object in your event listeners.

Creating custom events

Every event in Flex is inherited from the `flash.events.Event` class. The `Event` class is used as the base class for the creation of `Event` objects, which are passed as parameters to event listeners when an event occurs. The following table describes the properties of the `Event` class.

Property	Type	Description
`type`	`String`	The name of the event. For example, "click". The event constructor sets this property.
`target`	`EventDispatcher`	A reference to the component instance that dispatches the event. This property is set by the `dispatchEvent()` method; you cannot change this to a different object.
`currentTarget`	`EventDispatcher`	A reference to the component instance that is actively processing the `Event` object. The value of this property is different from the value of the target property during the event capture and bubbling phase.

Property	Type	Description
eventPhase	uint	The current phase in the event flow. The property might contain the following values: EventPhase.CAPTURING_PHASE: The capture phase EventPhase.AT_TARGET: The target phase EventPhase.BUBBLING_PHASE: The bubbling phase
bubbles	boolean	Whether the event is a bubbling event. If the event can bubble, the value for this property is true; otherwise, it is false. You can optionally pass this property as a constructor argument to the Event class. By default, most event classes set this property to false.
cancelable	boolean	Whether the event can be canceled. If the event can be canceled, the value for this property is true; otherwise, it is false. You can optionally pass this property as a constructor argument to the Event class. By default, most event classes set this property to false.

To create your own custom event, you need to extend the Event class as shown in the below example.

```
package cars.event
{
   import flash.events.Event;

   public class MyCustomEvent extends Event
   {
      public static const COLOR_CHANGED:String = "colorChanged";
      public var currentColor:String;

      public function MyCustomEvent(type:String, bubbles:
Boolean=false, cancelable:Boolean=false, currentColor:String = "Blue")
      {
         super(type, bubbles, cancelable);
         this.currentColor = currentColor;
      }
      //Creates and returns a copy of the current instance.
      public override function clone():Event
      {
         return new MyCustomEvent(this.type, this.bubbles, this.
cancelable, this.currentColor);
```

```
        }
        public override function toString():String
        {
            return formatToString("cars.event.MyCustomEvent",
"currentColor", "type", "bubbles", "cancelable");
        }
    }
}
```

By conventions in ActionScript 3.0, you must override the `clone` function which will be used by event framework, and optionally you can also override the `toString` method to print additional information about the class.

Along with other properties, you can define your own properties inside your event class, which will be available to the event listener through the `event` object instance; for example, we defined `currentColor` property in `MyCustomEvent` class.

To dispatch a custom event, simply use `dispatchEvent()` by passing an object instance of the custom event class. For example:

```
var myEvent:MyCustomEvent = new MyCustomEvent(MyCustomEvent.COLOR_
CHANGED, false, true, "Red");
dispatchEvent(myEvent);
```

Creating and using ActionScript components

You learned how to create and use MXML components in the last chapter. MXML components are used to create basic components mostly by utilizing existing components. In contrast, ActionScript 3.0 can be used to create advanced and completely new ActionScript components. You can also extend the existing component to enhance and customize its features to suit your needs. For example, Flex provides the `Panel` component—with window title bar and optional close button, and (if you need them) extra minimize and maximize buttons to minimize and maximize window operations. You can extend the existing `Panel` class and create your own custom component. ActionScript 3.0 provides very powerful drawing API which can be used to create entirely new components.

Creating custom component in ActionScript 3.0 is a very wide subject. To read more about it, visit `http://livedocs.adobe.com/flex/3/html/Part3_as_components_1.html`.

In Flex, all visual components are subclasses of the `UIComponent` class, and therefore visual components inherit properties, methods, and styles as defined by `UIComponent` class.

To create a custom component, you optionally override one or more of the `UIComponent` methods. You implement the basic component structure, the constructor, and one or more of the following methods of the `UIComponent` class:

UIComponent method	Description
`commitProperties()`	Commits changes to component properties, either to make the changes occur at the same time or to ensure that properties are set in a specific order.
`createChildren()`	Creates child components of the component. For example, the `ComboBox` control contains the `TextInput` control and the `Button` control as child components.
`layoutChrome()`	Defines the border area around the container for subclasses of the `Container` class.
`measure()`	Sets the default size and default minimum size of the component.
`updateDisplayList()`	Sizes and positions the children of the component on the screen based on all the previous property and style settings, and draws any skins or graphic elements used by the component. The parent container for the component determines the size of the component itself.

Basic structure of a custom component:

```
package components
{
    public class MyComponent extends UIComponent
    {
        ....
    }
}
```

You can also extend your custom component from any existing Flex component. Let's look at each of the above methods from the `UIComponent` class and their usage while creating a custom component.

The commitProperties() method

The `commitProperties()` method is used to commit/update component property changes before your component appears on the screen. The `commitProperties()` call can be scheduled for invocation by calling the `invalidateProperties()` method of Flex. Whenever you add a child to the container, Flex automatically calls the `invalidateProperties()` method. This method can be used to commit your custom component's styling- or sizing-related properties before it is rendered, so you can make use of these properties to determine style or size.

For example, you typically define component properties using setter and getter methods as the following code shows:

```
//Define private variable for holding text color information
private var _bottomTextColor:String;

//Define Boolean flag for checking if color is changed
private var bColorChanged:Boolean;

//Setter method of bottomLabelColor property
public function set bottomLabelColor(value:String):void {
   if(_bottomTextColor != value) {
      _bottomTextColor = value;
      bColorChanged = true;
      invalidateProperties();
   }
}

// Implement the commitProperties() method.
override protected function commitProperties():void {
    super.commitProperties();

    // Check whether the flag indicates a change to the
bottomLabelColor property.
    if (bColorChanged) {
   // Reset flag.
   bColorChanged = false;

   // Handle color change
   // In this case I am just forcing to update the display list
   invalidateDisplayList();
    }
}
```

In this example, if the user sets the `bottomLabelColor` property, it calls `invalidateProperties()` to schedule invocation of the `commitProperties()` method, which in turn calls `invalidateDisplayList()` to force update, or to render UI on the screen.

The createChildren() method

You can use the `createChildren()` method to create sub-components of your custom component. For example, the `Button` control has `Label` as its sub-component to display the button label on it, so you can use the `createChildren()` method to create any sub-components that are part of your custom component.

Unlike other methods such as `commitProperties()` and `updateDisplayList()`, you do not have to call any invalidate method. Instead, Flex calls this method automatically whenever a call to the `addChild()` method occurs.

For example, in the below example (apart from the `Button` control's default label to show button label), we will add one extra label called `bottomLabel` to show key code information.

```
//Define Label control to display extra Label on Button control
private var _bottomLabelField:Label;
//Define String to hold extra text for our new label
private var _bottomLabelText:String;

//Define Boolean flag for checking if text is changed
private var bLabelChanged:Boolean;

//Implement createChildren method to create and add extra Label
control to Button
override protected function createChildren():void
{
   super.createChildren();

   if (!_bottomLabelField)
   {
      _bottomLabelField = new Label();
      //Set new Label's text, style and other properties such as
        height, width, x and y position
      _bottomLabelField.setStyle("fontSize", "9");
      _bottomLabelField.setStyle("color", _bottomTextColor);
      _bottomLabelField.width = unscaledWidth;
      _bottomLabelField.height = unscaledHeight;
      _bottomLabelField.y = unscaledHeight - 18;
      _bottomLabelField.text = _bottomLabelText;

      addChild(_bottomLabelField);
   }
}
```

Notice that this example calls the `addChild()` method to add a newly created `Label` component as a child component of the `Button` component.

The layoutChrome() method

The `Container` class and some subclasses of container classes use the `layoutChrome()` method to define a border area around the container. Flex schedules a call to the `layoutChrome()` method when a call to the `invalidateDisplayList()` method occurs.

The `layoutContainer()` method is typically used to define and position the border area of a container and any additional elements you want to appear in the border area. For example, the `Panel` container uses the `layoutChrome()` method to define a title area including title text and close button. You can use the `RectangularBorder` class to define a border area of a container, and add it using the `addChild()` method.

The measure() method

The `measure()` method is used to set the default component size. You can use the `invalidateSize()` method to schedule a call to the `measure()` method. The `measure()` method is only called if you are making any changes to a component's default sizes.

You can set the following size-related properties of a component in the `measure()` method:

Properties	Description
`measuredHeight` `measuredWidth`	This specifies default height and width of a component. This is set to `0` until the `measure()` method is called.
`measuredMinHeight` `measuredMinWidth`	This specifies default minimum height and width of a component. Once this is defined, your component's height and width cannot be set less than its specified minimum size.

The following code overrides the `measure()` method to change the default size of the `Button` component.

```
override protected function measure():void {
   super.measure();

   measuredWidth=100;
   measuredHeight=50;

   measuredMinWidth=60;
   measuredMinHeight=30;
}
```

This example will set the button's default size to 100x50 pixels and minimum default size to 60x30 pixels.

The updateDisplayList() method

The `updateDisplayList()` method is used to manipulate graphical elements of your component including the sizing, styling, and positioning of any child components. This method can also be used to draw any graphic elements of your component. For example, you can use the drawing API of Flex to draw lines, fill colors, and so on.

You can call the `invalidateDisplayList()` method to schedule a call to the `updateDisplayList()` method. However, whenever you call the `addChild()` method, Flex automatically calls the `updateDisplayList()` method. This method is also responsible for rendering your component on-screen.

This function takes two implicit parameters:

- `unscaledWidth`: Specifies the width of the component, which is determined by its parent container
- `unscaledHeight`: Specifies the height of the component, which is determined by its parent container

In the following example, I have overridden the `updateDisplayList()` method to set the Y-axis of the default label of the `Button` control, and to set the color style of the `bottomLabel` control.

```
override protected function updateDisplayList(unscaledWidth:Number,
unscaledHeight:Number):void
{
    super.updateDisplayList(unscaledWidth, unscaledHeight);

    textField.y -= 3 - labelYOffset;

    _bottomLabelField.text = _bottomLabelText;
    _bottomLabelField.setStyle("color", _bottomTextColor);

    setChildIndex(_bottomLabelField, numChildren - 1);
}
```

This causes the default button label to move up a bit and make space for the additional bottom label in the Button control.

Now that you have understood each method from the `UIComponent` class and know where to use them in your custom component, it's time to put your knowledge to work.

In the following example, I will demonstrate how to add an extra label to Flex's `Button` control, which comes with only one default label. You must have seen buttons on a telephone keypad that have numeric and alphabet characters which allow you to input both numbers and letters. We will implement a similar button component. For this, we will need two labels; one below the other on the `Button` control, so our component extends Flex's `mx.controls.Button` class.

Let's start this step-by-step process and write our custom button component:

1. Click on **File | New | ActionScript Class** to create an ActionScript class using Flex Builder.
2. A **New ActionScript Class** dialog box will appear. Type in **Package, Name** as `cars.components`, **File Name** as `MyButton`, and **Superclass** as `mx.controls.Button`. The **Superclass** field specifies the component your component will be inherited from. Click the **Finish** button to create the ActionScript class. Use the file name `MyButton.as`.
3. Flex Builder will create a basic structure of your ActionScript component and open it in Editor View.

   The basic structure of your component is as follows:

   ```
   package cars.components
   {
      import mx.controls.Button;
      public class MyButton extends Button
     {
         public function MyButton()
         {
            super();
         }
      }
   }
   ```

   Now, as our basic component structure is ready, I will start defining necessary properties and methods required to create our custom component shown in the following code:

   `MyButton.as` file source:

   ```
   package cars.components
   {
      import mx.controls.Button;
      import mx.controls.Label;
      public class MyButton extends Button
      {
         public var labelYOffset:Number = 0; // Offsets the top label.
         private var _bottomLabelField:Label;
         private var _bottomLabelText:String;
         private var _bottomTextColor:String;
         private var bColorChanged:Boolean;
   ```

```
private var bLabelChanged:Boolean;

public function set bottomLabelColor(value:String):void {
   if(_bottomTextColor != value) {
      _bottomTextColor = value;
      bColorChanged = true;
      invalidateProperties();
   }
}

public function set bottomLabel(value:String):void {
   if (_bottomLabelText != value) {
       _bottomLabelText = value;
      bLabelChanged = true;
         invalidateSize();
         invalidateDisplayList();
   }
}

override protected function createChildren():void {
   super.createChildren();
   if (!_bottomLabelField) {
      _bottomLabelField = new Label();
       _bottomLabelField.setStyle("fontSize", "9");
      _bottomLabelField.width = unscaledWidth;
      _bottomLabelField.height = unscaledHeight;
       _bottomLabelField.y = unscaledHeight - 18;
       addChild(_bottomLabelField);
   }
}

// Implement the commitProperties() method.
override protected function commitProperties():void {
    super.commitProperties();

    // Check whether the flag indicates a change to the
       bottomLabelColor property.
    if (bColorChanged) {
        // Reset flag.
        bColorChanged = false;
        // Handle color change
        // In this case I am just forcing to update the
                                            display list
        invalidateDisplayList();
    }
}
//Sets default size and minimum size of Button control
override protected function measure():void {
```

```
            super.measure();
            measuredWidth=100;
            measuredHeight=50;
            measuredMinWidth=60;
            measuredMinHeight=30;
        }
        override protected function updateDisplayList(unscaledWidth:
        Number, unscaledHeight:Number):void {
            super.updateDisplayList(unscaledWidth, unscaledHeight);
            textField.y -= 3 - labelYOffset;
            _bottomLabelField.text = _bottomLabelText;
            _bottomLabelField.setStyle("color", _bottomTextColor);
            setChildIndex(_bottomLabelField, numChildren - 1);
        }
    }
}
```

4. I have defined two new properties called `bottomLabel` and `bottomLabelColor` to allow users of our custom button to set the second label and its color.
5. I have overridden the `createChildren()` method to create and add `bottomLabel` and to set its initial properties and style.
6. I have overridden the `commitProperties()` method to update the color change of `bottomLabel`. However, it is not required here, but to show you the concept of `commitProperties()` I have included it.
7. I have overridden the `measure()` method to set the default size and minimum size of the custom button control. When using this button, if you do not specify its size, it will be sized to its default size specified in this method.
8. And finally, I have overridden the `updateDisplayList()` method to manipulate the graphical elements. In this method, I am simply moving the default label's offset a bit up, so that I can place the extra label comfortably. I am also setting `bottomLabel's` text and color style in here so that whenever the user changes these two properties it automatically gets reflected on the UI.
9. Now create an MXML file to use our new custom button, as shown below.

```
<?xml version="1.0" encoding="utf-8"?>
<mx:Application xmlns:mx="http://www.adobe.com/2006/mxml" xmlns:
components="components.*">
    <mx:Panel id="btnPanel" title="Button Panel" height="150"
     width="150" verticalAlign="middle" horizontalAlign="center">
```

```
        <components:MyButton id="btn" bottomLabel="ABC" label="2"
         height="45" width="45" fontWeight="bold" fontSize="20"
         bottomLabelColor="black"/>
    </mx:Panel>

</mx:Application>
```

10. Now, compile your application and run it using Flex Builder. The output should be as follows:

Now, go ahead and create the complete telephone keypad by using a combination of `VBox` and `HBox` containers.

Summary

In this chapter, you learned about the general concepts, language features, and fundamentals of ActionScript 3.0. You also learned how to mix ActionScript and MXML code to write Flex applications and use events, create custom events, and create and use custom components.

In the next chapter, you will learn about using External API and LocalConnection. You will see how to enable communication between ActionScript and JavaScript and vice versa using External API. You will also learn how to establish communication between two Flex applications running in different browsers using LocalConnection.

4
Using External API and LocalConnection

SWF files are executed and rendered into Flash Player via a browser or desktop. This sometimes requires external communications with web scripting languages such as JavaScript or with other SWF applications running on different instances of Flash Player to exchange data. ActionScript 3.0 enables this type of communication by providing a set of APIs and classes.

This chapter will primarily focus on the following two points:

- Using External API
- Using LocalConnection

Using External API

The External API is a subset of ActionScript 3.0 and enables communication between a Flex application and the *container application* within which your Flex application is running. When you build a Flex application from Flex Builder, it also generates an HTML wrapper to execute your Flex `.swf` file into Flash Player instance. This HTML wrapper is known as the *container application* in this context.

This section gives you an overview of how the External API can be used to establish communication and exchange data between your ActionScript and JavaScript from HTML wrapper and vice versa.

An external API can be very useful in cases where you want to interact with container applications directly, or exchange data between JavaScript and ActionScript (and vice versa). A common example would be if you want to pass some data from an HTML page to your SWF file.

This chapter focuses on the following tasks:

- Communicating with JavaScript from the ActionScript code
- Communicating with ActionScript from the JavaScript code

ActionScript 3.0 provides an `ExternalInterface` class that gives you the ability to write a code to establish communication between Flex Application running under Flash Player and JavaScript from its hosted HTML file.

The `ExternalInterface` class can be used only in Flex application that is running in a browser. The following browsers are supported:

- Internet Explorer for Windows (5.0 and above).
- Any browser that has the support of NPRuntime interface, which currently includes:
    - Firefox 1.0 and above
    - Mozilla 1.7.5 and above
    - Netscape 8.0 and above
    - Safari 1.3 and above

The `ExternalInterface` class will not work with the Flex application that is running on standalone Flash Player on a desktop. To check if your application container environment supports `ExternalInterface`, you can use the `ExternalInterface.available` property which returns `true` or `false` based on whether or not your container application supports the `ExternalInterface` communication.

The External API can be used only to establish communication between a Flex application and its container application. You cannot use the External API to establish communication between two Flex applications or application containers.

Using the ExternalInterface class

You can use the `ExternalInterface` class in two different ways—to call JavaScript code in the application container from your ActionScript, or to call ActionScript code from JavaScript.

The `ExternalInterface` class provides static properties and methods. So to work with `ExternalInterface`, you need not create its instance. These properties and methods are mainly used to determine environment supportability for external communication and to make external calls. You can also expose the ActionScript methods for external communication so that they can be accessed from the JavaScript code. You will see examples of how to use these properties and methods to establish communication next in this chapter.

Getting information about external container

The `ExternalInterface.available` property can be used to determine if the container application that is hosting your Flash Player instance supports an external interface. If it supports an external interface, then this property is set to `true`; otherwise, it is set to `false`. It is always good practice to check if the current container supports an external interface before actually calling external methods, as shown in the following example:

```
if (ExternalInterface.available)
{
    //Call external method here.
}
```

The `ExternalInterface` class provides a property called `objectID`, which determines the identifier assigned to the Flash Player instance in the `<embed>` or `<object>` tag in the HTML page. This can be used to uniquely identify the current SWF document in case the HTML page contains multiple SWF documents. This property is null when the Flash Player is running on a standalone Flash Player.

Calling JavaScript code from ActionScript

You can use the `ExternalInterface.call()` method to call JavaScript method from the application container. The `call()` method accepts the name of the function that needs to be called from the container application as a parameter. You can pass in any number of additional parameters, which will be passed as arguments to the method from the container application.

By using `ExternalInterface`, you can do the following things in ActionScript:

- You can call JavaScript function and pass arguments to it
- Pass various data types such as Boolean, Number, String, and so on
- Receive JavaScript function return data

The following example shows you how to call a JavaScript method from ActionScript by using `ExternalInterface.call()`:

```
if(ExternalInterface.available)
{
   var title:String = "Flex 3 with Java";
   var pages:uint = 300;
   var result:String = ExternalInterface.call("printBookInfo", title,
pages);
   Alert.show(result);
} else {
   Alert.show("External Interface is not available");
}
```

In the above example, we are calling the `printBookInfo` JavaScript method by passing two additional `String` and `uint` type parameters to it from ActionScript. We are storing the returned string into a variable called `result` and showing an alert box with the returned value. The JavaScript method can be defined in the `script` element in the container HTML page.

For example, in your HTML page's `script` block, define a function called `printBookInfo` as follows:

```
<script language="JavaScript">
    function printBookInfo(title, price)
    {
      alert("Book Title: "+title+" is priced at: "+price);
      return ("JavaScript: Successfully printed the book information");
    }
</script>
```

You can write the above JavaScript code in your wrapper HTML file generated by Flex Builder that is found under your project's `bin` or `bin-debug` folder, and usually has the same name as your MXML application file name. If the external call fails or the JavaScript method does not return any value, then `null` is returned.

The external access from ActionScript to JavaScript and vice versa can be controlled by specifying the `AllowScriptAccess` property inside the `<embed>` and `<object>` tags of your container HTML page. The `allowScriptAccess` parameter determines whether or not an SWF file may call JavaScript methods. The `allowScriptAccess` property can have one of the three possible values—`always`, `sameDomain`, and `never`.

When `AllowScriptAccess` is set to `always`, the SWF file can always communicate with the HTML page in which it is embedded.

When `AllowScriptAccess` is set to `sameDomain`, the SWF file can communicate only with the HTML page in which it is embedded and is in the same domain as the SWF file.

When `AllowScriptAccess` is set to `never`, the SWF file cannot communicate with any HTML page. This is also a default configuration when the HTML wrapper is generated by Flex Builder.

To change the value of `allowScriptAccess` in a wrapper HTML page, you would need to edit the appropriate attribute in the `<object>` and `<embed>` tags as shown here:

```
<object id='MyMovie.swf' classid='clsid:D27CDB6E-AE6D-11cf-96B8-
444553540000' codebase='http://download.adobe.com/pub/shockwave/cabs/
flash/swflash.cab#version=9,0,0,0' height='100%' width='100%'>
```

```
<param name='AllowScriptAccess' value='sameDomain'/>
<param name='src' value=''MyMovie.swf'/>
<embed name='MyMovie.swf' pluginspage='http://www.adobe.com/go/
getflashplayer' src='MyMovie.swf' height='100%' width='100%' AllowScri
ptAccess='sameDomain'/>
</object>
```

Calling ActionScript code from JavaScript

You can call an ActionScript method by using the usual JavaScript method notation. By using JavaScript, you can do the following things:

- Call a registered ActionScript method and pass arguments
- Receive data returned by an ActionScript method

You can call an ActionScript method from JavaScript only if it is registered with the `ExternalInterface` class. Therefore, you must register and expose the ActionScript method to the `ExternalInterface` class. This would make it available to the container, which can be called from JavaScript.

The following ActionScript code block shows how to register a method with the `ExternalInterface` class:

```
private function init():void {
    ExternalInterface.addCallback("myFunction", sayHello);
}
private function sayHello(name:String):String
{
     return "Hello from ActionScript, "+name;
}
```

In the above code, we have defined an ActionScript method called `sayHello()`, which accepts a string argument and returns a string. In the `init()` method, we are registering the `sayHello()` method with `ExternalInterface` to make it accessible from the container application. The `addCallback()` method takes two parameters. The first parameter is a function name, which is a string and proxy name for the `sayHello()` method. It will be used by JavaScript to call the actual `sayHello()` ActionScript method. The second parameter is the actual ActionScript function that will be executed when the container calls the proxy function name. The proxy name technique is useful when the ActionScript function is anonymous, or the function to be called is determined at the runtime. For example, see the following code snippet:

```
//Declare variables
private var runTimeFunction:Function;
private var language:String = "English";
```

```
//Register method with ExternalInterface
private function init():void {
//Determine which function needs to be called based on language set.
   if(language=="Hindi") {
      runTimeFunction = sayNamaste;
   } else {
      runTimeFunction = sayHello;
   }
   ExternalInterface.addCallback("myFunction", runTimeFunction);
}

private function sayNamaste(name:String):String
{
    return "Namaste! from ActionScript, "+name;
}
private function sayHello(name:String):String
{
    return "Hello! from ActionScript, "+name;
}
```

The above ActionScript code decides which method to be called based on the value set to the language variable. In this way, JavaScript needs to call only the proxy function, and the underneath function call can be decided by ActionScript at runtime.

> The registration statement `ExternalInterface.addCallback()` should be a part of some function body. You can call this method in the application's `initialize` event.

Once an ActionScript function has been registered with the `ExternalInterface` class, JavaScript can call the function. For example, in JavaScript code in a HTML page, the ActionScript function is called using the proxy function name using Flash Player instance identifier, that is, `<object>` or `<embed>` tag's `name`, or `id` value.

For example, suppose you want to call a registered ActionScript method. Now you need to use the `id` of the `<embed>` tag from your HTML wrapper page, and then invoke the method as shown here:

```
<script language="JavaScript">
    //callResult gets the value "Hello from ActionScript, Satish"
    var callResult = flashObject.myFunction("Satish");
</script>
...
<object id="flashObject"...>
    ...
    <embed name="flashObject".../>
</object>
```

Make sure that you call the ActionScript method in JavaScript only after your SWF file is loaded; for example, the `onload` event of the `<body>` tag, on button click event, and so on. Any calls to the ActionScript method before loading the SWF file will result in failure without any errors or warning messages.

To read more about `ExternalInterface`, visit the Flex online documentation page at `http://livedocs.adobe.com/flex/3/html/19_External_Interface_09.html`.

Using LocalConnection

The `LocalConnection` class lets you enable communication between two different SWF files or Flex applications. The `LocalConnection` class can also be used to establish communication between SWF files created using an old version, such as ActionScript 1.0 or 2.0, and vice versa. Using `LocalConnection`, you can only communicate among SWF files that are running on the same physical computers, but they can execute in different applications (for example, two SWF files running in two different browsers or two different Flash Player instances).

For every `LocalConnection` communication, two SWF applications are involved. They are commonly known as a sender SWF file and a listener (or receiving) SWF file. You can easily communicate with two SWF files using `LocalConnection` if they are hosted in the same domain. For example, `www.domain1.com/app1.swf` can communicate with `www.domain1.com/app2.swf` using `LocalConnection` without any security concerns.

The applications that are served from different domains need to have cross-domain `LocalConnection` permissions granted. To grant permission, the receiver SWF file must give permission to the sender SWF using the `LocalConnection.allowDomain()` or `LocalConnection.allowInsecureDomain()` method.

Allowing an insecure communication using the `LocalConnection.allowInsecureDomain()` method is not recommended because this might compromise the security provided by HTTPS. It is best to allow only HTTPS to HTTPS SWF `LocalConnection`.

The sender SWF is the SWF which initiates the `LocalConnection` communication, and it must have the following things:

- It should contain the method that is to be invoked
- It should contain a `LocalConnection` class object
- It must call the `send()` method by passing the *connectionName*, *methodName*, and function arguments

The listener SWF is the SWF which receives the `LocalConnection` message, and it must have the following things:

- It should have the method which the sender SWF is invoking
- It should create the `LocalConnection` object and use the `connect()` method by passing the same connection name as specified in sender SWF's `send()` method

To show you how this works, an example showing two applications communicating over `LocalConnection` is listed next.

They are two completely separate Flex applications, each running in its own browser window under different Flash Player instances. They both use the `LocalConnection` class to communicate with each other on a single computer.

The sending application uses the `LocalConnection's send()` method to send the message over `LocalConnection`. We have also registered an event handler to receive status messages about the success or failure of the send.

Please notice that in the receiver application we are using the `connect()` method of the `LocalConnection` class to connect to `LocalConnection` by using the same connection string as it is defined in the sender application's `send()` method's first parameter.

`SenderApplication.mxml`:

```
<?xml version="1.0" encoding="utf-8"?>
<mx:Application xmlns:mx="http://www.adobe.com/2006/mxml" creationComp
lete="init()">
    <mx:Script>
        <![CDATA[
        import flash.net.LocalConnection;

        private var conn:LocalConnection;

        private function init():void{
            conn = new LocalConnection();
            conn.addEventListener(StatusEvent.STATUS, onStatus);
```

```
        }

        private function sendMessage():void {
            var bid:Object = new Object();
            bid.quantity = quantityTxt.text;
            bid.price = priceTxt.text
            conn.send("myBiddingChannel", "incomingBids", bid);
        }

        private function onStatus(event:StatusEvent):void {
            switch (event.level) {
                case "status":
                    statusLabel.text = "Bid sent successfully.";
                    break;
                case "error":
                    statusLabel.text = "Failed to send bid.";
                    break;
            }
        }
        ]]>
    </mx:Script>
    <mx:Panel title="LocalConnection Sender Application"
     horizontalCenter="0" verticalCenter="0">
        <mx:Form width="100%" height="100%" horizontalCenter="0"
         verticalCenter="0">
            <mx:FormItem label="Enter Quantity">
                <mx:TextInput id="quantityTxt"/>
            </mx:FormItem>
            <mx:FormItem label="Enter Price">
                <mx:TextInput id="priceTxt"/>
            </mx:FormItem>
            <mx:FormItem>
                <mx:Button id="btnBid" label="Send Bid"
                 click="sendMessage()"/>
            </mx:FormItem>
            <mx:ControlBar>
                <mx:Label id="statusLabel" text=""/>
            </mx:ControlBar>
        </mx:Form>
    </mx:Panel>
</mx:Application>
```

In the code above, we created a `LocalConnection` object in the `init()` method and registered an event listener to receive status messages as to the success or failure of the send. We have written a `sendMessage()` method to send a message over `LocalConnection` by using the `LocalConnection.send()` method. Please note that the send method of the LocalConnection class takes three parameters: the connection name (a unique name specified in the `LocalConnection.connect(connectionName)` method to establish communication), a method name (the name of the method to be invoked in the receiving `LocalConnection` object), and finally a ...`(rest)` parameter for passing additional optional function parameters to the specified method(in this case, we are using it to pass an object).

`ReceiverApplication.mxml:`

```
<?xml version="1.0" encoding="utf-8"?>
<mx:Application xmlns:mx="http://www.adobe.com/2006/mxml" creationComp
lete="init()">
   <mx:Script>
      <![CDATA[
         import mx.collections.ArrayCollection;
         import flash.net.LocalConnection;

          [Bindable]
         private var totalBids:ArrayCollection;
         private var conn:LocalConnection;

         private function init():void{
            totalBids = new ArrayCollection();

            conn = new LocalConnection();
            conn.client = this;
            try {
               conn.connect("myBiddingChannel");
            } catch (error:ArgumentError) {
               trace("Failed to connect to LocalConnection."
                     +error.message);
            }
         }

         public function incomingBids(bid:Object):void {
            totalBids.addItem(bid);
         }
      ]]>
   </mx:Script>
   <mx:Panel title="LocalConnection Receiver Application" height="300"
    width="500" paddingLeft="10" paddingRight="10" paddingBottom="10">
      <mx:Label text="Received Bids:"/>
      <mx:DataGrid id="bidGrid" dataProvider="{totalBids}"
       width="100%" height="100%"/>
   </mx:Panel>
</mx:Application>
```

The above receiver application code is fairly simple. It just creates a `LocalConnection` instance and uses the `LocalConnection.connect()` method by passing a unique connection name string, which is defined by the sender application in the `send()` method. In addition, it implements an `incomingBids()` method. This method is the one that is called by the sender application SWF file. When it's called, the bid object is passed to it which is displayed in `DataGrid`.

Run the `SenderApplication.mxml` and `ReceiverApplication.mxml` applications from Flex Builder, and make sure that they are running in two different browser windows. Then type the bidding information in the sender application and click on the **Send Bid** button. Clearly, this should send the message to the receiver application over `LocalConnection` and data should get displayed in `DataGrid`.

The following screenshot shows how these LocalConnection messages should appear in the application:

As shown in above screenshot, our sender application establishes `LocalConnection` and sends the bid details on to the **Send Bid** button's click and displays the status. Next, our receiver application will receive these details through `LocalConnection` and display them on the screen, as shown in the following screenshot:

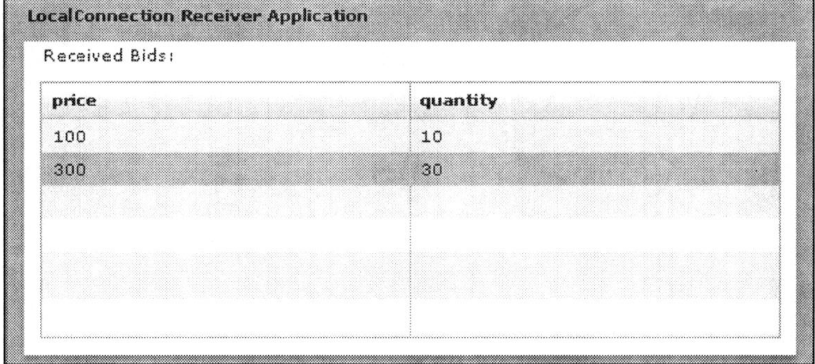

Summary

In this chapter, you learned how to make use of External API to establish communication between ActionScript and JavaScript, and vice versa. You also learned how to send and receive data between a Flex application and JavaScript from a container application. You also learned how to use the `LocalConnection` class to enable communication between two different SWF applications on a single computer.

In the next chapter, you will learn how to work with XML data using the E4X techniques and various XML classes provided by Flex E4X API. You will also learn how to load external XML data, and manipulate and use it as a data provider of your Flex components. We will also build a sample book explorer application using XML data and E4X techniques.

5

Working with XML

In today's world, many server-side applications make use of XML to structure data because XML is a standard way of representing structured information. It is easy to work with, and people can easily read, write, and understand XML without the need of any specialized skills. The XML standard is widely accepted and used in server communications such as Simple Object Access Protocol (SOAP) based web services. XML stands for eXtensible Markup Language. The XML standard specification is available at `http://www.w3.org/XML/`.

Adobe Flex provides a standardized ECMAScript-based set of API classes and functionality for working with XML data. This collection of classes and functionality provided by Flex are known as *E4X*. You can use these classes provided by Flex to build sophisticated **Rich Internet applications** using XML data.

This chapter covers the E4X approach to process XML data with a comprehensive example application using these techniques to process XML data.

XML basics

XML is a standard way to represent categorized data into a tree structure similar to HTML documents. XML is written in plain-text format, and hence it is very easy to read, write, and manipulate its data.

A typical XML document looks like this:

```
<book>
   <title>Flex 3 with Java</title>
   <author>Satish Kore</author>
   <publisher>Packt Publishing</publisher>
   <pages>300</pages>
</book>
```

Generally, XML data is known as XML documents and it is represented by tags wrapped in angle brackets (<>). These tags are also known as XML elements. Every XML document starts with a single top-level element known as the root element. Each element is distinguished by a set of tags known as the opening tag and the closing tag. In the previous XML document, `<book>` is the opening tag and `</book>` is the closing tag. If an element contains no content, it can be written as an empty statement (also called self-closing statement). For example, `<book/>` is as good as writing `<book></book>`.

XML documents can also be more complex with nested tags and attributes, as shown in the following example:

```
<book ISBN="978-1-847195-34-0">
   <title>Flex 3 with Java</title>
   <author country="India" numberOfBooks="1">
      <firstName>Satish</firstName>
      <lastName>Kore</lastName>
</author>
   <publisher country="United Kingdom">Packt Publishing</publisher>
   <pages>300</pages>
</book>
```

Notice that the above XML document contains nested tags such as `<firstName>` and `<lastName>` under the `<author>` tag. `ISBN`, `country`, and `numberOfBooks`, which you can see inside the tags, are called *XML attributes*.

To learn more about XML, visit the W3Schools' XML Tutorial at `http://w3schools.com/xml/`.

Understanding E4X

Flex provides a set of API classes and functionality based on the ECMAScript for XML (E4X) standards in order to work with XML data. The E4X approach provides a simple and straightforward way to work with XML structured data, and it also reduces the complexity of parsing XML documents.

Earlier versions of Flex did not have a direct way of working with XML data. The E4X provides an alternative to DOM (Document Object Model) interface that uses a simpler syntax for reading and querying XML documents. More information about other E4X implementations can be found at `http://en.wikipedia.org/wiki/E4X`.

The key features of E4X include:

- It is based on standard scripting language specifications known as ECMAScript for XML. Flex implements these specifications in the form of API classes and functionality for simplifying the XML data processing.

* It provides easy and well-known operators, such as the dot (.) and @, to work with XML objects.
* The @ and dot (.) operators can be used not only to read data, but also to assign data to XML nodes, attributes, and so on.
* The E4X functionality is much easier and more intuitive than working with the DOM documents to access XML data.

ActionScript 3.0 includes the following E4X classes: XML, XMLList, QName, and Namespace. These classes are designed to simplify XML data processing into Flex applications.

Let's see one quick example:

Define a variable of type XML and create a sample XML document. In this example, we will assign it as a literal. However, in the real world, your application might load XML data from external sources, such as a web service or an RSS feed.

```
private var myBooks:XML =
   <books publisher="Packt Pub">
      <book title="Book1" price="99.99">
         <author>Author1</author>
      </book>
      <book title="Book2" price="59.99">
         <author>Author2</author>
      </book>
      <book title="Book3" price="49.99">
         <author>Author3</author>
      </book>
   </books>;
```

Now, we will see some of the E4X approaches to read and parse the above XML in our application. The E4X uses many operators to simplify accessing XML nodes and attributes, such as dot (.) and attribute identifier (@), for accessing properties and attributes.

```
private function traceXML():void {
   trace(myBooks.book.(@price < 50.99).@title); //Output: Book3
   trace(myBooks.book[1].author); //Output: Author2
   trace(myBooks.@publisher); //Output: Packt Pub
   //Following for loop outputs prices of all books
   for each(var price in myBooks..@price) {
     trace(price);
   }
}
```

In the code above, we are using a conditional expression to extract the title of the book(s) whose price is set below 50.99$ in the first trace statement. If we have to do this manually, imagine how much code would have been needed to parse the XML. In the second trace, we are accessing a book node using index and printing its author node's value. And in the third trace, we are simply printing the root node's publisher attribute value and finally, we are using a `for` loop to traverse through prices of all the books and printing each price.

The following is a list of XML operators:

Operator	Name	Description
@	attribute identifier	Identifies attributes of an XML or `XMLList` object.
{ }	braces (XML)	Evaluates an expression that is used in an XML or `XMLList` initializer.
[ ]	brackets (XML)	Accesses a property or attribute of an XML or `XMLList` object, for example `myBooks.book["@title"]`.
+	concatenation (`XMLList`)	Concatenates (combines) XML or `XMLList` values into an `XMLList` object.
+=	concatenation assignment (`XMLList`)	Assigns `expression1`, which is an `XMLList` object, the value of `expression1 + expression2`.

There is no operator	delete (XML)	Deletes the XML elements or attributes specified by reference. For example:
		`delete myBooks.book[0].author;.`
		(The above code line deletes the `author` element from the `book` node.)
		OR
		`delete myBooks.book[0].@title;`
		(The above code line deletes the `title` attribute from the `book` node.)

..	descendant accessor	Navigates to descendant elements of an XML or `XMLList` object, or (combined with the @ operator) finds matching attributes of descendants.
.	dot (XML)	Navigates to child elements of an XML or `XMLList` object, or (combined with the @ operator) returns attributes of an XML or `XMLList` object.
( )	parentheses (XML)	Evaluates an expression in an E4X XML construct.
< >	XML literal tag delimiter	Defines an XML tag in an XML literal.

The @ and dot (.) operators can be used to read as well as assign data, as shown in following example:

```
myBooks.book[1].author = "Satish Kore";
myBooks.book.(@price < 50.99).@title = "Low Price Edition Book";
```

Now, let's look at the important classes used for working with XML data in Flex in the next section.

The XML object

An XML class represents an XML element, attribute, comment, processing instruction, or a text element.

We have used the XML class in our example above to initialize the myBooks variable with an XML literal. The XML class is included into an ActionScript 3.0 core class, so you don't need to import a package to use it.

The XML class provides many properties and methods to simplify XML processing, such as ignoreWhitespace and ignoreComments properties, used for ignoring whitespaces and comments in XML documents respectively. You can use the prependChild() and appendChild() methods to prepend and append XML nodes to existing XML documents. Methods such as toString() and toXMLString() allow you to convert XML to a string.

An example of an XML object:

```
private var myBooks:XML =
<books publisher="Packt Pub">
   <book title="Book1" price="99.99">
      <author>Author1</author>
   </book>
   <book title="Book2" price="120.00">
      <author>Author2</author>
   </book>
</books>;
```

In the above example, we have created an XML object by assigning an XML literal to it. You can also create an XML object from a string that contains XML data, as shown in the following example:

```
private var str:String = "<books publisher=\"Packt Pub\"> <book
title=\"Book1\" price=\"99.99\"> <author>Author1</author> </book>
<book title=\"Book2\" price=\"59.99\"> <author>Author2</author> </
book> </books>";
private var myBooks:XML = new XML(str);
trace(myBooks.toXMLString()); //outputs formatted xml as string
```

If the XML data in string is not well-formed (for example, a closing tag is missing), then you will see a runtime error.

You can also use binding expressions in the XML text to extract contents from a variable data. For example, you could bind a node's name attribute to a variable value, as in the following line:

```
private var title:String = "Book1"
var aBook:XML = <book title="{title}">;
```

To read more about XML class methods and properties, go through Flex 3 LiveDocs at `http://livedocs.adobe.com/flex/3/langref/XML.html`.

The XMLList object

As the class name indicates, `XMLList` contains one or more `XML` objects. It can contain full XML documents, XML fragments, or the results of an XML query.

You can typically use all of the `XML` class's methods and properties on the objects from `XMLList`. To access these objects from the `XMLList` collection, iterate over it using a `for each...` statement.

The `XMLList` provides you with the following methods to work with its objects:

- `child()`: Returns a specified child of every XML object
- `children()`: Returns specified children of every XML object
- `descendants()`: Returns all descendants of an XML object
- `elements()` : Calls the `elements()` method of each XML object in the `XMLList`. Returns all elements of the XML object
- `parent()` : Returns the parent of the `XMLList` object if all items in the `XMLList` object have the same parent
- `attribute(attributeName)`: Calls the `attribute()` method of each XML object and returns an `XMLList` object of the results. The results match the given `attributeName` parameter
- `attributes()`: Calls the `attributes()` method of each XML object and returns an `XMLList` object of attributes for each XML object
- `contains()`: Checks if the specified XML object is present in the `XMLList`
- `copy()`: Returns a copy of the given `XMLList` object
- `length()`: Returns the number of properties in the `XMLList` object
- `valueOf()`: Returns the `XMLList` object

For details on these methods, see the ActionScript 3.0 Language Reference.

Let's return to the example of the `XMLList`:

```
var xmlList:XMLList = myBooks.book.(@price == 99.99);
var item:XML;
for each(item in xmlList)
{
   trace("item:"+item.toXMLString());
}
```

Output:

item:<book title="Book1" price="99.99">
<author>Author1</author>
</book>

In the example above, we have used `XMLList` to store the result of the `myBooks.book.(@price == 99.99);` statement. This statement returns an `XMLList` containing XML node(s) whose price is 99.99$.

Working with XML objects

The XML class provides many useful methods to work with XML objects, such as the `appendChild()` and `prependChild()` methods to add an XML element to the beginning or end of an XML object, as shown in the following example:

```
var node1:XML = <middleInitial>B</middleInitial>
var node2:XML = <lastName>Kore</lastName>
var root:XML = <personalInfo></personalInfo>
root = root.appendChild(node1);
root = root.appendChild(node2);
root = root.prependChild(<firstName>Satish</firstName>);
```

The output is as follows:

<personalInfo>
<firstName>Satish</firstName>
<middleInitial>B</middleInitial>
<lastName>Kore</lastName>
</personalInfo>

You can use the `insertChildBefore()` or `insertChildAfter()` method to add a property before or after a specified property, as shown in the following example:

```
var x:XML = <count>
      <one>1</one>
      <three>3</three>
      <four>4</four>
   </count>;
x = x.insertChildBefore(x.three, "<two>2</two>");
x = x.insertChildAfter(x.four, "<five>5</five>");
trace(x.toXMLString());
```

The output of the above code is as follows:

<count>

<one>1</one>

<two>2</two>

<three>3</three>

<four>4</four>

<five>5</five>

</count>

Using XML as dataProvider

One of the powerful features of the XML object is to use it as a `dataProvider` for your component that allows you to tie XML directly with your component's data model. Let's see how we can use XML as the `dataProvider` of a `DataGrid` component to display complex data.

```
private var xmlData:XML =
<books>
   <book ISBN="184719530X">
      <title>Building Websites with Joomla! 1.5</title>
      <author>
         <lastName>Hagen</lastName>
         <firstName>Graf</firstName>
      </author>
      <image>../assets/images/184719530X.png</image>
      <pageCount>363</pageCount>
      <price>Rs.1,247.40</price>
      <description>The best-selling Joomla! tutorial</description>
```

```
    </book>
</books>;
private function getAuthorName(item:Object, column:DataGridColumn):
String {
    var xml:XML = XML(item);
    return item.author.firstName +" "+ item.author.lastName;
}
```

We have created an XML object with a complex XML structure. Now, we will tie this with the `DataGrid` component using data binding, as shown in the following example:

```
<mx:Panel title="XML dataProvider example" width="666" height="149">
    <mx:DataGrid id="dgGrid" dataProvider="{xmlData.book}"
     height="100%" width="100%">
        <mx:columns>
            <mx:DataGridColumn headerText="ISBN" dataField="@ISBN"/>
            <mx:DataGridColumn headerText="Title" dataField="title"/>
            <mx:DataGridColumn headerText="Author"
             labelFunction="getAuthorName"/>
            <mx:DataGridColumn headerText="Price" dataField="price"/>
            <mx:DataGridColumn headerText="Description"
             dataField="description"/>
        </mx:columns>
    </mx:DataGrid>
</mx:Panel>
```

In the code above, we have created a `DataGrid` component with a set of columns to display data from the XML object. Notice that we have used { } (curly braces) to bind the XML object's specific nodes with the `DataGrid`. This means `{xmlData.book}` specifies that the `DataGrid` will use the `book` node(s) and its children nodes as source of its data.

We have used the `DataGridColumn`'s `dataField` property. The `dataField` property is the name of the element or attribute in the XML data provider item associated with the column. For example, to display the book's title, the `dataField` property is set to `title`.

The `labelFunction` function is used to specify the name of a function. The function will be called and the return value is used to display in this column. For example, sometimes you might need to customize how your data gets displayed. In this case, `labelFunction` is used to concatenate the `firstName` and `lastName` element's values and return them as a single string.

The `labelFunction` function takes two parameters: the DataGrid item as an object and the DataGrid column.

The output looks as follows:

XML dataProvider example

ISBN	Title	Author	Price	Description
184719530X	Building Websites witl	Graf Hagen	Rs.1,247.40	The best-selling Joon

You can also use the `XMLListCollection` object as the `dataProvider` of your component. The `XMLListCollection` object can hold the `XMLList` objects and provides a set of methods that lets you access, sort, filter, and modify the data items in that data object. This is very helpful if you are working with dynamic XML data. It can be used to dynamically add and remove items from the data provider and its representation in the UI control.

The following example shows how to work with `XMLListCollection` and dynamically add new elements in it:

```
private var xmlData:XML =
    <books>
        <book ISBN="184719530X">
            <title>Building Websites with Joomla! 1.5</title>
            <author>
                <lastName>Hagen</lastName>
                <firstName>Graf</firstName>
            </author>
            <image>../assets/images/184719530X.png</image>
            <pageCount>363</pageCount>
            <price>Rs.1,247.40</price>
            <description>The best-selling Joomla! tutorial</description>
        </book>
    </books>;

private var newBookElement:XML =
    <book ISBN="1847196160">
        <title>Drupal 6 JavaScript and jQuery</title>
        <author>
            <lastName>Matt</lastName>
            <firstName>Butcher</firstName>
        </author>
```

```
        <image>../assets/images/1847196160.png</image>
        <pageCount>250</pageCount>
        <price>Rs.1,108.80</price>
        <description>Drupal 6 modules and themes</description>
    </book>;

private var xmlListCollection:XMLListCollection =
new XMLListCollection(xmlData.book);
```

Note that `xmlData.book` returns an `XMLList` object with all book elements.

You can use the `addItem()` method of the `XMLListCollection` class to add `newBookElement` to it, as shown here:

```
xmlListCollection.addItem(newBookElement);
```

And you can set the `xmlListCollection` object as the `dataProvider` of your `DataGrid` using { } (curly braces) data-binding expression.

Loading external XML documents

You can use the `URLLoader` class to load external data from a URL. The `URLLoader` class downloads data from a URL as text or binary data. In this section, we will see how to use the `URLLoader` class for loading external XML data into your application. You can create a `URLLoader` class instance and call the `load()` method by passing `URLRequest` as a parameter and register for its *complete* event to handle loaded data. The following code snippet shows how exactly this works:

```
private var xmlUrl:String = "http://www.foo.com/rssdata.xml";
private var request:URLRequest = new URLRequest(xmlUrl);
private var loader:URLLoader = new URLLoader(;
private var rssData:XML;

loader.addEventListener(Event.COMPLETE, completeHandler);

loader.load(request);

private function completeHandler(event:Event):void {
    rssData = XML(loader.data);
    trace(rssData);
}
```

Let's see one quick complete sample of loading RSS data from the Internet:

```
<?xml version="1.0" encoding="utf-8"?>
<mx:Application xmlns:mx="http://www.adobe.com/2006/mxml"
 creationComplete="loadData();">

   <mx:Script>
      <![CDATA[
         import mx.collections.XMLListCollection;

         private var xmlUrl:String = "http://sessions.adobe.com/
                                      360FlexSJ2008/feed.xml";
         private var request:URLRequest = new URLRequest(xmlUrl);
         private var loader:URLLoader = new URLLoader(request);
          [Bindable]
         private var rssData:XML;

         private function loadData():void {
            loader.addEventListener(Event.COMPLETE, completeHandler);
            loader.load(request);
         }
         private function completeHandler(event:Event):void {
             rssData = new XML(loader.data);
         }

      ]]>
   </mx:Script>
   <mx:Panel title="RSS Feed Reader" width="100%" height="100%">
      <mx:DataGrid id="dgGrid" dataProvider="{rssData.channel.item}"
                                         height="100%" width="100%">
         <mx:columns>
            <mx:DataGridColumn headerText="Title" dataField="title"/>
            <mx:DataGridColumn headerText="Link" dataField="link"/>
            <mx:DataGridColumn headerText="pubDate"
                              dataField="pubDate"/>
            <mx:DataGridColumn headerText="Description"
             dataField="description"/>
         </mx:columns>
      </mx:DataGrid>
      <mx:TextArea width="100%" height="80"
       text="{dgGrid.selectedItem.description}"/>
   </mx:Panel>
   </mx:Application>
```

In the code above, we are loading RSS feed from an external URL and displaying it in `DataGrid` by using data binding.

Output:

RSS Feed Reader

Title	Link	pubDate	Description
Implementing BlazeDS by Andrew Powell	http://link.brightcove.com/services/link/bcpic	Mon, 10 Nov 2008 12:43:29 -0800	This session is a survey of implementing BlazeDS witl
Encrypting Flex & Protecting Revenue by Andr	http://link.brightcove.com/services/link/bcpic	Tue, 19 Aug 2008 00:00:00 -0700	So your dreaming about the ALL the new customers y
How to make your AIR app blow up with Mera	http://link.brightcove.com/services/link/bcpic	Mon, 10 Nov 2008 12:51:02 -0800	How to make your AIR app blow up with Merapi with A
Creating an MMO w/ Flex 3 in 59 Min by Sam	http://link.brightcove.com/services/link/bcpic	Mon, 10 Nov 2008 12:56:20 -0800	Creating an MMO with Adobe Flex 3 in 59 Minutes!
Promoting your Flex and AIR applications by	http://link.brightcove.com/services/link/bcpic	Mon, 10 Nov 2008 12:59:05 -0800	Now that you've built something cool with Flex and AII
Creating Flex Components by Jeffry Houser	http://link.brightcove.com/services/link/bcpic	Mon, 10 Nov 2008 13:01:30 -0800	An introductory presentation on creating Flex Compor
High Definition Video & Flex Hands On by Ch	http://link.brightcove.com/services/link/bcpic	Mon, 10 Nov 2008 13:02:31 -0800	This session covers the tools and workflows you need
Versioning Support for Large Apps & Portals b	http://link.brightcove.com/services/link/bcpic	Mon, 10 Nov 2008 13:04:40 -0800	Many large applications and most portals are architec
Cairngorm For Beginners by Neil Webb	http://link.brightcove.com/services/link/bcpic	Mon, 10 Nov 2008 13:05:22 -0800	Cairngorm For Beginners - Making A Molehill Out Of A
Advanced Analytics for Flex and Flash RIAs b	http://link.brightcove.com/services/link/bcpic	Mon, 10 Nov 2008 13:07:13 -0800	Web analytics is no longer just click-throughs and pag
Data Visualization and Dashboards by Thoma	http://link.brightcove.com/services/link/bcpic	Mon, 10 Nov 2008 13:10:21 -0800	This session discusses approaches and techniques to
Day 3 Keynote with Tom, John and company	http://link.brightcove.com/services/link/bcpic	Mon, 10 Nov 2008 13:11:32 -0800	Tom Ortega and John Wilker present awards for past
Using Item Renderers in Flex by Mary Mcdon	http://link.brightcove.com/services/link/bcpic	Mon, 10 Nov 2008 13:13:15 -0800	Discusses using item renderers and item editors in Fl
AIR SQLite: an optimization conversa by H. F	http://link.brightcove.com/services/link/bcpic	Mon, 10 Nov 2008 13:13:46 -0800	How can I optimize my indexes? What's the best way
PatchPanel/SwitchBoard: Connect SWF/AIR w	http://link.brightcove.com/services/link/bcpic	Mon, 10 Nov 2008 13:14:31 -0800	Bernd Paradies: PatchPanel is a Flex library called cs3
Adv Video Streaming & Mgmt Techs w/ Flex &	http://link.brightcove.com/services/link/bcpic	Mon, 10 Nov 2008 13:25:23 -0800	David Hassoun: This session will be a deeper dive lo
Learning Flex from Scratch (LFFS) by Flater &	http://link.brightcove.com/services/link/bcpic	Mon, 10 Nov 2008 13:27:05 -0800	Adam Flater & Scott Sheridan: The Learning Flex fror
Flex and Acrobat by Joel Geraci	http://link.brightcove.com/services/link/bcpic	Mon, 10 Nov 2008 13:28:33 -0800	This session will make you rethink everything you kn

Tom Ortega and John Wilker present awards for past 360|Flex events, give updates on the future and offer others time to share their business updates. Ted Patrick gives sneak preview of Adobe's latest 'Sessions' project.

An example: Building a book explorer

By this time, you would be comfortable in writing Flex applications by using many features of Flex and ActionScript, which you have learned in the previous chapters. In this section, we will build something more complicated and interesting by using many features, including custom components, events, data binding, E4X, loading external XML data, and so on.

We will build a sample books explorer, which will load a books catalog from an external XML file and allow the users to explore and view details of books. We will also build a simple shopping cart component, which will list books that a user would add to cart by clicking on the **add to cart** button.

Create a new Flex project using Flex Builder. Once the project is created, create an `\assets\images\` folder under its `src` folder. This folder will be used to store images used in this application. Now start creating the following source files into its source folder.

Let's start by creating a simple book catalog XML file as follows:

`bookscatalog.xml`:

```
<books>
   <book ISBN="184719530X">
      <title>Building Websites with Joomla! 1.5</title>
      <author>
         <lastName>Hagen</lastName>
         <firstName>Graf</firstName>
      </author>
      <image>../assets/images/184719530X.png</image>
      <pageCount>363</pageCount>
      <price>Rs.1,247.40</price>
      <description>The best-selling Joomla! tutorial guide updated for
the latest 1.5 release </description>
   </book>
   <book ISBN="1847196160">
      <title>Drupal 6 JavaScript and jQuery</title>
      <author>
         <lastName>Matt</lastName>
         <firstName>Butcher</firstName>
      </author>
      <image>../assets/images/1847196160.png</image>
      <pageCount>250</pageCount>
      <price>Rs.1,108.80</price>
      <description>Putting jQuery, AJAX, and JavaScript effects into
your Drupal 6 modules and themes</description>
   </book>
   <book ISBN="184719494X">
      <title>Expert Python Programming</title>
      <author>
         <lastName>Tarek</lastName>
         <firstName>Ziadé</firstName>
      </author>
      <image>../assets/images/184719494X.png</image>
      <pageCount>350</pageCount>
      <price>Rs.1,247.4</price>
      <description>Best practices for designing, coding, and
distributing your Python software</description>
   </book>
   <book ISBN="1847194885">
      <title>Joomla! Web Security</title>
      <author>
         <lastName>Tom</lastName>
```

```
            <firstName>Canavan</firstName>
        </author>
        <image>../assets/images/1847194885.png</image>
        <pageCount>248</pageCount>
        <price>Rs.1,108.80</price>
        <description>Secure your Joomla! website from common security
threats with this easy-to-use guide</description>
    </book>
</books>
```

The above XML file contains details of individual books in an XML form. You can also deploy this file on your web server and specify its URL into `URLRequest` while loading it.

Next, we will create a custom event which we will be dispatching from our custom component. Make sure you create an `events` package under your `src` folder in Flex Builder called *events*, and place this file in it.

`AddToCartEvent.as`

```
package events
{
    import flash.events.Event;

    public class AddToCartEvent extends Event
    {
        public static const ADD_TO_CART:String = "addToCart";
        public var book:Object;

        public function AddToCartEvent(type:String, bubbles:
Boolean=false, cancelable:Boolean=false)
        {
                    super(type, bubbles, cancelable);
        }

    }
}
```

This is a simple custom event created by inheriting the `flash.events.Event` class. This class defines the `ADD_TO_CART` string constant, which will be used as the name of the event in the `addEventListener()` method. You will see this in the `BooksExplorer.mxml` code. We have also defined an object to hold the reference of the book which the user can add into the shopping cart. In short, this object will hold the XML node of a selected book.

Next, we will create the MXML custom component called `BookDetailItemRenderer.mxml`. Make sure that you create a package under your src folder in Flex Builder called `components`, and place this file in it and copy the following code in it:

```
<?xml version="1.0" encoding="utf-8"?>
<mx:HBox xmlns:mx="http://www.adobe.com/2006/mxml"
 cornerRadius="8" paddingBottom="2" paddingLeft="2"
 paddingRight="2" paddingTop="2">
   <mx:Metadata>
       [Event(name="addToCart", type="flash.events.Event")]
   </mx:Metadata>

   <mx:Script>
      <![CDATA[
         import events.AddToCartEvent;
         import mx.controls.Alert;

          [Bindable]
          [Embed(source="../assets/images/cart.gif")]
         public var cartImage:Class;

         private function addToCardEventDispatcher():void {
         var addToCartEvent:AddToCartEvent = new AddToCartEvent
         ("addToCart", true, true);
            addtoCartEvent.book = data;
            dispatchEvent(addtoCartEvent);
         }
      ]]>
   </mx:Script>
   <mx:HBox width="100%" verticalAlign="middle" paddingBottom="2"
    paddingLeft="2" paddingRight="2" paddingTop="2" height="100%"
    borderStyle="solid" borderThickness="2" borderColor="#6E6B6B"
    cornerRadius="4">
      <mx:Image id="bookImage" source="{data.image}" height="109"
       width="78" maintainAspectRatio="false"/>
      <mx:VBox height="100%" width="100%" verticalGap="2"
       paddingBottom="0" paddingLeft="0" paddingRight="0"
       paddingTop="0" verticalAlign="middle">
         <mx:Label id="bookTitle" text="{data.title}"
          fontSize="12" fontWeight="bold"/>
         <mx:Label id="bookAuthor" text="By: {data.author.
          lastName},{data.author.firstName}" fontWeight="bold"/>
         <mx:Label id="coverPrice" text="Price: {data.price}"
          fontWeight="bold"/>
         <mx:Label id="pageCount" text="Pages: {data.pageCount}"
          fontWeight="bold"/>
```

```
            <mx:HBox width="100%" backgroundColor="#3A478D"
             horizontalAlign="right" paddingBottom="0" paddingLeft="0"
             paddingRight="5" paddingTop="0" height="22"
             verticalAlign="middle">
               <mx:Label text="Add to cart  " color="#FFFFFF"
                fontWeight="bold"/>
               <mx:Button icon="{cartImage}" height="20" width="20"
                click="addToCardEventDispatcher();"/>
            </mx:HBox>
         </mx:VBox>
      </mx:HBox>
   </mx:HBox>
```

The above custom component will be used as an `itemRenderer` to display books' details from an XML file. In this example, we have created a custom MXML-based component. This custom component dispatches a custom event called `AddToCartEvent` when a user clicks on the **add to cart** button. Notice that when we are dispatching an event, we are setting its `bubbles` argument (second argument in the `AddToCartEvent` constructor, which is inherited from the `flash.events.Event` class) to `true`. This is very important in order to bubble this event up to its parent where we will write an event listener for it. (For information on bubbling, please see the *Event propagation* section in Chapter 3). You will see how to write an event listener on the parent to handle the event dispatched by its children in the `BooksExplorer.mxml` code. At the end, this custom component will be used as `ItemRenderer` of the `TileList` component to display books. So we are using the `data` property of the `itemRenderer` instance to access XML nodes and properties using the E4X technique. The `data` property is implicitly available in item renderers that can be used to access content locally. For information on `ItemRenderers` and how to use its `data` property, please see the *Understanding Flex item renderers* section in Chapter 2.

Next, we will create the main application and layout the book explorer user interface, and then we will write business logic for loading XML data and display it in the custom component, and so on.

`BooksExplorer.mxml`:

```
   <?xml version="1.0" encoding="utf-8"?>
   <mx:Application xmlns:mx="http://www.adobe.com/2006/mxml" creationCom
   plete="init()"
      xmlns:components="components.*" layout="horizontal">

      <mx:Script>
         <![CDATA[
            import mx.collections.XMLListCollection;
            import mx.formatters.CurrencyFormatter;
            import mx.collections.ArrayCollection;
```

```
            import mx.effects.Blur;
            import events.AddToCartEvent;
            import components.BookDetailItemRenderer;
            import mx.controls.Alert;

            private var loader:URLLoader;
            private var request:URLRequest;

             [Bindable]
            private var xmlData:XML;

             [Bindable]
            private var selectedBook:XML;
             [Bindable]
            private var shoppingCart:ArrayCollection;

            private function init():void {
               tileList.addEventListener(AddToCartEvent.ADD_TO_CART,
               addToCartHandler);
               shoppingCart = new ArrayCollection();

               request = new URLRequest("./bookscatalog.xml");

               loader = new URLLoader();
               loader.addEventListener(Event.COMPLETE, completeHandler);

               try {
                  loader.load(request);
               } catch (error:SecurityError) {
                    trace("A SecurityError has occurred.");
               } catch(error:Error) {
                  trace("An Unknown Error has occurred. ["+error.
                         message+"]");
               }
            }

            private function completeHandler(event:Event):void {
               xmlData = new XML(loader.data);
            }
            private function addToCartHandler(event:AddToCartEvent):void
{
               shoppingCart.addItem(XML(event.book));
            }
            private function itemSelected(event:Event):void {
               selectedBook = XML(tileList.selectedItem);
            }
         ]]>
      </mx:Script>
      <mx:VBox width="100%" height="100%" verticalAlign="bottom">
         <mx:HBox width="100%" height="70%">
```

```
    <mx:Panel title="Products Explorer" width="70%" height="100%"
     layout="horizontal">
       <mx:TileList id="tileList" variableRowHeight="false"
        itemRenderer="components.BookDetailItemRenderer"
          dataProvider="{xmlData.book}"
          change="itemSelected(event)" columnCount="2"
          height="100%" width="100%"/>
    </mx:Panel>
    <mx:Panel width="30%" height="100%" title="Details">
          <mx:Form width="100%" height="100%">
          <mx:FormItem label="Book Name:">
             <mx:Label id="bookName" text="{selectedBook.title}"/>
          </mx:FormItem>
          <mx:FormItem label="ISBN:">
             <mx:Label id="isbnNumber"
              text="{selectedBook.@ISBN}"/>
          </mx:FormItem>
          <mx:FormItem label="Author:">
             <mx:Label id="authorName">
                <mx:text>{selectedBook.author.firstName}
                 {selectedBook.author.lastName}</mx:text>
             </mx:Label>
          </mx:FormItem>
          <mx:FormItem label="Pages:">
             <mx:Label id="pageNumber"
              text="{selectedBook.pageCount}"/>
          </mx:FormItem>
          <mx:FormItem label="Price:">
             <mx:Label id="bookPrice"
              text="{selectedBook.price}"/>
          </mx:FormItem>
          <mx:FormItem label="Description:">
             <mx:Text id="bookDesc"
              text="{selectedBook.description}" width="200"/>
          </mx:FormItem>
          <mx:FormItem label="Cover Page:">
             <mx:Image width="138"
              height="146" source="{selectedBook.image}"/>
          </mx:FormItem>
       </mx:Form>
    </mx:Panel>
</mx:HBox>
<mx:HBox width="100%" height="30%">
    <mx:Panel width="100%" height="100%" title="Shopping Cart">
```

```
            <mx:DataGrid id="dgGrid" dataProvider="{shoppingCart}"
             height="100%" width="100%" editable="true">
                <mx:columns>
                    <mx:DataGridColumn headerText="Book Name"
                     dataField="title" editable="false"/>
                    <mx:DataGridColumn headerText="Price"
                     dataField="price" editable="false"/>
                    <mx:DataGridColumn headerText="Qty."
                     dataField="quantity" editable="true"/>
                </mx:columns>
            </mx:DataGrid>
            <mx:ControlBar>
                <mx:Button label="Checkout"
                 click="Alert.show(,Not yet implemented.');"/>
                <mx:Button label="Remove"
                 click="Alert.show(,Not yet implemented.');"/>
            </mx:ControlBar>
        </mx:Panel>
    </mx:HBox>
</mx:VBox>

</mx:Application>
```

In the code above, we have used the `HBox`, `VBox`, and `Panel` containers to lay out the main user interface. We have also added a `TileList` component to display books using a custom component, that is, `BookDetailItemRenderer.mxml` as its `itemRenderer`. Next, we have added another `Panel` container to display the selected book's details using a `Form` container. We have used data binding to bind the selected book's details with individual labels in the `Form` container, for example, `text="{selectedBook.title}"`. The `selectedBook` is an XML object which will be populated with the selected book's details when you select an item in the `TileList` component using its `change` event.

> The `TileList` control displays a number of items laid out in tiles. It displays a scroll bar to access all items in the list. You can use its `direction` property to control the direction in which this control lays out its children. To know more about the `TileList` control, see Flex 3 language reference at `http://livedocs.adobe.com/flex/3/langref/mx/controls/TileList.html`.

Next, we have created another `Panel` container to create the shopping cart user interface and added a `DataGrid` component to display cart details. The `DataGrid` component is using data binding to display information from the `shoppingCart ArrayCollection` object, which will contain individual selected book nodes. We will populate the `shopppingCart` array in the `addToCartHandler()` method, which is the event handler for the `addToCart` custom event.

In the ActionScript code block, we have defined a method called `init()` to initialize the application's resources and variables. This method is called in the `application` tag's `creationComplete` event. In this method, we have registered an event handler for the `addToCart` event which will be dispatched by the `BookDetailItemRenderer.mxml` custom component.

Notice that `BookDetailItemRenderer.mxml` is acting as an `itemRenderer` of a `TileList` component, so there is no straight way to add an event listener to it. Therefore, to handle events from the `itemRenderer` component in its parent, you need to dispatch an event from custom component by setting its `bubble` argument to `true`. When an event is dispatched with the `bubble` argument set to `true`, Flex searches for event listeners in the bottom to top order—that is, from event target to root display object. When it finds an appropriate event listener anywhere in its display hierarchy, it delivers an event to it. This is a simple way to communicate with your application from itemRenderers.

Next, we are loading XML file using `URLLoader` and setting its result to the `xmlData` XML object, which is used as the `dataProvider` of the `TileList` component. `xmlData.book` refers to individual `<book>` node(s) from the XML file.

Now we are ready with our application. Once we compile and execute this application, you would see the following screen:

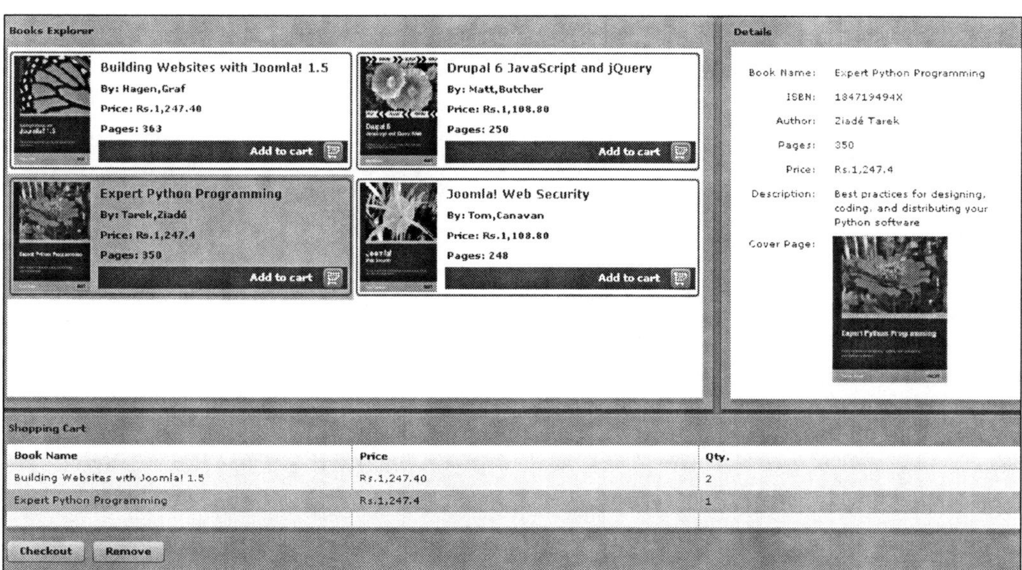

You can play with this application. You can try selecting different items from the `TileList` control and see how it changes display in the **Details** panel, and see what happens when you click on the **Add to cart** button.

Summary

In this chapter, you learned what E4X is and how to use it to work with XML data. You also learned various Flex classes to work with XML data, and how to load external XML files and use XML as a data provider. You also created a sample books explorer application using various concepts such as custom component, event creation, data binding, and E4X.

In the next chapter, you will learn about Adobe's LiveCycle Data Services and what is the BlazeDS platform.

6
Overview of LiveCycle Data Services and BlazeDS

Let's begin this chapter by understanding the real meaning of the term Rich Internet applications (RIAs). RIAs are web-based applications that are rich in presenting dynamic content that goes beyond the traditional request and response model. Flex is a presentation technology, which means that it sits over many existing middleware technologies such as Java, .NET, ColdFusion, and PHP. The purpose of Flex is to build data-intensive applications that provide richer and engaging experience to the end user.

You can leverage your existing server-side infrastructure and choose Flex as your presentation layer. Flex integrates well with J2EE (Enterprise Edition) or server-side Java technologies using an additional server-side layer known as LiveCycle Data Services or BlazeDS deployed on your application server. This additional layer facilitates your Flex application to invoke and communicate directly with Java classes on the server so that they can be called and accessed from the Flex application.

Many third-party remoting and messaging implementations are available to communicate with different server-side technologies such as AMFPHP (`www.amfphp.org`) for PHP, AMF.NET (`www.sourceforge.net/projects/amfnet/`) for .NET, and there are some alternatives to BlazeDS for Java such as GraniteDS (`www.graniteds.org`), WebORB(`http://www.themidnightcoders.com/products/weborb-for-java`), and so on. In this chapter, I will focus only on Adobe's LiveCycle Data Services and BlazeDS technologies.

The following diagram shows its deployment architecture:

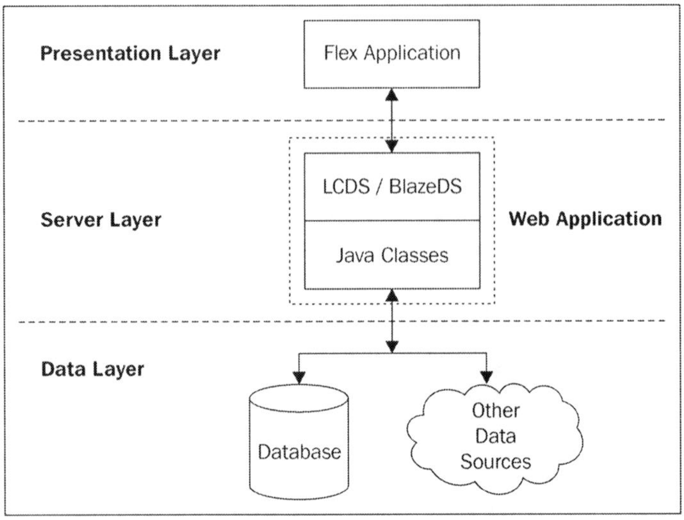

Adobe provides Java remoting and web messaging technology known as LiveCycle Data Services and BlazeDS. You can choose any one of these technologies to work with server-side Java. Let's take a look at each one of them and understand their features.

LiveCycle Data Services

Adobe LiveCycle Data Services is the high-performance, scalable, and flexible server-side framework that provides a powerful data service API to simplify critical data management problems such as data synchronization, paging, and conflict management.

The LiveCycle Data Services provides an entire set of data management features such as data synchronization, paging, real-time messaging, and conflict management to help you build real-time enterprise Flex applications. LiveCycle Data Services is deployed as a standard J2EE web application.

LiveCycle Data Services is a commercial product from Adobe. You can download the trial version from Adobe's web site: `http://www.adobe.com/go/trylivecycle_dataservices`.

LiveCycle Data Services features can be categorized into three main categories, as shown in the following table:

Service	Description
Data Management Services	The services such as real-time data synchronization, data conflict management, and data paging are a part of this category
Remote Procedure Call (RPC) Services	RPC services provide data access methods to communicate with external data sources using HTTP, SOAP, or remote objects using AMF
Messaging Services	These services enable your Flex application to communicate with Java Messaging Service (JMS) to send and receive real-time messages

Adobe LiveCycle Data Services can help you to:

- Build and deploy data-intensive rich enterprise applications that can be easily integrated with LiveCycle document and process services
- Speed up the development and deployment process by leveraging built-in data management capabilities without worrying about the underlying complexities
- Build your application in a scalable and reliable manner by utilizing robust publish and subscribe messaging services that work with Flex and Java Messaging Service (JMS)
- Exploit innovative real-time and binary data access methods, such as HTTP, SOAP, and Remote Object over AMF3 to create seamless and data-intensive applications
- Integrate your application with existing server-side Java infrastructure.
- Generate PDF documents based on pre-authored templates that include graphical assets
- Minimize complexity and error possibility from data synchronization process by using a high-performance and robust synchronization process between the client and the server
- Provide data synchronization between multiple clients and server-side data resources
- Provide client-side offline data persistence for occasionally-connected clients

- Allow integratation of your Flex application data using the Hibernate framework
- Allow Flex applications to use messaging infrastructure by allowing them to use publish and subscribe messaging format between Flex and Java applications

For the complete set of features and capabilities provided by LiveCycle Data Service, see `http://www.adobe.com/products/livecycle/dataservices/features.html`.

BlazeDS

BlazeDS is a free, open source version that provides a subset of the functionality provided by LiveCycle Data Services. BlazeDS is a server-side remoting and messaging technology. Remoting simplifies communication between Flex and server-side Java by automatically serializing and de-serializing objects between Flex and Java, and vice versa. In simple words, by using BlazeDS, developers can call server-side Java methods and classes from a Flex application. By using BlazeDS, developers can create data-rich Flex applications by easily integrating with server-side Java technology and push data in real time to the Flex application.

BlazeDS, along with the Action Message Format (AMF) protocol specification, are open source. The source code is available under the Lesser General Public License (LGPL v3) from `http://opensource.adobe.com/blazeds`. The AMF is a compact binary data transfer protocol which increases application's data-loading performance. AMF binary data format is up to 10 times faster than text-based formats such as XML or SOAP. This was previously available only with LiveCycle Data Services, but now Adobe has released this as part of BlazeDS under the Lesser General Public License version three (LGPL v3).

Adobe has also published the AMF binary data protocol specification, on which BlazeDS remoting and messaging implementation is based.

The following is the list of features available in BlazeDS:

- Integrates and collaborates your Flex application with your existing server-side Java infrastructure without writing plumbing code.
- Allows you to develop a high-performance and faster data delivery application by using AMF format.
- Enables your Flex applications to utilize, publish, and subscribe messaging over standard HTTP. This gives you the ability to push data to your web application from server.
- Most importantly, it is free and open source.

- Allows you to utilize remoting services to access external data sources from your Flex application. Developers can create applications to make asynchronous requests to remote services, including HTTP services, SOAP-based web services, and direct invocation of Java objects on the server.
- Provides transparent data serialization and de-serialization between Java and Flex, which supports mapping between Java and ActionScript data types, including data structures that use Java 5 enumerations.
- Allows you to build high-performance, scalable applications by utilizing binary data transfer between the client and the server, which is faster than text-based protocols such as HTTP, SOAP, or XML.
- Provides Proxy service to get around browser sandbox limitations such as cross-domain restrictions.

Apart from BlazeDS and LiveCycle Data Services, Adobe also offers certified builds of BlazeDS as LiveCycle Data Services, Community Edition, which can be downloaded from `http://www.adobe.com/support/programs/livecycle_dataservices/`.

LiveCycle Data Service Community Edition is a subscription-based offering that provides access to the latest rigorously tested certified builds of BlazeDS open source technologies. Subscriptions allow organizations to take advantage of open source BlazeDS software, but with all the trust and support required for business-critical applications. In short, this has the same features as BlazeDS, but it comes with reliable support for business-critical applications.

BlazeDS vs LiveCycle Data Services

In comparison, LiveCycle Data Services offers more features than BlazeDS. But when it comes to choosing between LiveCycle Data Services and BlazeDS, consider the following comparison points.

LiveCycle Data Services

LiveCycle Data Services offers the following features:

- **High scalability and performance**: If your application offers services for a very large number of concurrent users and requires the ability to send and receive data in real time
- **Data management**: If you are building real-time data collaboration application services, which require data management abilities such as conflict management, change management, and so on
- **Enterprise document integration**: If your application involves reporting and document generation (such as PDF documents) that include graphical assets from Flex applications (such as graphs and charts)

BlazeDS

BlazeDS offers the following features:

- **Remoting**: Remoting over AMF offers faster data-loading performance and the ability to call server-side Java business logic from your Flex client.
- **Messaging**: Messaging offers the ability to push content to your Flex client over HTTP. Unlike LCDS, BlazeDS does not support Real Time Messaging Protocol (RTMP), but it provides the publish and subscribe model to push content in real time over HTTP protocol.
- **It is free and open source**: BlazeDS is free and open source. You do not need to purchase any commercial license to start building data-rich applications.

BlazeDS uses **Comet** style (`http://en.wikipedia.org/wiki/Comet_(programming)`) long polling technique for data push over HTTP and it supports a modest number of concurrent users (several hundreds). But the actual number depends on the server's threading configuration, CPU, and JVM heap memory size. BlazeDS's ability to support a number of concurrent connections depends on your application server's ability to handle and hold a number of asynchronous, non-blocking IO connection threads over HTTP. BlazeDS, combined with the new Servlet 3.0 API (which offers NIO/suspend/resume API), can be used to overcome this limitation. Using this technique can increase the number of concurrent connections from several hundreds to several thousands.

Unlike HTTP, Real Time Messaging Protocol (RTMP) maintains a dedicated socket connection from the client to the server. The same connection is used for data push and handling request and responses.

The following table shows feature comparison of BlazeDS and LiveCycle Data Services:

Features	BlazeDS	LiveCycle Data Services
Data Management Services		
Client-server synchronization	×	✓
Conflict resolution	×	✓
Data paging	×	✓
SQL adapter	×	✓
Hibernate adapter	×	✓

Features	BlazeDS	LiveCycle Data Services
Document Services		
LiveCycle remoting	×	✓
RIA-to-PDF file generation	×	✓
Enterprise-class Flex application services		
Data access/remoting	✓	✓
Proxy service	✓	✓
Automated testing support	×	✓
Software clustering	✓	✓
Enterprise Integration		
WSRP generation	×	✓
Ajax Data Services	✓	✓
Flex-Ajax Bridge (FABridge)	✓	✓
Runtime configuration	✓	✓
Open adapter architecture	✓	✓
Java Message Service adapter	✓	✓
Server-side component framework integration	✓	✓
ColdFusion® integration	×	✓
Offline Application Support		
Offline data cache	×	✓
Local message queuing	×	✓
Real-time Data		
Publish and subscribe messaging	✓	✓
Real-time data quality of service	×	✓
RTMP tunneling	×	✓

Moving ahead in this book, we will use BlazeDS as our primary framework for integrating Flex applications with server-side Java.

Understanding AMF

LiveCycle Data Services and BlazeDS both support remoting over the AMF protocol. AMF is a compact binary format, which increases an application's data loading speed up to 10 times when compared with text-based format protocols such as HTTP, SOAP, and so on.

The AMF format is used by Flash Player for data storage (`SharedObjects`) and data exchange (`RemoteObject`, `LocalConnection`, and so on). AMF uses a compact binary format to serialize and deserialize ActionScript objects allowing you to directly invoke and access server-side code without worry about data type mismatch between your server technology and ActionScript.

The AMF format is now open source and can be downloaded from `http://opensource.adobe.com/wiki/download/attachments/1114283/amf3_spec_05_05_08.pdf`. However, using AMF in your Flex application is abstract; you need not write any of the serialization or deserialization logic inside your application. You will learn how to use it in your Flex application in the next chapter.

Summary

In this chapter, you learned about LiveCycle Data Services and BlazeDS technologies for integrating Flex applications with service-side Java. You also understood detailed features offered by BlazeDS and LCDS.

In the next chapter, you will learn about various data access methods with code examples along with the Flash Player security model. You will also get an overview of various data types mapping between Java to ActionScript during serialization/deserialization, which will help you to get started with Flex and server-side Java communication.

7
Flex Data Access Methods

So far in this book, you have learned the basics of Flex, such as how to lay out simple and complex user interfaces in your application, working with local data, using data binding, handling events, loading and working with XML data, and so on.

We have also discussed Adobe LiveCycle Data Services and BlazeDS that enable developers to leverage the existing server-side Java infrastructure. Flex takes care of the presentation part of your application, but it does not have native access to any databases.

Flex provides a range of data access components to work with server-side remote data. These components are also commonly called Remote Procedure Call or RPC services. The Remote Procedure Call allows you to execute remote or server-side procedure or method, either locally or remotely in another address space without having to write the details of that method explicitly. (For more information on RPC, visit `http://en.wikipedia.org/wiki/Remote_procedure_call`.) The Flex data access components are based on Service Oriented Architecture (SOA). The Flex data access components allow you to call the server-side business logic built in Java, PHP, ColdFusion, .NET, or any other server-side technology to send and receive remote data.

In this chapter, you will learn how to interact with a server environment (specifically built with Java) and access backend data sources to send and receive remote data in your Flex application.

Flex data access components

Flex data access components provide call-and-response model to access remote data. There are three methods for accessing remote data in Flex: via the `HTTPService` class, the `WebService` class (compliant with Simple Object Access Protocol, or SOAP), or the `RemoteObject` class.

The HTTPService class

The HTTPService class is a basic method to send and receive remote data over the HTTP protocol. It allows you to perform traditional HTTP GET and POST requests to a URL. The HTTPService class can be used with any kind of service-side technology, such as JSP, PHP, ColdFusion, ASP, and so on. The HTTP service is also known as a REST-style web service.

REST stands for Representational State Transfer. It is an approach for getting content from a web server via web pages. Web pages are written in many languages such as JSP, PHP, ColdFusion, ASP, and so on that receive POST or GET requests. Output can be formatted in XML instead of HTML, which can be used in Flex applications for manipulating and displaying content. For example, RSS feeds output standard XML content when accessed using URL. For more information about REST, see www.ics.uci.edu/~fielding/pubs/dissertation/rest_arch_style.htm.

Using the HTTPService tag in MXML

The HTTPService class can be used to load both static and dynamic content from remote URLs. For example, you can use HTTPService to load an XML file that is located on a server, or you can also use HTTPService in conjunction with server-side technologies that return dynamic results to the Flex application. You can use both the HTTPS and the HTTP protocol to access secure and non-secure remote content.

The following is the basic syntax of a HTTPService class:

```
<mx:HTTPService
   id="instanceName"
   method="GET|POST|HEAD|OPTIONS|PUT|TRACE|DELETE"
   resultFormat="object|array|xml|e4x|flashvars|text"
   url="http://www.mydomain.com/myFile.jsp"
   fault="faultHandler(event);"
   result="resultHandler(event)"
/>
```

The following are the properties and events:

- id: Specifies instance identifier name
- method: Specifies HTTP method; the default value is GET
- resultFormat: Specifies the format of the result data
- url: Specifies the complete remote URL which will be called

- `fault`: Specifies the event handler method that'll be called when a fault or error occurs while connecting to the URL
- `result`: Specifies the event handler method to call when the `HttpService` call completed successfully and returned results

When you call the `HTTPService.send()` method, Flex will make the HTTP request to the specified URL. The HTTP response will be returned in the `result` property of the `ResultEvent` class in the result handler of the `HTTPService` class. You can also pass an optional parameter to the `send()` method by passing in an object. Any attributes of the object will be passed in as a URL-encoded query string along with URL request. For example:

```
var param:Object = {title:"Book Title", isbn:"1234567890"}
myHS.send(param);
```

In the above code example, we have created an object called `param` and added two string attributes to it: `title` and `isbn`. When you pass the `param` object to the `send()` method, these two string attributes will get converted to URL-encoded http parameters and your http request URL will look like this: `http://www.domain.com/myjsp.jsp?title=Book Title &isbn=1234567890`. This way, you can pass any number of http parameters to the URL and these parameters can be accessed in your server-side code. For example, in a JSP or servlet, you could use `request.getParameter("title")` to get the http request parameter.

An example of HTTPService

`HTTPService` is a simple, yet powerful way to work with remote data such as XML data. For example, you can use `HTTPService` to work with your server-side technologies, such as JSP, PHP, and so on to retrieve dynamic content and display it in your Flex application. You can call your JSP or servlet using `HTTPService`, and your JSP or servlet can connect to your database or any other data source to retrieve the data. The results can be formatted as XML and returned as a response. Then, you can use Flex's E4X techniques to manipulate and display the result in your Flex application. The following example shows you how to load XML data using the `HTTPService` class and display it in your Flex application.

Flex application:

```
<?xml version="1.0" encoding="utf-8"?>
<mx:Application xmlns:mx="http://www.adobe.com/2006/mxml"
creationComplete="myHS.send();">

    <mx:Script>
        <![CDATA[
            import mx.rpc.events.ResultEvent;
```

```
            import mx.rpc.events.FaultEvent;
            import mx.controls.Alert;

            private function faultHandler(event:FaultEvent):void
            {
               Alert.show(""+event.message);
            }
            private function resultHandler(event:ResultEvent):void
            {
               dgGrid.dataProvider = event.result.book;
            }
            private function getAuthorName(item:Object,
            column:DataGridColumn):String {
               return item.author.firstName+" "+item.author.lastName;
            }
         ]]>
      </mx:Script>

      <mx:HTTPService
         id="myHS"
         method="GET"
         resultFormat="e4x"
         url="http://localhost:8180/bookscatalog.xml"
         fault="faultHandler(event);"
         result="resultHandler(event)"
      />

      <mx:Panel width="100%" height="100%" title="Books Catalog">
         <mx:DataGrid id="dgGrid" height="100%" width="100%">
            <mx:columns>
               <mx:DataGridColumn headerText="ISBN" dataField="@ISBN"/>
               <mx:DataGridColumn headerText="Book Name"
                dataField="title"/>
               <mx:DataGridColumn headerText="Author"
                labelFunction="getAuthorName"/>
               <mx:DataGridColumn headerText="Price" dataField="price"/>
               <mx:DataGridColumn headerText="Description"
                dataField="description"/>
            </mx:columns>
         </mx:DataGrid>
      </mx:Panel>
   </mx:Application>
```

The above MXML code defines the `HTTPService` tag with the `id` property set to `myHS`. This will be used to reference the `HTTPService` object instance. It also specifies the `url` property to point to `localhost` where I have hosted the `bookscatalog.xml` file. You can change this with the URL of your own web server where you will be hosting the `bookscatalog.xml` file. The `resultFormat` property is set to `e4x`, so that the value is returned as an XML object, which can be accessed using ECMAScript for XML (E4X) expressions. The following are the valid `resultFormat` property values:

- `object`: The HTTPService will parse the returned XML and return an ActionScript Object, which is the default value
- `array`: The HTTPService will parse and return the result in the Array form, and if the `makeObjectsBindable` property is set to `true`, then it will return ArrayCollection
- `xml`: The HTTPService will parse the XML result and return the XMLNode object
- `flashvars`: The HTTPService will return plain text containing name-value pairs separated by ampersands, which are parsed into an ActionScript object
- `text`: The HTTPService will return plain text
- `e4x`: The HTTPService will return ECMAScript-E4X-compliant XML

We have also registered two event listeners for two of `HTTPService`'s events, namely `result` and `fault`. The `result` event occurs on successful invocation and execution of URL, and it will return an event object of the `ResultEvent` type. The resulted data can be accessed using the `result` property of the `ResultEvent` object, for example `event.result`.

The `result` property can be used to manipulate result data and display it on Flex controls, such as it is used here as `dataProvider` of the `DataGrid` control. You can also use `HTTPService`'s `lastResult` property to access result data. The `lastResult` property provides access to the result of last invocation and it can be used as the source of data binding of Flex controls. For example, you can bind the `DataGrid`'s `dataProvider` property with `HTTPService`'s `lastResult` property to show response data into `DataGrid`.

```
<mx:DataGrid id="dgGrid" height="100%" width="100%"
 dataProvider="{myHS.lastResult.book}">
```

The `fault` event occurs on any failure case, such as connection failure, timeout, and so on. It returns an event object of the `FaultEvent` type, which can be used to handle and display an error message to the user.

The HTTP call can be invoked by calling `HTTPService`'s `send()` method. Notice that the `creationComplete` event of the `Application` tag is used to invoke the `myHS.send()` method.

`bookscatalog.xml:`

```
<books>
   <book ISBN="184719530X">
      <title>Building Websites with Joomla! 1.5</title>
      <author>
         <lastName>Hagen</lastName>
         <firstName>Graf</firstName>
      </author>
      <image>../assets/images/184719530X.png</image>
      <pageCount>363</pageCount>
      <price>Rs.1,247.40</price>
      <description>The best-selling Joomla! tutorial guide updated for
       the latest 1.5 release </description>
   </book>
   <book ISBN="1847196160">
      <title>Drupal 6 JavaScript and jQuery</title>
      <author>
         <lastName>Matt</lastName>
         <firstName>Butcher</firstName>
      </author>
      <image>../assets/images/1847196160.png</image>
      <pageCount>250</pageCount>
      <price>Rs.1,108.80</price>
      <description>Putting jQuery, AJAX, and JavaScript effects into
       your Drupal 6 modules and themes</description>
   </book>
   <book ISBN="184719494X">
      <title>Expert Python Programming</title>
      <author>
         <lastName>Tarek</lastName>
         <firstName>Ziadé</firstName>
      </author>
      <image>../assets/images/184719494X.png</image>
      <pageCount>350</pageCount>
      <price>Rs.1,247.4</price>
      <description>Best practices for designing, coding,
       and distributing your Python software</description>
   </book>
   <book ISBN="1847194885">
      <title>Joomla! Web Security</title>
```

```
        <author>
            <lastName>Tom</lastName>
            <firstName>Canavan</firstName>
        </author>
        <image>../assets/images/1847194885.png</image>
        <pageCount>248</pageCount>
        <price>Rs.1,108.80</price>
        <description>Secure your Joomla! website from common security
         threats with this easy-to-use guide</description>
    </book>
</books>
```

The above is a simple XML file that contains details of various books in the form of XML elements. I have used hardcoded XML to demonstrate the concept, but in a real-time scenario, you can write Java code to connect to your database or any other data source and then form dynamic XML and return it. You will learn more about how to do this in the next chapter.

The program output should look like the following screen:

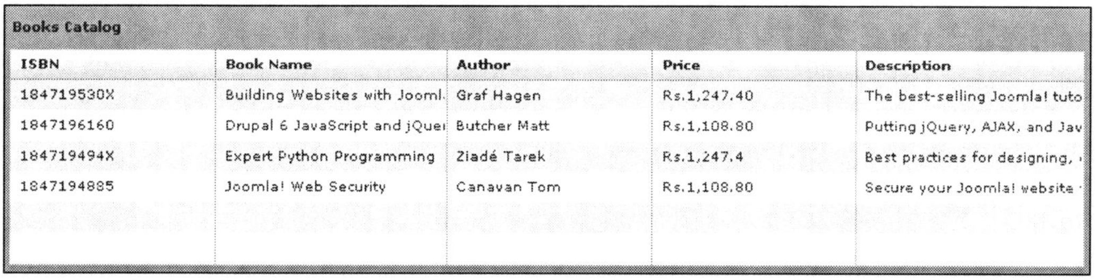

Books Catalog

ISBN	Book Name	Author	Price	Description
184719530X	Building Websites with Jooml	Graf Hagen	Rs.1,247.40	The best-selling Joomla! tuto
1847196160	Drupal 6 JavaScript and jQue	Butcher Matt	Rs.1,108.80	Putting jQuery, AJAX, and Jav
184719494X	Expert Python Programming	Ziadé Tarek	Rs.1,247.4	Best practices for designing,
1847194885	Joomla! Web Security	Canavan Tom	Rs.1,108.80	Secure your Joomla! website

After the above example, you must now be familiar with the general way of using the `HTTPService` tag for loading remote data in an MXML file. Now, you will learn how to work with the `HTTPService` class in ActionScript.

Using the HTTPService class in ActionScript

As you already know, every MXML tag represents an ActionScript class. For example, the `<mx:HTTPService>` tag has a corresponding `HTTPService.as` ActionScript class. This means that you will be able to create a class instance of corresponding ActionScript class in ActionScript code as shown here:

```
//Import required classes
import mx.rpc.http.HTTPService;
import mx.rpc.events.ResultEvent;
import mx.rpc.events.FaultEvent;
```

```
//Define HTTPService
var myHS:HTTPService = new HTTPService();
myHS.url = "http://192.168.0.3:8180/bookscatalog.xml";
myHS.resultFormat = "e4x";
myHS.addEventListener(ResultEvent.RESULT, resultHandler);
myHS.addEventListener(FaultEvent.FAULT, faultHandler);
myHS.send();
```

In the above example, we have created an instance of the `mx.rpc.http.HTTPService` class. We've set its `url` and `resultFormat` properties. We have registered two event listeners for its `result` and `fault` events. Finally, we're calling the `myHS.send()` method to invoke the http request.

You will learn more about how to use the `HTTPService` class to send and receive dynamic content via server-side scripting languages in the next chapter.

The WebService class

As the name indicates, the `WebService` class allows you to communicate with web services. Unlike using JSP, PHP, or ColdFusion to load data, it uses a web service endpoint. The `WebService` class communicates with web services using standard Simple Object Access Protocol (SOAP) 1.1 compliant requests and responses. The Flex web service API supports (SOAP) 1.1, XML Schema 1.0, and WSDL 1.1 with the following WSDL-to-SOAP binding styles:

- RPC/encoded
- RPC/literal
- Document/literal

Based on Web Service Description Language (WSDL) specification, a web service determines the format in which data has to be sent and received (a contract between client and server). Today, web services are most commonly used when communication is needed across many different technologies. It aims to provide a standard and interoperable way of communicating (for example, a web service written in .Net should be callable from a Java class).

A Flex application can interact with a web service only if it is defined in a Web Services Description Language (WSDL) file, and if requests and responses are formatted using the SOAP message format.

Using the WebService tag in MXML

The `<mx:WebService>` tag has the following basic attributes and events:

```
<mx:WebService
   id="No default."
   wsdl="No default."
   fault="No default."
   result="No default."
/>
```

It has the following properties and events:

- `id`: Specifies an instance identifier name
- `wsdl`: Specifies the web service's WSDL URI
- `fault`: Specifies an event handler if a fault or error occurs while connecting to the URL
- `result`: Specifies an event handler for successful execution and returns the result to it

A `<mx:WebService>` tag can have multiple `<mx:operation>` tags. The `<mx:operation>` tag specifies the actual web service operation or method details. The `operation` tag has the following basic attributes and events:

```
<mx:operation
   name="No default, required."
   resultFormat="object|xml|e4x"
   fault=No default.
   result=No default.
/>
```

It has the following properties and events:

- `name`: Specifies the name of the actual web service method or operation
- `resultFormat`: Specifies the format of the result data
- `fault`: Specifies an event handler if fault or error occurs while connecting to the URL
- `result`: Specifies an event handler for successful execution and returns the result to it

You can call `operation` in two different ways: you can invoke the function of the same name as operation on the `WebService` object, or access operation name as a property of the `WebService` object and then call the `send()` method. Similar to `HTTPService`, you can also pass arguments to the web service method/operation by passing arguments directly into the `send()` method, or by passing it in a function invoked on the `WebService` object. Any arguments will be passed in as a part of the method call. The following code snippet shows you how to pass arguments:

```
webServiceInstance.operationName(param1, param2,...);
```

Or

```
webServiceInstance.operationName.send(param1, param2,...);
```

Flash Player's security sandbox does not allow Flex/Flash applications (`.swf` files) to access the resources outside of its own domain. So, accessing any data other than its own domain requires special handling known as proxy implementation. To read more about the security sandbox and how to use a proxy, read the *Understanding the Flash Player security sandbox* section of this chapter.

An example of WebService

The following example application uses a `<mx:WebService>` tag to invoke web service operations:

MXML code:

```
<?xml version="1.0" encoding="utf-8"?>
<mx:Application xmlns:mx="http://www.adobe.com/2006/mxml" >

   <mx:Script>
   <![CDATA[
         import mx.controls.Alert;
         import mx.rpc.events.FaultEvent;
         import mx.rpc.events.ResultEvent;

         private function getAvailableBooksResult(event:ResultEvent):
void {
            dgGrid.dataProvider = event.result;
         }
         private function handleFault(event:FaultEvent):void {
            Alert.show("Fault: "+event.message);
         }
      ]]>
   </mx:Script>
```

```
    <mx:WebService
         id="webService"
         wsdl="http://www.satishkore.com/WebServiceProject/services/
BooksSearchService?wsdl">
        <mx:operation
           name="getAvailableBooks"
           resultFormat="object"
            fault="handleFault(event)"
            result="getAvailableBooksResult(event)"/>
    </mx:WebService>

    <mx:Panel title="Web Service Example" width="100%" height="100%">

       <mx:DataGrid id="dgGrid" width="100%" height="100%"/>
       <mx:ControlBar width="100%">
          <mx:Button label="Available Books" click="webService.
getAvailableBooks(); "/>
       </mx:ControlBar>
    </mx:Panel>

</mx:Application>
```

In the above code, we have defined a `<mx:WebService>` tag and specified its `id` and `wsdl` properties. You can change the `wsdl` property value according to your web service's WSDL URL.

We have defined one `<mx:operation>` tag under the `WebService` tag that specifies the web service method details such as its name, result format, fault handler, and result handler. The `resultFormat` property supports three different options: `object`, `xml`, and `e4x`. A value `object` specifies that the web service result will be decoded into an object structure as specified by the WSDL document. `xml` specifies that the web service result will be returned as `XMLNode`. `e4x` specifies that the web service result will be accessible using ECMAScript for XML (E4X) expressions.

We have registered a handler for the `result` event of the `<mx:operation>` tag called `getAvailableBooksResult()`. It handles returned data and displays it in the `DataGrid` component. In this case, we are just setting `DataGrid`'s `dataProvider` property to `event.result` because the data returned by the `getAvailableBooks` operation is in Object format. The `DataGrid` control can automatically display Object's attributes as columns and respective values in rows, as shown in the following screenshot:

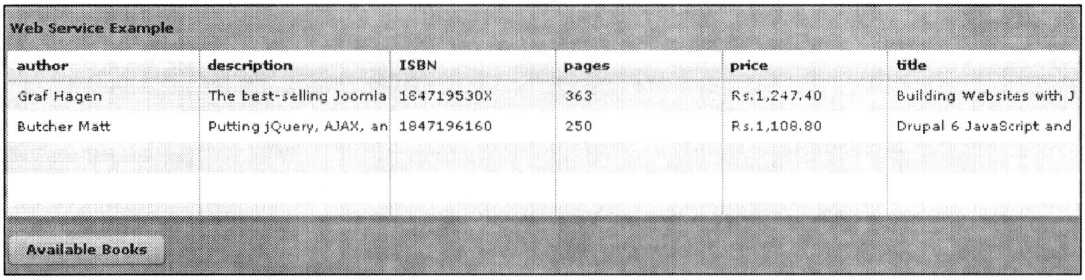

Web Service Example

author	description	ISBN	pages	price	title
Graf Hagen	The best-selling Joomla	184719530X	363	Rs.1,247.40	Building Websites with J
Butcher Matt	Putting jQuery, AJAX, an	1847196160	250	Rs.1,108.80	Drupal 6 JavaScript and

Available Books

WSDL document

The Web Service Description Language (WSDL) is an XML-based language used for describing the remote service operations using SOAP. In short, the WSDL describes the format of the request and response of the remote method.

Many tools are available in a variety of languages for building web services, such as Eclipse plugin Web Tools Platform (WTP) for developing Java web services found at `http://www.eclipse.org/webtools/`.

The following is an example of a WSDL document that defines the web service API:

```
<?xml version="1.0" encoding="UTF-8"?>
<wsdl:definitions targetNamespace="http://service.com" xmlns:
apachesoap="http://xml.apache.org/xml-soap" xmlns:impl="http://
service.com" xmlns:intf="http://service.com" xmlns:soapenc="http://
schemas.xmlsoap.org/soap/encoding/" xmlns:tns1="http://beans.
service.com" xmlns:wsdl="http://schemas.xmlsoap.org/wsdl/" xmlns:
wsdlsoap="http://schemas.xmlsoap.org/wsdl/soap/" xmlns:xsd="http://
www.w3.org/2001/XMLSchema">
<!--WSDL created by Apache Axis version: 1.4
Built on Apr 22, 2006 (06:55:48 PDT)-->
 <wsdl:types>
  <schema targetNamespace="http://beans.service.com"
   xmlns="http://www.w3.org/2001/XMLSchema">
   <import namespace="http://service.com"/>
   <import namespace="http://schemas.xmlsoap.org/soap/encoding/"/>
   <complexType name="Book">
    <sequence>
     <element name="ISBN" nillable="true" type="xsd:string"/>
     <element name="author" nillable="true" type="xsd:string"/>
     <element name="description" nillable="true" type="xsd:string"/>
     <element name="pages" nillable="true" type="xsd:string"/>
     <element name="price" nillable="true" type="xsd:string"/>
     <element name="title" nillable="true" type="xsd:string"/>
    </sequence>
```

```
    </complexType>
   </schema>
   <schema targetNamespace="http://service.com" xmlns="http://www.
w3.org/2001/XMLSchema">
    <import namespace="http://beans.service.com"/>
    <import namespace="http://schemas.xmlsoap.org/soap/encoding/"/>
    <complexType name="ArrayOf_tns1_Book">
     <complexContent>
      <restriction base="soapenc:Array">
       <attribute ref="soapenc:arrayType" wsdl:arrayType="tns1:
Book[]"/>
      </restriction>
     </complexContent>
    </complexType>
   </schema>
  </wsdl:types>
    <wsdl:message name="getAvailableBooksRequest">
    </wsdl:message>
    <wsdl:message name="getBookByNameResponse">
       <wsdl:part name="getBookByNameReturn" type="tns1:Book"/>
    </wsdl:message>
    <wsdl:message name="getBookByNameRequest">
       <wsdl:part name="bookName" type="xsd:string"/>
    </wsdl:message>
    <wsdl:message name="getAvailableBooksResponse">
       <wsdl:part name="getAvailableBooksReturn" type="impl:ArrayOf_
tns1_Book"/>
    </wsdl:message>
    <wsdl:portType name="BooksSearchService">
       <wsdl:operation name="getBookByName" parameterOrder="bookName">
          <wsdl:input message="impl:getBookByNameRequest" name="getBook
ByNameRequest"/>
          <wsdl:output message="impl:getBookByNameResponse" name="getBo
okByNameResponse"/>
       </wsdl:operation>
       <wsdl:operation name="getAvailableBooks">
          <wsdl:input message="impl:getAvailableBooksRequest" name="get
AvailableBooksRequest"/>
          <wsdl:output message="impl:getAvailableBooksResponse" name="g
etAvailableBooksResponse"/>
       </wsdl:operation>
    </wsdl:portType>
    <wsdl:binding name="BooksSearchServiceSoapBinding" type="impl:
BooksSearchService">
```

```
        <wsdlsoap:binding style="rpc" transport="http://schemas.xmlsoap.
org/soap/http"/>
        <wsdl:operation name="getBookByName">
            <wsdlsoap:operation soapAction=""/>
            <wsdl:input name="getBookByNameRequest">
                <wsdlsoap:body encodingStyle="http://schemas.xmlsoap.org/
soap/encoding/" namespace="http://service.com" use="encoded"/>
            </wsdl:input>
            <wsdl:output name="getBookByNameResponse">
                <wsdlsoap:body encodingStyle="http://schemas.xmlsoap.org/
soap/encoding/" namespace="http://service.com" use="encoded"/>
            </wsdl:output>
        </wsdl:operation>
        <wsdl:operation name="getAvailableBooks">
            <wsdlsoap:operation soapAction=""/>
            <wsdl:input name="getAvailableBooksRequest">
                <wsdlsoap:body encodingStyle="http://schemas.xmlsoap.org/
soap/encoding/" namespace="http://service.com" use="encoded"/>
            </wsdl:input>
            <wsdl:output name="getAvailableBooksResponse">
                <wsdlsoap:body encodingStyle="http://schemas.xmlsoap.org/
soap/encoding/" namespace="http://service.com" use="encoded"/>
            </wsdl:output>
        </wsdl:operation>
    </wsdl:binding>
    <wsdl:service name="BooksSearchServiceService">
        <wsdl:port binding="impl:BooksSearchServiceSoapBinding" name="Bo
oksSearchService">
            <wsdlsoap:address location="http://www.satishkore.com/
WebServiceProject/services/BooksSearchService"/>
        </wsdl:port>
    </wsdl:service>
</wsdl:definitions>
```

Using the WebService class in ActionScript

Till now, you saw how to call a web service in MXML using an `<mx:WebService>` tag. Now, in the following example, you will see how to call a web service in ActionScript:

```
//Import web service
import mx.rpc.soap.WebService;

//Define web service in ActionScript
Var ws: WebService = new WebService();
```

```
ws.wsdl = "http://www.satishkore.com/WebServiceProject/services/BooksS
earchService?wsdl";
ws.getAvailableBooks.addEventListener("result",
getAvailableBooksResult);
ws.getAvailableBooks.addEventListener("fault", handleFault);
ws.loadWSDL();

//Call web service operation
ws.getAvailableBooks();
```

Working with SOAP headers

Sometimes, you need to send additional header information along with web service calls to send application-specific data to the web service. You can add an SOAP header to the operation or to the web service by calling the `WebService` or `Operation` object's `addHeader()` or `addSimpleHeader()` method.

In order to add a header, the following steps are required:

1. Create a `SOAPHeader` class object. The following is the constructor of the `SOAPHeader` class: `SOAPHeader(qname:QName, content:Object)`.
2. To create a `SOAPHeader` class object, you need to pass a `QName` in the first parameter. The following is the constructor for `QName`: `QName(uri:String, localName:String)`.
3. The second parameter of `SOAPHeader` is content object which constructs a set of name-value pairs as shown in the following snippet: `{name1:value1, name2:value2,...}`.
4. You can also use the `addSimpleHeader()` method for adding SOAP headers. This is just a simple way of creating name-value headers. Its constructor is as shown here: `addSimpleHeader(qnameLocale:String, qnameNamespace:String, headerName:String, headerValue:String)`.

These are the parameters:

- `qnameLocal`: Specifies the local name for the header `QName`
- `qnameNamespace`: Specifies the namespace for the header `QName`
- `headerName`: Specifies the header name
- `headerValue`: Specifies the header value

The following code snippet shows you how to use the `addHeader()` and `addSimpleHeader()` methods:

```
var q1:QName = new QName("http://service.com", "Header1");
var header1:SOAPHeader = new SOAPHeader(q1, {uname:"fooUser",
attempt:"3"});
ws.addHeader(header1);
ws.addSimpleHeader("Header1", "http://service.com", "uname",
"fooUser");
```

To remove the added header, you can use the `clearHeaders()` method on a web service or operation object.

The RemoteObject class

Unlike `HTTPService` and `WebService`, the `RemoteObject` class is used to send and receive binary data over HTTP. The `RemoteObject` class uses Adobe's Action Message Format (AMF), a binary object format to send and receive remote data in its native form. The `RemoteObject` method is 10 times faster than `HTTPService`, or `WebService`, or any other text-based remote data access methods. Typically, it uses the AMF3 libraries to serialize and deserialize objects between the client and the server. This allows you to write an application that can interact with your existing server-side business logic and invoke their object natively.

To use `RemoteObject`, you would need an additional server-side layer mainly responsible for serializing and deserializing objects between ActionScript and your server-side technology. You can use Adobe's open source BlazeDS or the commercially offered LiveCycle Data Services (LCDS) to work with `RemoteObject` over AMF3.

The BlazeDS and LCDS offer you the Java remoting capabilities. However, you can find many freely available remoting gateways (AMF3) to work with other server-side technologies, such as PHP, .NET, and so on. Adobe recommends the following third-party remoting gateways:

- Zend Framework 1.7 or above: `http://framework.zend.com/`
- AMFPHP: `http://sourceforge.net/projects/amfphp/`
- SabreAMF: `http://www.osflash.org/sabreamf`
- Midnight Coders WebORB: `http://www.themidnightcoders.com/`

Using the RemoteObject tag in MXML

You can use a `RemoteObject` in conjunction with BlazeDS or LCDS to invoke methods on your server-side Java classes, and send and receive ActionScript and Java value objects without worrying about their serialization and deserialization process. Java classes can typically return any data type including primitive data types, objects, collections, and so on. These data types are deserialized into matching ActionScript data types or objects by AMF gateway (BlazeDS or LCDS).

The following is the basic syntax of the `RemoteObject` tag:

```
<mx:RemoteObject
   destination="No default."
   id="No default."
   fault="No default."
   result="No default."
/>
```

These are the properties and events:

- `id`: Specifies the unique identifier for the service
- `destination`: Specifies the destination of the service. The value is configured in the `services-config.xml` file of BlazeDS or LCDS
- `fault`: Specifies the error handler method to call if any error occurs during invocation
- `result`: Specifies the result handler method that handles the result data returned by the method call

The `RemoteObject` tag can have multiple `<mx:method>` tags to represent individual methods of a server-side object (for example, a Java class object). The `<mx:method>` syntax is as shown here:

```
<mx:method
  name="No default, required."
  fault="No default."
  result="No default."
 />
```

These are the properties and events:

- `name`: Specifies the server-side object's method name
- `fault`: Specifies the error handler method if any error occurs during invocation
- `result`: Specifies the result handler method to handle the result data returned by the method call

An example of RemoteObject

The following example shows how to use the `<mx:RemoteObject>` tag to invoke a method on the server-side Java class and consume the return value in the Flex application. This program requires you to have the BlazeDS infrastructure in place on your server to be able to communicate with Java objects using `RemoteObject`.

Follow these steps to set up and create a Flex remoting application:

1. Make sure that you have downloaded BlazeDS. If you have not done so yet, you can download it from `http://opensource.adobe.com/wiki/display/blazeds/BlazeDS/`. You get two choices for download. You can download BlazeDS with an integrated Tomcat server and pre-built sample web applications. This version is known as **BlazeDS Turnkey**. Secondly, you can download the BlazeDS Binary Distribution package which doesn't include Tomcat. In this example, I have downloaded BlazeDS Binary Distribution and I assume that you have already installed the Tomcat server. If you do not have Tomcat installed, then you can download and install it from `http://tomcat.apache.org/`.
2. The next step is to set up a project. We will create a Flex and Java combined project. This is only possible if you have installed the Flex Builder Eclipse plugin on top of an Eclipse installation with WTP (Web Tools Platform), or if you have WTP installed on top of Flex Builder. Open Flex Builder and choose **File | New | Flex Project** from the **Eclipse** menu.
3. Enter **Project name** as **RemotingExample** and leave **Project location** to its default.
4. Make sure that your **Application type** is selected as **Web application**, and choose **Application server type** as **J2EE**.
5. Make sure that the **Use remote object access service** and **LiveCycle Data Services** options are selected.
6. Select **Create combined Java/Flex project using WTP** and enter the **Java source folder** name. This is where you will keep your Java source files. This step will allow you to maintain your Flex and Java source files separately. Click on **Next**.
7. Next, you will have to configure J2EE (Enterprise Edition) server settings. Choose **Target runtime**; this is your tomcat server. You can configure your own server using the **New...** button displayed next to the field.

8. Enter **Context root** and **Content folder** and make sure they are set to the same name as that of your project name. In this case, they are set to **RemotingExample**. This is required to assemble all your compiled code (Flex and Java) under one output directory, which can be then deployed on Tomcat server as your web application.
9. Enter or browse the `Flex WAR file` location. This is the location of the `blazeds.war` file which you have downloaded as a part of **BlazeDS Binary Distribution** package or **BlazeDS Turnkey**.
10. Make sure the **Compile application locally in Flex Builder** option is selected.
11. Change **Output folder** to the `RemotingExample` root of your application. This step is required to make sure that your Flex application binaries (`.swf`) file and other related files are copied under this folder. Later, we can deploy this folder under Tomcat's `webapps` directory. Click on the **Next** button.
12. Leave all settings as they are if there is no change. If needed, change **Output folder URL** as per your Tomcat server Internet Protocol (IP) address and port. Click on the **Finish** button to create a Flex/Java project. Now, we are ready to write server-side Java classes.
13. Make sure that you switch Flex Builder to **Java perspective**. Now select the project from **Package Explorer** and then click on **File | New | Class** to create a new Java class file. Enter **exampleas** as the package name and **BookVO** as the file name. Now click on the **Finish** button and implement the Java class as follows:

```
package example;

public class BookVO {
   private String ISBN;
   private String title;
   private String author;
   private int pages;
   private String description;

   public String getISBN() {
      return ISBN;
   }
   public void setISBN(String isbn) {
      ISBN = isbn;
   }
   public String getDescription() {
      return description;
   }
   public void setDescription(String description) {
```

```
        this.description = description;
    }
    public String getTitle() {
        return title;
    }
    public void setTitle(String title) {
        this.title = title;
    }
    public String getAuthor() {
        return author;
    }
    public void setAuthor(String author) {
        this.author = author;
    }
    public int getPages() {
        return pages;
    }
    public void setPages(int pages) {
        this.pages = pages;
    }
}
```

14. Now follow the same process for creating the `BookServiceDAO.java` file under the same package and implement it as follows:

```
package example;

import java.util.ArrayList;
import java.util.List;

public class BookServiceDAO {

    public List<BookVO> getAvailableBooks(String name) {

        ArrayList<BookVO> theArray = new ArrayList<BookVO>();

        BookVO theBook = new BookVO();

        theBook.setISBN("1847196160");
        theBook.setTitle("Drupal 6 JavaScript and jQuery");
        theBook.setAuthor("Butcher Matt");
        theBook.setPages(250);
        theBook.setDescription("Putting jQuery, AJAX, and JavaScript
        effects into your Drupal 6 modules and themes");
        theArray.add(theBook);

        theBook = new BookVO();
        theBook.setISBN("184719530X");
```

```
        theBook.setTitle("Building Websites with Joomla! 1.5");
        theBook.setAuthor("Graf Hagen");
        theBook.setPages(363);
        theBook.setDescription("The best-selling Joomla! tutorial
        guide updated for the latest 1.5 release");
        theArray.add(theBook);

        return theArray;
    }

    public boolean isBookAvailable(BookVO book) {
        System.out.println("#### Book Availability Search ####");
        System.out.println("Received object of ["+book.
        getClass()+"]");
        System.out.println(book.getISBN());
        System.out.println(book.getTitle());
        System.out.println(book.getAuthor());
        System.out.println(book.getDescription());
        System.out.println(book.getPages());

        return true;
    }
}
```

In the code above, I have defined two methods. The first method is `getAvailableBooks()`, which accepts a parameter string parameter called `name`. This method returns an `ArrayList` containing two `BookVO` objects. I am returning the hardcoded results for demonstration purposes. But in a real-world scenario, the results would be generated dynamically by connecting with a database and returning dynamically-generated VO objects. I am not using the method parameter `name` here, but it's added just to demonstrate how to pass parameters to the Java function through a `RemoteObject`. The second method `isBookAvailable()` accepts a `BookVO` class object as a parameter, and this will be used to demonstrate how to work with strongly-typed objects between Java and Flex.

15. Now compile the Java source code while you are in **Java perspective**. This will compile Java source files and place the compiled code into our project's output folder under the `/WEB-INF/classes/` folder.

16. The next step is to define a remoting destination. The remoting destination exposes a Java class to your Flex application so that its method can be invoked remotely using the `RemoteObject` service. Switch back to **Flex Development Perspective** and open the `remoting-config.xml` file located under your project's `\RemotingExample\WEB-INF\flex\` folder. Add the following remote destination entry in it and save the file:

    ```
    <destination id="myROService">
        <properties>
            <source>example.BookServiceDAO</source>
        </properties>
    </destination>
    ```

    In the above remoting XML configuration, `id` is a unique identifier for the destination service which will be used by your Flex application to refer to the Java class. Notice that I have mentioned a full class name including its package under the `<source>` tag. This specifies the Java class that needs to be exposed for remoting.

> The destinations are the way to dynamically configure your server-side objects, remote URLs, and endpoints. They will be referenced by `RemoteObject`, `HTTPService`, or `WebService` to access the remote data. Going ahead, we will use this method to declare and expose Java objects or define remote URLs or endpoints to use with remote data access methods.

17. Next, we will create a Flex application which invokes the Java method using `RemoteObject`. Open `RemotingExample.mxml` from your `flex_src` folder and implement it as follows:

    ```
    <?xml version="1.0" encoding="utf-8"?>
    <mx:Application xmlns:mx="http://www.adobe.com/2006/mxml">

        <mx:Script>
            <![CDATA[
                import mx.controls.Alert;
                import mx.rpc.events.FaultEvent;
                import mx.rpc.events.ResultEvent;

                private function faultHandler(event:FaultEvent):void {
                    Alert.show(event.fault.faultString, "ERROR");
                }
                private function getAvailableBooksResultHandler(event:
                ResultEvent):void {
                    dgGrid.dataProvider = event.result;
                }
    ```

```
        ]]>
    </mx:Script>

    <mx:RemoteObject
        id="myRO"
        destination="myROService">
        <mx:method
            name="getAvailableBooks"
            fault="faultHandler(event)"
            result="getAvailableBooksResultHandler(event)"/>
    </mx:RemoteObject>

    <mx:Panel title="RemoteObject Example"
     width="100%" height="100%">
        <mx:DataGrid id="dgGrid" width="100%" height="100%"/>
        <mx:ControlBar width="100%">
            <mx:Button label="Get Available Books"
             click="myRO.getAvailableBooks('fooBook');"/>
        </mx:ControlBar>
    </mx:Panel>
</mx:Application>
```

In the above MXML code, we have defined one `<mx:RemoteObject>` tag and specified its `id` property as `myRO` and the `destination` property as `myROService`. Notice that the destination name is the same as specified in the `remoting-config.xml` file in step 16.

We have also defined a `<mx:method>` tag representing a remote Java method defined in `BookServiceDAO.java`. We have also specified the `fault` and `result` event handlers for the method. You can invoke a Java method on `RemoteObject`, for example `myRO.getAvailableBooks('fooBook')`. This would call the Java method and return the result into the result handler, that is, `getAvailableBooksResultHandler()`. In the result handler, we are assigning the result to `DataGrid` which displays the result into rows and columns.

18. Compile your source code by selecting the project from the **Flex Navigator** view and click on the **Project | Build Project** menu.

> Make sure that your project is pointing to the correct BlazeDS service configuration by right-clicking on your project and selecting **Properties | Flex Compiler**. Also, make sure that **Additional compiler arguments:** includes the `-services` parameter, which should point to the correct `services-config.xml` file from your project's output folder—that is, the `/RemotingExample/WEB-INF/flex/` folder.

19. Now, you are ready for application deployment. Go to your project's root folder and copy the **/RemotingExample** folder and deploy it under your tomcat server's `webapps` directory. This folder contains all your Flex and Java binaries along with the BlazeDS configuration and library `.jar` files. Flex Builder copies all BlazeDS configuration and library `.jar` files behind the scene into your output folder when you specify the `blazeds.war` file in step 9. Alternatively, you can also write Ant Build Script to build the `.war` file and deploy it.

20. Now, run the application by accessing its URL in a browser. Open the browser and type your web application's URL, for example `http://localhost:8180/RemotingExample/RemotingExample.html`, and press the *Enter* button. The application output will look like the following screenshot:

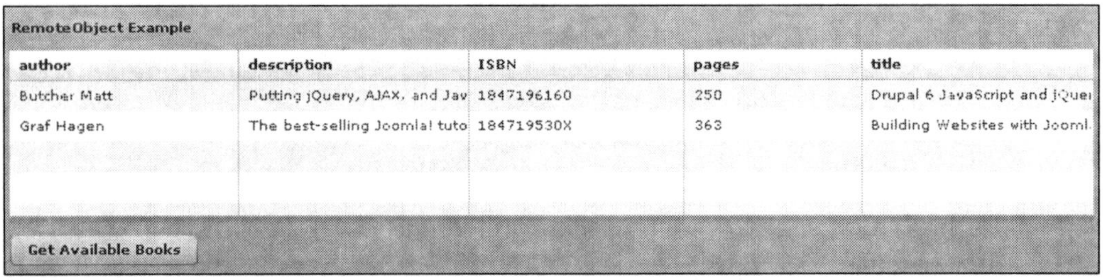

RemoteObject Example

author	description	ISBN	pages	title
Butcher Matt	Putting jQuery, AJAX, and Jav	1847196160	250	Drupal 6 JavaScript and jQuei
Graf Hagen	The best-selling Joomla! tuto	184719530X	363	Building Websites with Jooml

Get Available Books

Working with strongly-typed objects

If you have noticed the above Flex code, we have not mentioned any specific type for the object returned by the `getAvailableBooks()` method. By default, ActionScript deserializes the result into a dynamically typed object. (In other words, a generic object without any specific type.) There are situations when you need to send and receive strongly-typed objects, for example a Java method that accepts a strongly-typed Java class object as a parameter.

To work with strongly-typed objects, you must define the ActionScript version of Java class (`BookVO.java`). Follow the steps given here:

1. Under the **RemotingExample** project's `flex_src` folder, create an ActionScript class by clicking on the **File | New | ActionScript Class** menu. Specify `BookVO` as the file name and click on **Finish.**

2. Implement the `BookVO.as` class as follows:

```
package
{
   [Bindable]
    [RemoteClass(alias="example.BookVO")]
   public class BookVO
```

```
        {
        public var ISBN:String;
        public var title:String;
        public var author:String;
        public var pages:uint;
        public var description:String;
    }
}
```

3. In the above ActionScript class file, notice that we are using the `[RemoteClass(alias="example.BookVO")]` metadata tag to map ActionScript class with server-side `example.BookVo` Java class. This metadata tag causes the result of the `getAvailableBooks()` method to be deserialized into ActionScript version of the `BookVO` class or vice versa.
4. Change the `RemotingExample.mxml` code as follows:

```
<?xml version="1.0" encoding="utf-8"?>
<mx:Application xmlns:mx="http://www.adobe.com/2006/mxml">

    <mx:Script>
        <![CDATA[
            import mx.controls.Alert;
            import mx.rpc.events.FaultEvent;
            import mx.rpc.events.ResultEvent;

            private function faultHandler(event:FaultEvent):void {
                Alert.show(event.fault.faultString, "ERROR");
            }
            private function getAvailableBooksResultHandler(event:
            ResultEvent):void {
                dgGrid.dataProvider = event.result;
            }
            private function isBookAvailableResultHandler(event:
            ResultEvent):void {
                if(event.result == true) {
                    Alert.show("The book is available for sale now!");
                }
            }
            private function checkAvailability():void {
                var aBook:BookVO = new BookVO();

                aBook.title = "Flex 3 with Java";
                aBook.author = "Satish Kore";
                aBook.ISBN = "1234567890";
                aBook.description = "Getting started with Flex 3 with
                Java";
                aBook.pages = 300;
```

```
            myRO.isBookAvailable(aBook);
        }
    ]]>
</mx:Script>

<mx:RemoteObject
    id="myRO"
    destination="myROService">
    <mx:method
        name="getAvailableBooks"
        fault="faultHandler(event)"
        result="getAvailableBooksResultHandler(event)"/>
    <mx:method
        name="isBookAvailable"
        fault="faultHandler(event)"
        result="isBookAvailableResultHandler(event)"/>
</mx:RemoteObject>

<mx:Panel title="RemoteObject Example"
 width="100%" height="100%">
    <mx:DataGrid id="dgGrid" width="100%" height="100%"/>
    <mx:ControlBar width="100%">
        <mx:Button label="Get Available Books"
         click="myRO.getAvailableBooks('fooBook');"/>
        <mx:Button label="Check Flex 3 with Java Book
         Availability" click="checkAvailability();"/>
    </mx:ControlBar>
</mx:Panel>
</mx:Application>
```

5. In the above code, we have added a new `<mx:method>` tag to add the additional Java method `isBookAvailable()`, which accepts a strongly-typed `BookVO` Java class object. Now let's pass the ActionScript version of `BookVO` to the Java method `isBookAvailable()` to see if Java can read the ActionScript class and its properties.
6. We have implemented the new ActionScript method `checkAvailability()` which creates the `BookVO` ActionScript class object and sets its properties. It then invokes the `isBookAvailable()` remote method and passes the `BookVO` ActionScript object as a parameter.
7. Now recompile and redeploy the **RemotingExample** application as shown in step 18 and open the application URL in a browser and click on the **Check Flex 3 with Java Book Availability** button on your Flex application. It calls the `checkAvailability()` ActionScript method, which in turn invokes a remote Java method, for example `myRO.isBookAvailable(aBook)`. The output would be printed in your Tomcat server console logs.

Tomcat console output:

Book Availability Search

Received object of [class example.BookVO]

1234567890

Flex 3 with Java

Satish Kore

Getting started with Flex 3 with Java

300

Notice the Java class name. It is `example.BookVO`, a Java version of VO class. Also notice that all properties are deserialized into their native data types. Similarly, you can also return Java objects to Flex, and they can be serialized and deserialized into ActionScript objects by AMF.

Understanding the Flash Player security sandbox

Flex applications are essentially `.swf` files that are loaded and executed in the Adobe Flash Player. Adobe Flash player is a runtime environment to execute Flash applications (`.swf` files).

Adobe Flash Player operates within a strict security sandbox that limits how Flex applications access remote data. A sandbox is a security model exposed by the runtime environment to restrict any malicious code to cause any potential damage or attack.

By default, Flash Player does not allow access to the resources outside of its own domain. This means that the `.swf` files hosted on `http://www.domain1.com` cannot access data from `http://www.domain2.com` unless domain2 has the `crossdomain.xml` file to allow remote access to its resources explicitly. This security restriction is applicable for any Flex/ActionScript API which is used to access remote data such as `HTTPService`, `WebService`, `RemoteObject`, and so on.

Please note that the security restrictions are applied by Flash Player, and not by Flex or ActionScript API. Adobe is constantly improving security to make it more secure and robust. The security restrictions applied to your application depend on the Flash Player version and it may vary from version to version.

The following two methods can be used for accessing data from a different domain:

- Use a cross-domain policy file that allows configuring different domain names that are allowed to access the resources
- Use BlazeDS or LCDS Proxy Services

Understanding the cross-domain policy file

A cross-domain policy file is an XML-based configuration file that allows web site owners to control the access of the resources hosted on their web site. The resources could be any data hosted on the web site such as RSS feeds, images, HTML or static text, and so on. The important thing which many developers get confused with is where to host the cross-domain policy file. Please note that the cross-domain policy file is hosted on the domain from where the data is being requested (destination domain), and not on the domain from which the request is being made (source domain).

When a Flex application (`.swf` file) makes a request for the content hosted on another domain than its own, Flash Player checks if the other domain contains a cross-domain policy (`crossdomain.xml`) file that explicitly grants access permissions to the domain from which the request is made. If it does not find a cross-domain policy file or appropriate permissions, then it blocks the request and returns a security error.

The cross-domain policy file allows you to grant read permissions for the resources as well as control whether clients can include http headers information in requests from a specific domain.

Typically, the `crossdomain.xml` file will be hosted in the root folder of your server, for example `http://www.domain.com/crossdomain.xml`. This is the default location which Flash player checks before making any requests for other resources. The following is the general format of a cross-domain policy file:

```
<?xml version="1.0"?>
<!DOCTYPE cross-domain-policy SYSTEM
"http://www.adobe.com/xml/dtds/cross-domain-policy.dtd">

<cross-domain-policy>
   <site-control permitted-cross-domain-policies="master-only"/>
   <allow-access-from domain="Domain name or IP address"/>
   <allow-http-request-headers-from domain="*" headers="*"/>
</cross-domain-policy>
```

The cross-domain policy file format should be a valid XML file. The `<site-control>` tag specifies that this cross-domain policy file should be considered as the master and the only policy file on that domain. The `<allow-access-from>` tag specifies the name of the domain that is allowed to access the content from this domain. You can have multiple `<allow-access-from>` tags to specify multiple domain names.

Please note that Flash Player does not try to resolve the IP address of a given domain name, so `www.domain.com` and its IP address and subdomains are treated as different domains. Hence, they require different `allow-access-domain` permissions. However, you can use a (*) wildcard to specify multiple declarations in the same line, for example `<allow-access-from domain="*.domain.com"/>` or `<allow-access-from domain="192.0.238.*"/>`. This will allow requests from all subdomains of `www.domain.com` and all IP addresses in the `192.0.238` subnet.

The `<allow-http-request-headers-from>` tag grants permission to the domain to send user-defined headers with the request. The `header` attribute can be used to specify a comma-separated header list that is allowed by the domain specified in the `domain` attribute.

The cross-domain policy definition is a very vast subject. To read more about its configuration and how to use it to control access, check the specification at `http://www.adobe.com/devnet/articles/crossdomain_policy_file_spec.html`.

Creating a proxy service

If you are using BlazeDS or LCDS, you can use their proxy services to access remote resources and eliminate the need to implement a cross-domain policy file on the server which hosts the resources.

The proxy services provide two kinds of proxy services:

- HTTP proxy to work with normal HTTP requests
- Web service proxy to work with SOAP-based requests

The proxy services intercept the requests from the client and forward them to the remote web server. The proxy services also read the response and return it back to the client.

The following example shows you how to use a BlazeDS proxy service via an `HTTPService` class to access a third-party URL which does not host a cross-domain policy file. Follow these steps:

1. First, we will create an `HTTPService` class without using proxy services and see how Flash Player security sandbox behaves.
2. Create a new Flex project with J2EE as application server type or use the previously created Flex project.

3. Now create a new Flex application file and name it `HTTPServiceExample.mxml` and implement it as follows:

```
<?xml version="1.0" encoding="utf-8"?>
<mx:Application xmlns:mx="http://www.adobe.com/2006/mxml">

   <mx:Script>
      <![CDATA[
         import mx.controls.Alert;
         import mx.rpc.events.FaultEvent;

         private function faultHandler(event:FaultEvent):void {
         Alert.show(event.fault.faultString+"\n"+event.fault.
         rootCause.text);
         }
      ]]>
   </mx:Script>

   <mx:HTTPService id="httpSvc" url="http://newsrss.bbc.co.uk/rss/
    newsonline_world_edition/front_page/rss.xml"
    fault="faultHandler(event)"/>
   <mx:DataGrid dataProvider="{httpSvc.lastResult.rss.channel.
    item}" width="100%"/>
   <mx:Button label="Fetch Feed" click="httpSvc.send();"/>

</mx:Application>
```

4. Compile and deploy the above application under your application server and access it in a browser using its URL, for example `http://localhost:8180/YourApp/HTTPServiceExample.html`. Click on the **Fetch Feed** button. Please note that in order to see security sandbox error, you need to deploy your application on the server. Locally executed applications are allowed to access any data without restrictions.
5. Instead of showing results, Flash Player will show the following security error while accessing the URL:

   Error #2048: Security sandbox violation: http://localhost:8180/YourApp/HTTPServiceExample.swf cannot load data from http://newsrss.bbc.co.uk/rss/newsonline_world_edition/front_page/rss.xml.

   This is because the URL you have specified—`http://newsrss.bbc.co.uk`—does not have a cross-domain policy file, or its cross-domain policy does not specify permissions to grant access to the `http://localhost:8180` domain.
6. Now let's modify the same application and use the BlazeDS proxy service to load data from the same URL. To do this, you need to move the `HTTPService`'s `url` property value to BlazeDS's proxy configuration file, `proxy-config.xml`.

7. Open the `proxy-config.xml` file located under your project's `/WEB-NF/flex/` folder and add the following entry in it just before the `</service>` tag:

```
<destination id="BBCNewsFeed">
   <properties>
   <url>http://newsrss.bbc.co.uk/rss/newsonline_world_edition/
        front_page/rss.xml</url>
   </properties>
</destination>
```

8. The above destination configuration specifies the same URL that we used in the previous example. The above code specifies the destination identifier `BBCNewsFeed`, which is pointing to the URL specified under the `<url>` tag.
9. Now modify the `HTTPServiceExample.mxml` code and implement it as follows:

```
<?xml version="1.0" encoding="utf-8"?>
<mx:Application xmlns:mx="http://www.adobe.com/2006/mxml">

   <mx:Script>
      <![CDATA[
         import mx.controls.Alert;
         import mx.rpc.events.FaultEvent;

         private function faultHandler(event:FaultEvent):void {
         Alert.show(event.fault.faultString+
         "\n"+event.fault.rootCause.text);
         }
      ]]>
   </mx:Script>

   <mx:HTTPService id="httpSvc" destination="BBCNewsFeed"
    useProxy="true" fault="faultHandler(event)"/>
   <mx:DataGrid dataProvider="{httpSvc.lastResult.rss.channel.
    item}" width="100%"/>
   <mx:Button label="Fetch Feed" click="httpSvc.send();"/>

</mx:Application>
```

10. The only thing I changed in the above code is the definition of the `<mx:HTTPService>` tag which is now using the `destination` property instead of `url` to specify where to look for URL. The `destination` property is now pointing to the destination defined in the `proxy-config.xml` file, that is, `BBCNewsFeed`. Also notice that the `useProxy` property is set to `true`. The `useProxy` property specifies that this request should be routed through proxy service defined in BlazeDS or LCDS proxy configuration file.

11. Now compile and deploy this application under your application server and access it through the browser and click on the **Fetch Feed** button again. This time it loads the feed data from `http://newsrss.bbc.co.uk` and displays it in `DataGrid`. This works because this time the request you made from the `HTTPService` class does not directly go to `http://newsrss.bbc.co.uk`. Instead, it is routed through a proxy service of BlazeDS or LCDS. The proxy service forwards the same request to `http://newsrss.bbc.co.uk` and reads its response, and then returns it to the client. This whole process works because the proxy services are also deployed under the same domain under your application context. The following illustration shows how this works:

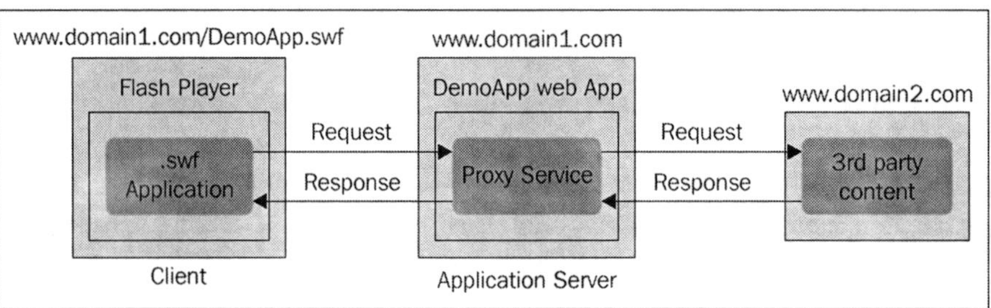

Summary

In this chapter you learned the various data access methods such as `HTTPService`, `WebService`, and `RemoteObjects` with code examples. Now you know how to use them to send and receive remote data. Along with this, you also learned the Flash Player security sandbox model and cross-domain policy files, and their usage. You also learned how to use BlazeDS or LCDS proxy services to access data without needing a cross-domain policy file.

In the next chapter, you will learn how to use Flex and data access methods to communicate with traditional JavaServer Pages (JSP) with examples.

8

Communicating with Server-side Java

In the previous chapter, you saw three main methods for accessing data from Flex applications. Most Flex applications you would develop will communicate with server using one of the three data access methods provided by the Flex 3 SDK. In this chapter, we will mainly focus on how to develop Flex applications to communicate with server-side Java objects or JSP, and process the data sent by the server into your Flex application.

Flex provides three main methods for accessing server-side data: `HTTPService`, `WebService`, and `RemoteObject`. Although we have discussed these three methods in our earlier chapter, in this chapter we will concentrate on the `HTTPService` data access method. We will learn how to use it in conjunction with JSP on the server to send and fetch dynamic results in your Flex application.

In this chapter, we will discuss two common data formats which can be used to send and fetch data over HTTP from a Flex application to a JSP, that is, XML and JSON (JavaScript Object Notation).

The HTTPService class

As you know, a `HTTPService` class can be used to make HTTP calls to your server-side business logic to send and load plain-text results into your Flex application.

Typically, JavaServer Pages (JSP) is used for processing and building dynamic results, and returning presentation HTML code/an HTML page which is rendered by your web browser. But in this chapter, you will learn how to use JSP to build dynamic results and let it return an XML document or JSON object instead of the HTML code. Let's understand how the `HTTPService` class can be used to load XML and JSON data.

Working with XML data

The following example illustrates how to use a `HTTPService` class to communicate with JavaServer Pages (JSP) to send and load dynamic XML data.

`XMLHTTPServiceExample.mxml`:

```
<?xml version="1.0" encoding="utf-8"?>
<mx:Application xmlns:mx="http://www.adobe.com/2006/mxml">

   <mx:Script>
      <![CDATA[
         import mx.rpc.events.ResultEvent;
         import mx.controls.Alert;
         import mx.rpc.events.FaultEvent;

      private function faultHandler(event:FaultEvent):void {
            Alert.show(event.fault.message);
         }
         private function resultHandler(event:ResultEvent):void {
            dgGrid.dataProvider = event.result.book;
         }

         private var myXml:XML =
            <book>
                 <ISBN>184719530X</ISBN>
                 <title>Building Websites with Joomla! 1.5</title>
                 <author>Graf Hagen</author>
                 <pages>363</pages>
                 <description>The best-selling Joomla! tutorial guide
                  updated for the latest 1.5 release</description>
             </book>;
      ]]>
   </mx:Script>

   <mx:HTTPService id="httpSvc"
      url="http://localhost:8180/XMLSearchService.jsp"
      resultFormat="e4x"
      result="resultHandler(event)"
      fault="faultHandler(event)"/>

   <mx:Panel title="XML HTTPService Example"
    width="100%" height="100%">

      <mx:DataGrid id="dgGrid" height="100%" width="100%">
         <mx:columns>
            <mx:DataGridColumn headerText="ISBN" dataField="ISBN"/>
```

```
            <mx:DataGridColumn headerText="Book Name"
             dataField="title"/>
            <mx:DataGridColumn headerText="Author"
             dataField="author"/>
            <mx:DataGridColumn headerText="Pages" dataField="pages"/>
            <mx:DataGridColumn headerText="Description"
             dataField="description"/>
         </mx:columns>
      </mx:DataGrid>

      <mx:ControlBar width="100%">
         <mx:Button label="Search" click="httpSvc.send({myParameter:
          myXml});"/>
      </mx:ControlBar>
   </mx:Panel>
</mx:Application>
```

In the above code, we have defined the `HTTPService` tag with the `resultFormat` property set to `e4x`, and the `url` property pointing to `XMLSearchService.jsp` deployed on a web server. Make sure that you change the `url` property to your web server address. We have written the `result` and `fault` event handlers for `HTTPService`. On the `result` event, we are setting the result of `HTTPService` to the `DataGrid` component's `dataProvider` property. We are invoking a JSP page on the `click` event of a button by passing an XML object as a parameter. Next, you will see how to write a simple JSP page and read the parameter passed by the Flex application using the `httpSvc.send({myParameter:myXml})` method and return XML data. Let's understand the JSP code.

`XMLSearchService.jsp`:

```
<?xml version="1.0" encoding="UTF-8"?>
<%@page import="example.BookSearchService"%>
<%@page import="java.util.List"%>
<%@page import="example.BookVO"%>
<%
   //Reading Parameter sent by Flex and printing it.
   System.out.println(request.getParameter("myParameter"));
%>
<result>
<%
    BookSearchService srv = new BookSearchService();
    List results = srv.getAvailableBook();

    for (int i = 0; i < results.size(); i++) {
        BookVO aBook = (BookVO)results.get(i);
```

```
%>
    <book>
        <ISBN><%= aBook.getISBN() %></ISBN>
        <title><%= aBook.getTitle() %></title>
        <author><%= aBook.getAuthor() %></author>
        <pages><%= aBook.getPages() %></pages>
        <description><%= aBook.getDescription() %></description>
    </book>
<%
    }
%>
</result>
```

The above code is a simple JSP page. It gets dynamic results by invoking the `BookSearchService` Java class's `getAvailableBook()` method, and then outputs it into a formatted XML document. We are also reading the HTTP parameter passed by the Flex application using `request.getParameter("myParameter")`. In this scenario, we are just printing it. But in a real-world scenario, you can make use of it to retrieve conditional data from the database and return the results as XML. Next, we will see the `BookSearchService.java` class code.

`BookSearchService.java`:

```
package example;

import java.util.ArrayList;
import java.util.List;

public class BookSearchService {

   public List<BookVO> getAvailableBook()
   {
      //Connect to DB and build and return dynamic results

      List<BookVO> theArray = new ArrayList<BookVO>();
      BookVO theBook = new BookVO();
      theBook.setISBN("184719530X");
      theBook.setTitle("Building Websites with Joomla! 1.5");
      theBook.setAuthor("Graf Hagen");
      theBook.setPages(363);
      theBook.setDescription("The best-selling Joomla! tutorial guide
      updated for the latest 1.5 release");
      theArray.add(theBook);

      theBook = new BookVO();
      theBook.setISBN("1847196160");
      theBook.setTitle("Drupal 6 JavaScript and jQuery");
```

```
        theBook.setAuthor("Butcher Matt");
        theBook.setPages(250);
        theBook.setDescription("Putting jQuery, AJAX, and JavaScript
        effects into your Drupal 6 modules and themes");
        theArray.add(theBook);
        return theArray;
    }
}
```

The above code is the simple Java DAO class. In this example, we are building results from hardcoded values. But in the real world, you may connect to a database and then generate dynamic results and return it. The `getAvailableBook()` method uses the `BookVO.java` class containing simple setter and getter methods to generate book details object, and returns the `ArrayList` object containing two `BookVO` objects. Please note that both `BookSearchService.java` and `BookVO.java` are defined under a package called `example`. So make sure you maintain the same package structure while deploying it on your web server.

`BookVO.java`:

```
package example;

public class BookVO {
   private String ISBN;
   private String title;
   private String author;
   private int pages;
   private String description;

   public String getISBN() {
      return ISBN;
   }
   public void setISBN(String isbn) {
      ISBN = isbn;
   }
   public String getDescription() {
      return description;
   }
   public void setDescription(String description) {
      this.description = description;
   }
   public String getTitle() {
      return title;
   }
   public void setTitle(String title) {
      this.title = title;
```

```
        }
        public String getAuthor() {
            return author;
        }
        public void setAuthor(String author) {
            this.author = author;
        }
        public int getPages() {
            return pages;
        }
        public void setPages(int pages) {
            this.pages = pages;
        }
    }
```

The above class is self-explanatory. It is a simple Value Object (VO) class with setter and getter methods for accessing its properties.

Now compile the Flex and Java source code and deploy it on your web server. Launch the Flex application using Flex Builder and click on the **Search** button to see the result.

You would see the following output in the browser:

XML HTTPService Example

ISBN	Book Name	Author	Pages	Description
184719530X	Building Websites with Jooml	Graf Hagen	363	The best-selling Joomla! tuto
1847196160	Drupal 6 JavaScript and jQue	Butcher Matt	250	Putting jQuery, AJAX, and Jav

Search

Working with JSON data

JSON (JavaScript Object Notation) is the text format used for serializing and deserializing complex object structures into human-readable text that can be converted back to the object. JSON has become a more popular choice for many RIA technologies because of its compact text format and its ability to exchange data between many languages such as Java, C#, PHP, and so on. To know more about JSON format, visit `http://www.json.org/`.

In the following example, we will use some third-party open source libraries to encode and decode JSON objects in Flex and JSP. They are as follows:

- json-simple (`http://code.google.com/p/json-simple/`): A Java open source library for encoding and decoding JSON objects in Java
- as3corelib (`http://code.google.com/p/as3corelib/`): An ActionScript open source library for encoding and decoding JSON objects in Flex/ActionScript

Before we start writing code, we will have to copy the `as3corelib.swc` file into our project's `libs` folder. This ensures that all JSON-related API classes are available during coding and compilation. So make sure that you have downloaded **AS3CoreLib** from the URL specified above.

The `.swc` files are library files used in Flex or ActionScript programming. Think of them as Java's `.jar` files which contain all your compiled class files. Similarly, the `.swc` files contain all your precompiled definitions which can be referenced by your `.swf` application. To know more about `.SWC`, visit `http://livedocs.adobe.com/flex/3/html/help.html?content=compilers_30.html`.

We will start with writing the Flex MXML code, which will use `HTTPService` to invoke a JSP page that builds and returns a JSON object.

The MXML code:

```
<?xml version="1.0" encoding="utf-8"?>
<mx:Application xmlns:mx="http://www.adobe.com/2006/mxml" creationComp
lete="init();">

    <mx:Script>
        <![CDATA[
            import com.adobe.serialization.json.JSONDecoder;
            import mx.rpc.events.FaultEvent;
            import mx.controls.Alert;
            import mx.rpc.events.ResultEvent;

            private function init():void {
                httpSrv.send();
            }

            private function resultHandler(event:ResultEvent):void {
                var jd:JSONDecoder = new JSONDecoder(String(event.result));
                dgGrid.dataProvider = jd.getValue();
            }
```

```
        private function faultHandler(event:FaultEvent):void {
            Alert.show(event.fault.message);
        }

    ]]>
  </mx:Script>

  <mx:HTTPService id="httpSrv" url="http://192.168.0.2:8180/
   JSONService.jsp"
     result="resultHandler(event)" fault="faultHandler(event)"/>

  <mx:DataGrid id="dgGrid" width="100%" height="100%"/>

</mx:Application>
```

In the above code, we have defined `HTTPService` with the `url` property set to the `JSONService.jsp` file deployed on your web server. You can change this value to your web server address. We are handling the `result` event of `HTTPService` via the registered event handler method `resultHandler()`. In this method, we have created a JSONDecoder ActionScript object (provided by the open source library **as3corelib).** The `JSONDecoder` class reads the result of `HTTPService` and decodes it into an ActionScript object by using the `getValue()` method. This method returns an object we can set as `dataProvider` of the `DataGrid` component.

We are invoking HTTP service in the `init()` method which is called on the `creationComplete` event of our application.

Next, we will see how to write the JSP code. Here, I assume that you are aware of how to create a Java project and add **json-simple** as a library to your project in Eclipse, or in your favourite IDE. Once you copy the `json-simple` library JAR file into your project, start writing the following JSP code and deploy it on your web server. Please note that you will have to specify this web server address as the `url` of your `HTTPService` in MXML code.

`JSONService.jsp`:

```
<%@ page language="java" import="java.util.*" pageEncoding="UTF-8"%>
<%@ page import="org.json.simple.JSONObject" %>
<%
      JSONObject obj = new JSONObject();

      obj.put("title","BookTitle1");
      obj.put("pages",new Integer(300));
      obj.put("price",new Double(99.99));
      obj.put("isAvailable",new Boolean(true));
      obj.put("description","BookDescription1");
%>
<%= obj %>
```

In the above JSP code, we created `JSONObject` provided by the **json-simple** library and we set its various properties using the `obj.put(Object, Object)` method. Lastly, we wrote `JSONObject` as the output of our JSP file.

Now, we are all set to test our application. Make sure that you deploy the above JSP file in your web server along with the **json-simple** library JAR file, and then run the Flex application using Flex Builder. You will see following screen as output:

description	isAvailable	pages	price	title
BookDescription1	true	300	99.99	BookTitle1

Summary

In this chapter, you learned how to develop Flex applications in conjunction with JSP. You also learned how to send and return dynamic XML documents and JSON objects instead of the typical HTML code from JSPs, and use them in you Flex application.

In the next chapter, you will learn various debugging techniques used for developing Flex applications. We will also discuss about Flex Builder's profiler and debugger views and how to use them along with some of the third-party tools used for debugging Flex requests and responses.

9
Debugging Techniques

It is very important to understand the debugging techniques and tooling available with any Software Development Kit (SDK), and Flex is no different. Traditionally, debugging web applications—especially the client-side code—has been a cumbersome task. One of the core strengths of Flex is its ability to debug client-side Flex application code. The Flex SDK provides built-in debugging tools for speeding up the development of web applications.

The Flex SDK includes a fully-featured command line debugging tool called `FDB` (Flash Player Debugger). This tool can be used to debug your application. Although you can use the Flex Builder to do the same thing, it is good to have a free debugging tool as part of the SDK itself. We will not be covering this command line tool in depth. To know more about this tool, visit `http://livedocs.adobe.com/flex/3/html/debugging_01.html`.

The Flex Builder IDE provides a set of very powerful and easy-to-use tools to debug your Flex application. In this chapter, we will discuss various debugging techniques possible with Flex Builder's debugger and some third-party tools to help you with debugging your application in the production environment.

Flash Debug Player

In order to debug your Flex application, you need to install a debug version of Flash Player known as Flash Debug Player. When you install Flex Builder, it installs the debug version of Flash Player. But if for some reason you do not have it, you can download and install the latest version from the Adobe web site `http://www.adobe.com/support/flashplayer/downloads.html`. Make sure that you uninstall the older version of Flash Player before installing the latest Flash Debug Player.

If you aren't sure whether you have the Flash Debug Player installed or not, then follow the steps below to find out.

Visit `http://www.adobe.com/products/flash/about/` and right-click on any Flash content, and see if the **Debugger** menu appears in the list. This web page also displays the version of your currently installed Flash Player.

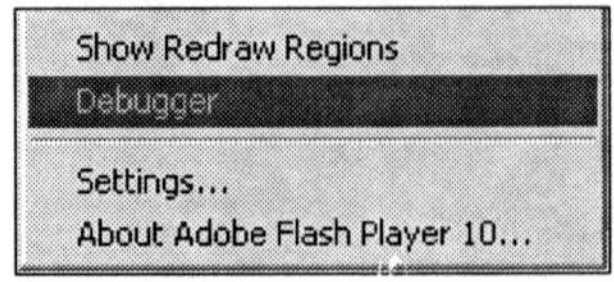

If you see the **Debugger** menu, then you have Flash Debug Player installed. But if you don't see it, then you should download Flash Debug Player from the above URL.

Once you install Flash Debug Player, we are all set to start debugging our Flex application. We will start by configuring client-side logging so that the debug information is put into a log file created by Flash Debug Player.

Running an application in a debug mode in Flash Debug Player may affect your application's performance, and so it should be used only in the development environment.

Using client-side logging

Flex SDK and Flex Builder provide you advanced tooling and debugging capabilities. But you can use a simple client-side logging technique to print debug information from your Flex application in a log file, which can be used to debug your application.

In order to use logging, you need to set up Flash Debug Player's configuration file called `mm.cfg`. This configuration file is typically found in the following directories:

Windows 2000/XP	`C:\Documents and Settings\<username>`
Windows Vista	`C:\Users\<username>`

If this file is not present, then you can create a new file with the name `mm.cfg` and add the following entries in it to enable logging using Flash Debug Player:

`TraceOutputFileEnable`	Turns logging on or off. Use `0` to turn it off (default) and `1` to turn it on.
`ErrorReportingEnable`	Turns logging of error messages on or off. Use `0` to turn it off (default) and `1` to turn it on.
`MaxWarnings`	Maximum number of warnings to record. Default is set to `100`. You can increase it and set it to `0` for unlimited.

The `mm.cfg` file should look like this:

```
TraceOutputFileEnable=1
ErrorReportingEnable=1
MaxWarnings=100
```

Now we are all set to print debug information from our Flex application using the global `trace()` method. The `trace()` method is used to print debug information from Flex application into the `flashlog.txt` log file created by Flash Debug Player at the following location:

Windows 200/XP	`C:\Documents and Settings\<username>\Application Data\Macromedia\Flash Player\Logs`
Windows Vista	`C:\Users\<username>\AppData\Roaming\Macromedia\Flash Player\Logs`

Let's see one simple example of using the `trace()` method to print various kinds of information to the log file. Create a simple MXML application file and copy the following code into it:

```
<?xml version="1.0" encoding="utf-8"?>
<mx:Application xmlns:mx="http://www.adobe.com/2006/mxml" creationComp
lete="printDebugLogs()">

   <mx:Script>
      <![CDATA[
         import mx.utils.ObjectUtil;
         private function printDebugLogs():void {
            var str:String = "Flex Debugging Example";
            var obj:Object = {title:"Flex Debugging", pages:100};

            trace("This is debug line 1");
            trace("Printing variable: "+str);
            trace("Printing object: "+ObjectUtil.toString(obj));
         }
      ]]>
   </mx:Script>

</mx:Application>
```

In the above code example, we have defined a simple method called `printDebugLogs()`, which demonstrates how to use the `trace()` method to print various data to a log file. We are printing three different debug lines using the `trace()` method—the first one prints a simple string, the second one appends a string variable value with debug information, and the third one prints the `Object`'s properties using the `ObjectUtil` class's `toString()` method.

Now, run this application using Flex Builder and open your `flashlog.txt` file from the appropriate location. You should see the following lines in it:

This is debug line 1

Printing variable: Flex Debugging Example

Printing object: (Object)#0

pages = 100

title = "Flex Debugging"

Please note that the `flashlog.txt` file is a common file used by Flash Debug Player to write logs. So if you are running two Flex applications' printing debug information, then log statements from both the applications will be written into the same `flashlog.txt` file.

If you do not see the `flashlog.txt` file generated by your Flash Debug Player for some reason, you can visit `http://kb.adobe.com/selfservice/viewContent.do?externalId=tn_19323&sliceId=2` for troubleshooting tips.

Flex Builder Debugger

Flex Builder provides a full-blown modern debugger perspective that allows you to add breakpoints in your code, step through the code, evaluate expressions, and watch runtime variables and objects, and change their values in real time. If you have ever used Eclipse's Java debugger, then you will find this very familiar.

By default, Flex Builder compiles all `.swf` files with the debug mode enabled, and they are stored under `\bin-debug` folder under your project path. You can disable this behavior by setting the `-debug=false` compiler option in the `Additional compiler arguments` field of your project's properties. The debug version of the `.swf` file is only recommended for development purposes, and is never to be used in the production environment. To know how to generate a non-debug `.swf` file, read Chapter 6.

With Flex Builder Debugger, you can set breakpoints in your code. To set a breakpoint, just open your MXML or ActionScript source file and double-click on the left margin area (highlighted in a green box in the following screenshot) of your code editor. Alternatively, you can also right-click on it and select the **Toggle Breakpoint** menu option as shown in the following screenshot:

Source | Design

```
<?xml version="1.0" encoding="utf-8"?>
<mx:Application xmlns:mx="http://www.adobe.com/2006/mxml">

    <mx:Script>
        <![CDATA[
            import mx.utils.ObjectUtil;
            private function printDebugLogs():void {
                var str:String = "Flex Debugging Example";
                var obj:Object = {title:"Flex Debugging", pages:100};

                trace("This is debug line 1");
                trace("Printing variable: "+str);
                trace("Printing object: "+ObjectUtil.toString(obj));
            }
        ]]>
    </mx:Script>

    <mx:Button label="click" click="printDebugLogs();"/>
</mx:Application>
```

This will add the breakpoint. Flex Builder puts a blue dot on that line number indicating that the debug breakpoint has been added, as shown in the above screenshot.

Now you can debug your application by clicking on the **Debug As...** button on your Flex Builder's toolbar, as shown in following screenshot:

Choose debug as **Flex Application** if prompted, and then Flex Builder will launch your application in a debug mode.

Your application will run until it reaches the first breakpoint in your code. Once it reaches the breakpoint, Flex Builder will switch to the debugger perspective and open a few views which are useful for debugging your application. It should generally look like the following:

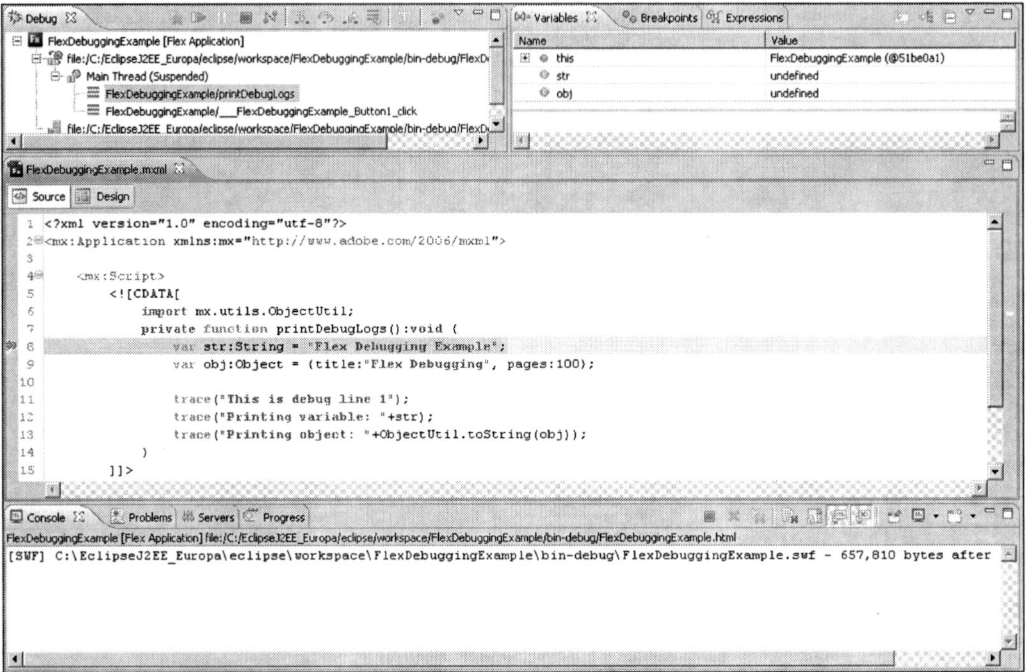

You can also switch to the Flex Debugger perspective by choosing **Windows | Perspective | Flex Debugging**. The Flex Debugging perspective contains different views that are discussed in the sections that follow.

The Debug view

The Debug view allows you to manage the debugging session. It displays a list of suspended threads of targets that you are currently debugging. It also provides the following options to control the execution:

	`Resume`	Resumes the suspended thread
	`Suspend`	Pauses the current debugging thread
	`Terminate`	Terminates the selected debugging thread
	`Disconnect`	Disconnects the debugger from the current debugging thread

	`Step Into`	Steps into the currently highlighted statement and continues debugging
	`Step Over`	Steps over the currently highlighted statement and executes the next line of code in a debug mode
	`Step Return`	Steps out of the current debugging thread and stops debugging after exiting the current method

The following screenshot shows the Debug view:

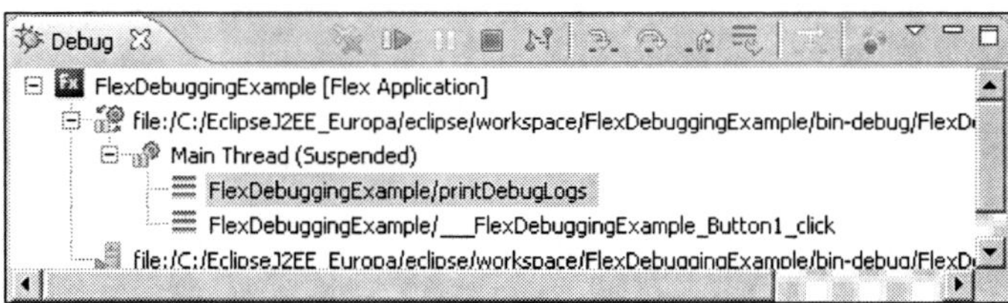

To speed up debugging, Flex Builder offers some handy keyboard shortcuts for debugging, as shown here:

- `Step Into` (*F5*)
- `Step Over` (*F6*)
- `Step Return` (*F7*)
- `Resume` (*F8*)
- `Terminate` (*Ctrl+F2*)

The Variables view

The Variables view displays information about the variables associated with the object that is being debugged. The variable view is split into two parts. The top part displays a list of variables in a tree structure. You can expand the tree structure and go into the variable details. The bottom part displays the selected variable's value. You can also change the variable's value by right-clicking on the variable and selecting **Change Value...** from the menu. This is very helpful while debugging any logical problem in your code. The following screenshot shows the Variable view:

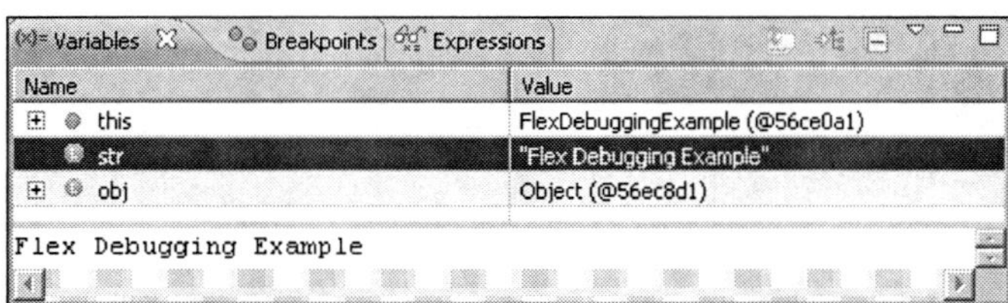

The Breakpoints view

The Breakpoints view lists all the breakpoints that you have set in your Flex Builder's workspace with the line number. You can double-click on the breakpoint to go to the source code where you have set that breakpoint. The following screenshot shows the Breakpoints view:

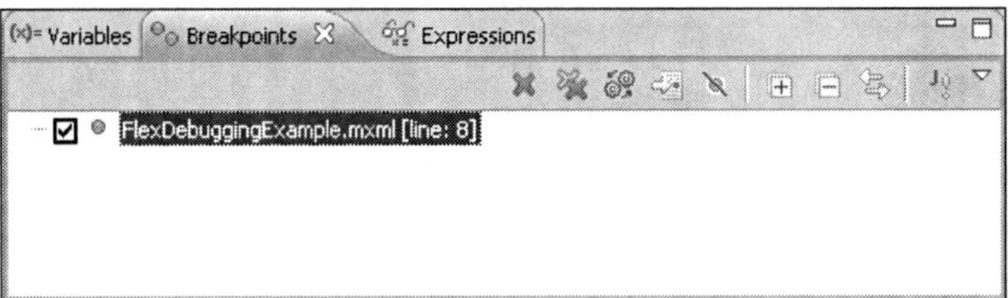

The Expressions view

The Expressions view is used to inspect the runtime data. You can select any variable, expression, or object from your source code, right-click on it, and select the **Watch <selected expression>** menu item to add an expression, variable, or an object into the Expressions view. You can also right-click on the Expressions view area and select the **Add Watch Expression...** menu item to add custom expressions that you want to evaluate at runtime. The following screenshot shows the Expressions view:

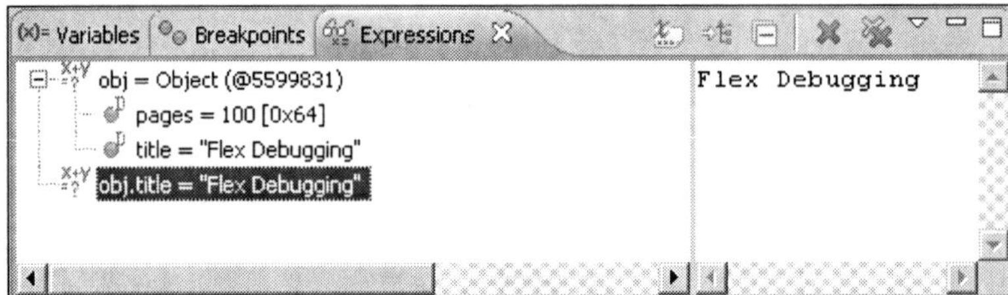

These are the main debugging views provided by Flex Builder in the Debugger perspective. Apart from these, you have the Console view which displays errors and warnings, and debugs the `trace()` messages printed by your application or compiler.

Network monitoring

Network monitoring is a very important aspect while debugging any web application. Network monitoring tools provide you with information about the requests and responses sent and received by your application. This is very important to understand because applications mostly fail due to network-related issues such as wrong data being sent or received, latency in loading data, and so on. This also helps you to figure out the response time taken by every remote call made by your application. This information is important when you are benchmarking your application performance in a production mode.

There are many network-monitoring tools available that work for plain HTTP or Socket requests and responses. When using Flex these tools may not work, especially when you're using `RemoteObject` that uses the AMF encoding. But there are a couple of tools available that capture Flex remoting or AMF requests and responses, and provide you with detailed results that will help you to nail down the problem.

ServiceCapture

ServiceCapture is specially designed to work with Rich Internet applications to help developers in debugging, analysis, and testing their applications. This is one of the best tools available for monitoring Flex remoting AMF traffic.

ServiceCapture provides a very intuitive and easy-to-use user interface, which provides detailed information about network traffic generated by the application including HTTP, AMF, SOAP, XML, JSON-RPC, and so on. It includes the following important features:

Remote service deserialization	Decodes Flex/Flash Remoting or AMF traffic and shows it in an easy-to-use interface.
Bandwidth simulation	Allows developers to simulate different bandwidths to test their application even when it is running locally.
Map URLs to files	Allows you to replace a server response with the data from a local file. This allows you to test server operations with different sets of data.
Unit testing	Allows you to replay/resend any request from the UI. This is a good way to test specific server operation without actually using web applications every time.
Flash trace logging	Displays all your `trace()` logs within the same UI.
Monitor any log file	You can load any log file and watch it in real time. This is very useful while reading the `flashlog.txt` output.

ServiceCapture currently works only on Windows, supports Internet Explorer (IE) and Firefox, and requires Java 1.5. ServiceCapture costs $34 US for a single user license, but there is an option to download a 30-day evaluation copy for your test run. Please visit `http://www.kevinlangdon.com/serviceCapture/` for its download and purchase details.

Charles Web Debugging Proxy

This is another good, network traffic monitoring tool available which supports capturing HTTP, JSON, JSON-RPC, XML, SOAP, and Flex/Flash remoting or AMF traffic. Charles proxy can also simulate different bandwidths to test your application under dial-up or broadband connection speed.

Charles proxy currently works on Windows, Mac OS X, and Linux/Unix; and it supports Internet Explorer (IE), Firefox, and Safari (on both Mac OS X and Windows); and requires Java 1.4 or above.

To read the complete set of features and download Charles proxy, visit `http://www.charlesproxy.com/download.php`.

Charles Web Debugging Proxy costs $50 US for a single user license, but there is an option that you can download a 30-days evaluation copy for your test run.

Both tools are more or less the same in features, and they are relatively easy to work with. These tools allow you to export the results as a `.cvs` file, and the resulted data is easy to read and understand.

There are many other free network traffic monitoring tools available such as Fiddler (`http://www.fiddlertool.com/Fiddler2/`), WireShark (previously known as Ethereal, `http://sourceforge.net/projects/wireshark/`), and Firebug-Firefox browser add-on (`https://addons.mozilla.org/en-US/firefox/addon/1843`). But none of these are found to be capturing Flex/Flash remoting or AMF traffic.

Summary

In this chapter, you learned about Flex application's debugging techniques and tools available in Flex Builder along with some third-party network monitoring tools to help you with debugging your Flex application. We also saw how to use Flash Debug Player and the `trace()` method to output debug information into the `flashlog.txt` file.

In the next chapter, you will learn how to customize your application's look and feel using external CSS and how to utilize runtime CSS to dynamically change an application's look and feel.

10
Styling your Application

If you have worked on web designing using modern web technologies and tools, then it is more than likely you have used Cascading Style Sheets (CSS) for changing the look and feel of your web application. Using CSS is the most common way of personalizing your application. CSS enables you to separate your content from presentation logic.

It is very important for any web programming language to exploit the CSS framework to provide a flexible and standard way for customizing application appearance. This includes simple changes such as color, font, or text size to more detailed changes such as an individual component's look and feel, alignment, and properties such as background image, shape and size, and so on.

Flex extends the concept of CSS and it enables web developers to utilize their existing knowledge about CSS to customize the Flex applications. One of the cool things about Flex is it lets you customize the look and feel of your entire application and its individual components using CSS, such as application color scheme, font, alignment, shape and size, and so on.

Flex lets you customize the look and feel of your application in the following ways:

- Using inline styles
- Using external CSS files
- Loading stylesheets at runtime

Using inline styles

In Flex, every component provides a set of properties that can be categorized into **Properties, Methods, Events,** and **Styles**. In this section, what we are interested in is the last category of properties—**Styles**. To read about styles that every component provides you, open the Flex language reference from your Flex Builder by pressing the shortcut key *Shift+F2*, or by choosing the **Help | Find in Language Reference** menu item and opening the documentation for the `Label` class. You can find the **Styles** category on top of the page. Click on it to navigate to the **Style** section of the `Label` class as shown in the following screenshot:

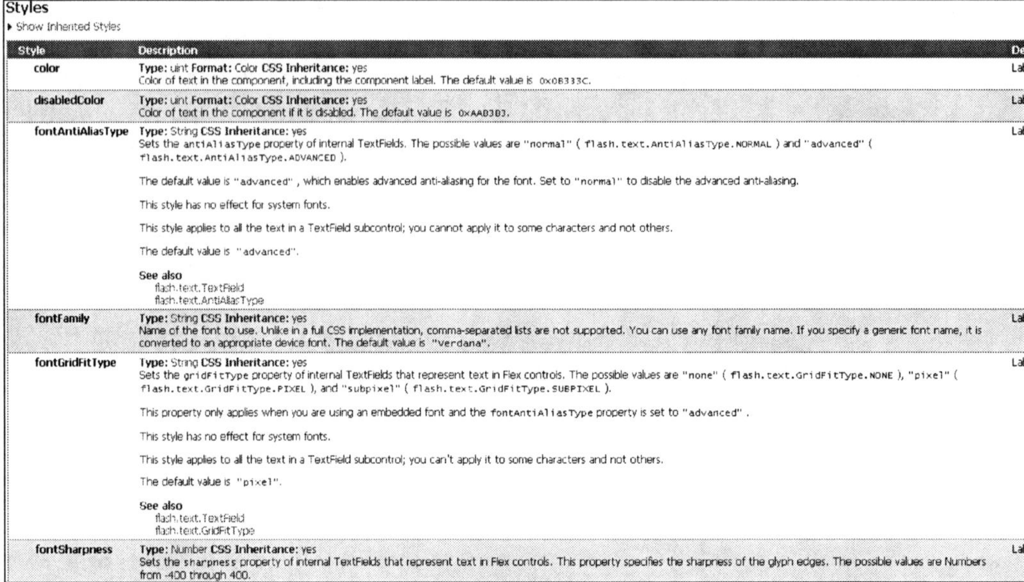

Styles

▸ Show Inherited Styles

Style	Description	De
color	**Type:** uint **Format:** Color **CSS Inheritance:** yes Color of text in the component, including the component label. The default value is `0x0B333C`.	Lab
disabledColor	**Type:** uint **Format:** Color **CSS Inheritance:** yes Color of text in the component if it is disabled. The default value is `0xAAB3B3`.	Lab
fontAntiAliasType	**Type:** String **CSS Inheritance:** yes Sets the `antiAliasType` property of internal TextFields. The possible values are `"normal"` (`flash.text.AntiAliasType.NORMAL`) and `"advanced"` (`flash.text.AntiAliasType.ADVANCED`). The default value is `"advanced"` , which enables advanced anti-aliasing for the font. Set to `"normal"` to disable the advanced anti-aliasing. This style has no effect for system fonts. This style applies to all the text in a TextField subcontrol; you cannot apply it to some characters and not others. The default value is `"advanced"`. **See also** flash.text.TextField flash.text.AntiAliasType	Lab
fontFamily	**Type:** String **CSS Inheritance:** yes Name of the font to use. Unlike in a full CSS implementation, comma-separated lists are not supported. You can use any font family name. If you specify a generic font name, it is converted to an appropriate device font. The default value is `"verdana"`.	Lab
fontGridFitType	**Type:** String **CSS Inheritance:** yes Sets the `gridFitType` property of internal TextFields that represent text in Flex controls. The possible values are `"none"` (`flash.text.GridFitType.NONE`), `"pixel"` (`flash.text.GridFitType.PIXEL`), and `"subpixel"` (`flash.text.GridFitType.SUBPIXEL`). This property only applies when you are using an embedded font and the `fontAntiAliasType` property is set to `"advanced"` . This style has no effect for system fonts. This style applies to all the text in a TextField subcontrol; you can't apply it to some characters and not others. The default value is `"pixel"`. **See also** flash.text.TextField flash.text.GridFitType	Lab
fontSharpness	**Type:** Number **CSS Inheritance:** yes Sets the `sharpness` property of internal TextFields that represent text in Flex controls. This property specifies the sharpness of the glyph edges. The possible values are Numbers from -400 through 400.	Lab

The **Styles** section lists all the styles and inherited styles that are supported by this component. You can use these individual style properties, such as `color`, `fontSize`, `fontStyle`, and so on, to customize specific appearance of your components.

You can also access a component's style properties from Flex Builder in the **Flex Properties** view. Make sure you have selected the **Category** view button from the top-right corner of the **Flex Properties** window, as shown in following screenshot:

The following example shows you how to use these properties to customize the appearance of your application:

```
<?xml version="1.0" encoding="utf-8"?>
<mx:Application xmlns:mx="http://www.adobe.com/2006/mxml">
   <mx:Label text="Hello!" color="red"
    fontSize="20" fontStyle="italic"/>
   <mx:Label text="Bonjour!" color="blue"
    fontSize="20" fontFamily="Arial" />
   <mx:Label text="Namaste!" color="#ffff00"
    fontSize="20" fontWeight="bold"/>
</mx:Application>
```

In the above example, we have used three `Label` controls and set different style properties to each one of them—`color` for setting the color of the text, `fontSize` to set the size of the font, `fontStyle` to set the font style, such as italic or normal; and `fontWeight` to set the font weight, such as bold or normal. If you run this application, you will see the following output:

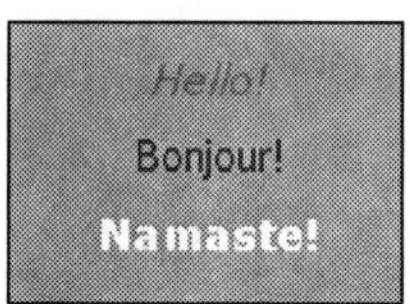

Alternatively, you can also use the `setStyle()` ActionScript method to set the style of your component, as shown in the following example:

```
myLabel.setStyle("fontSize",20);
myLabel.setStyle("color",0xffff00);
```

The style properties of every component are the easiest way to start customizing their look and feel. Flex provides various style properties for every visual component to customize individual component's appearance. To read more about styles, visit the Flex language reference.

Using external CSS files

The default Flex application look is called Halo. Flex includes a default stylesheet (`default.css`) that defines the default look of your Flex application in the `framework.swc` file found under the FLEX_HOME `\frameworks\libs` folder. The `default.css` file defines the look and feel of all Flex components, and is explicitly bundled with your application when you compile it.

The default Flex application color theme is called `haloBlue`. A color theme defines the default color scheme used for Flex components, such as a Button's mouse over, mouse click text color, focus rectangle color, and so on. You can change the default theme color by using `Application` tag's `themeColor` property, for example `themeColor="haloGreen"`, `themeColor="haloOrange"`, or `themeColor="haloSilver"`, or you can set it to the color of your own choice.

Flex supports the use of external CSS. You can define your own stylesheet file with the `.css` extension. The general style declaration syntax is as follows:

```
selector_name {
    style_property: value;
    [...]
}
```

Once the CSS file and styles are declared, you can set it as the application's style using the `<Style>` tag. This overrides the default look of your application, for example:

```
<mx:Style source="../assets/mystyle.css"/>
```

The `Style` tag's `source` property specifies the URL of the stylesheet file that contains the style declaration. The following CSS declaration is used in the `mystyle.css` file:

```
Label
{
    color: #ffff00;
```

```
    fontSize: 20;
    fontWeight: bold;
}
```

In the above CSS code, we are styling the `Label` component. Therefore, our selector name starts with the name of the component that we want to style and then encloses the actual style properties inside curly braces, as shown in the above CSS example. You can also define styles within the `Style` tag. In this case, the `source` property must not be specified, for example:

```
<mx:Style>
    Label
    {
        color: #ffff00;
        fontSize: 20;
        fontWeight: bold;
    }
</mx:Style>
```

You can use the above method to locally define styles for instances of individual component or controls. Both of the methods used above will have the same effect on the look of your application. The only difference is that mentioning an external CSS file path in the `source` property decouples your style declaration from your UI and allows you to dynamically change it anytime.

You can mention any Flex component's name as the selector name in your CSS style declaration in order to apply that style for all instances of that component. For example, the above CSS defines a new style that applies to all instances of the `Label` control in your application. If you need to apply a style only to a specific instance of that component, you will need to define a custom style declaration and specify that custom style selector name in your component's `styleName` property. The following example shows you how to define a custom style for individual components:

```
<mx:Style>
Label
{
    color: #ffff00;
    fontSize: 20;
    fontWeight: bold;
}
Label.helloStyle
{
    color: red;
    fontSize: 20;
    fontStyle: italic;
```

```
}
Label.bonjourStyle
{
   color: blue;
   fontFamily: Arial;
   fontSize: 20;
}
</mx:Style>
```

The above CSS style declaration declares three styles—the first style applies to all `Label` controls that have not set any style explicitly, and the second and third custom style declarations will be used in our application to apply to specific `Label` instances, as shown in the following example:

```
<mx:Label text="Hello!" styleName="helloStyle"/>
<mx:Label text="Bonjour!" styleName="bonjourStyle"/>
<mx:Label text="Namaste!"/>
```

As you can see in the above code, we have three instances of `Label` controls—the first `Label` control's `styleName` property is set to `helloStyle` and the second `Label` control's `styleName` property is set to `bonjourStyle`, which specifies the name of the custom styles declared in CSS. The third `Label` control does not specify any style name, so it will be applied with the style declared using the `Label` selector name in CSS.

You can set the global style by defining the style declaration using a `global` selector and declare the style that you want to apply to all components and controls that do not explicitly override that style. For example, if you want to apply the same font and font color for all controls in your application, you can declare the `global` style as shown in the following code snippet:

```
<mx:Style>
   global
   {
      color: blue;
      fontFamily: Arial;
   }
</mx:Style>
```

Most of the styles you define are inheritable by nature and they automatically get applied to the children. For example, you can use the `Application` type selector to declare styles that will be automatically applied to all its containers and their children, such as fonts, color schema, and so on.

Some styles that are specific to the `Application` tag will only be applied to `Application`, and non-inheritable styles will not be inherited by its children. For example, if you set the `Application` tag's `backgroundGradientColors`, `paddingTop`, or `paddingBottom` styles, it will not be inherited by its children. To read more about the inheritance of style, see `http://livedocs.adobe.com/flex/3/html/help.html?content=styles_04.html`. The following syntax shows how to use the `Application` type selector to define style for your application:

```
<mx:Style>
    Application
    {
        style_definition;
        [...]
    }
</mx:Style>
```

However, using many stylesheets in your application and components may cause your application to behave unexpectedly. Hence, it is not recommended. Instead, you can have a single CSS file under your `Application` tag level.

Creating and designing Cascading Style Sheets

You can use Flex Builder for creating and designing Cascading Style Sheets. Flex Builder provides a specialized editor for editing CSS code in the Design view and the Code view. The following example shows the steps for creating and designing CSS styles for your application and components:

1. Create a new Flex project using Flex Builder and name it `StylingExample`.
2. Add three `Label` components in your MXML file, as shown in following code snippet:

   ```
   <mx:Label text="Hello!"/>
   <mx:Label text="Bonjour!"/>
   <mx:Label text="Namaste!"/>
   ```

3. Create a new CSS file by selecting the **File | New | CSS file** menu and name it `mystyle.css`. Now click on the **Finish** button to create the CSS file.
4. Flex Builder opens a code editor for editing the blank CSS file. It gives you two options—**Source** and **Design**—in the top-left corner of your code editor to edit CSS in the Code view or the Design view. You can use the Code view and start typing style declarations. But in this section, we will use the Design mode for editing the CSS file.

5. Click on the **Design** button shown in the top left corner of your code editor. It opens the Design view as shown in following screenshot:

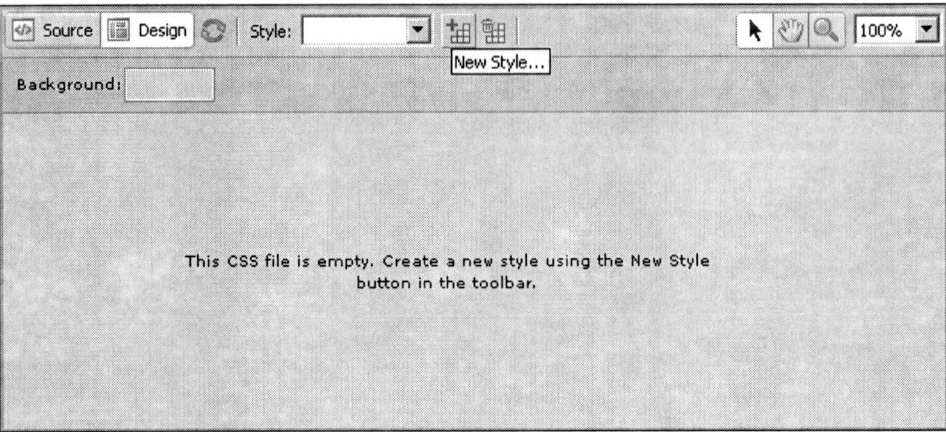

6. Click on the **New Style...** button in the toolbar of your design editor as highlighted in the above screenshot. It opens the **New Style** dialog box as shown in following screenshot:

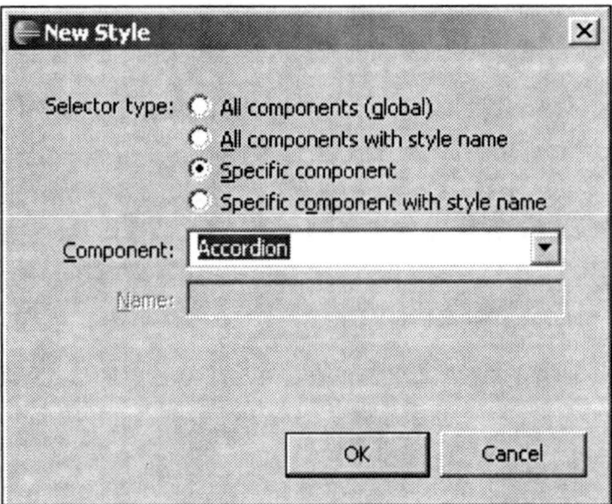

7. The **New Style** dialog box gives you many options such as creating a global style, all component style with name, create style for specific component, or specific component with custom style name, and so on. Go on and explore these options yourself. In this example, we will use the **Specific component** option to create a new style.

8. Select the component name from the **Component** dropdown for which you want to declare a style. Go ahead and select the `Label` component from the dropdown and click on **OK**.

9. Now Flex Builder shows the `Label` control's style properties in **Flex Properties**, as shown in the following screenshot:

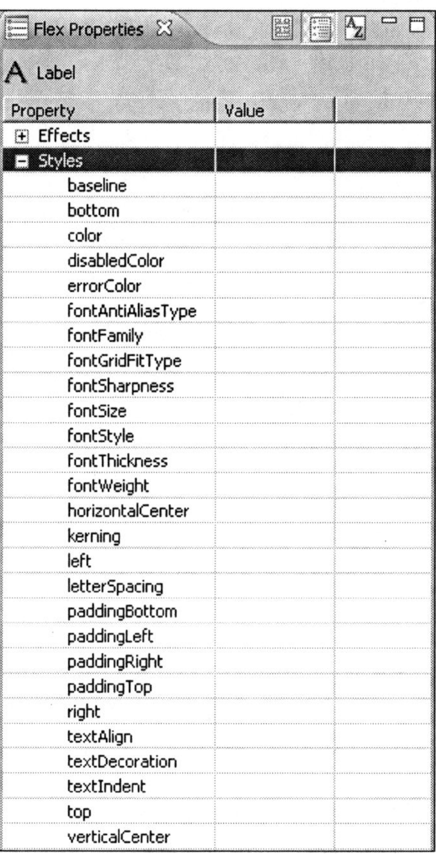

10. Now you can start defining styles using **Flex Properties** such as `color`, `fontStyle`, `fontFamily`, and so on. Flex Builder shows a live preview of your component in the design area.
11. Once you are done with defining style for the `Label` control, click on the **Source** button in the top left corner of the code editor view to view a generated CSS code. Flex Builder generates CSS code in background.
12. Now open your application's MXML file (in this case, it is `StylingExample.mxml`), add the `<mx:Style>` tag, and point its source property to the `mystyle.css` file as shown in this code snippet:

```
<mx:Style source="mystyle.css"/>
```

13. Run the application and you should see that the `Label` style is applied to all three labels from your application.

You can also use Flex Builder to export your component's inline style declarations into a CSS file. For example, if you have the `Label` control that uses inline style to define its appearance, just go to Flex Builder's Design view and **Flex Properties** view, select **Standard view**, and click on the **Convert to CSS...** button. This opens the **New Style Rule** dialog box, which gives you an option to select or create the CSS file to export inline styles, as shown in following screenshot:

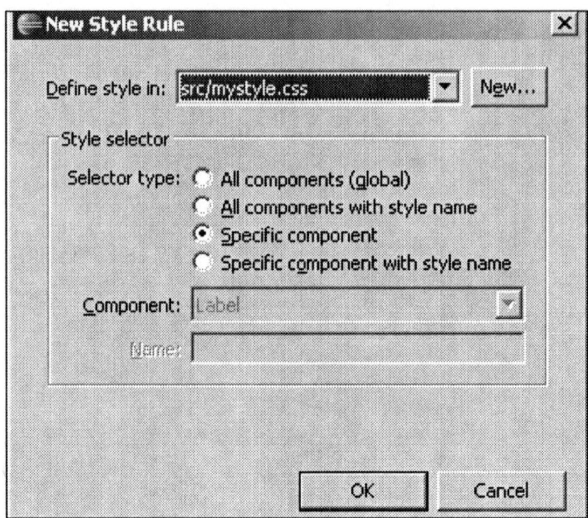

You can also check out Adobe's online CSS builder tool called **Flex Style Explorer**, which allows you to design CSS for Flex components online and preview it. It also generates CSS code that can be copied into your application's CSS file. You can access the **Flex Style Explorer** tool at `http://examples.adobe.com/flex3/consulting/styleexplorer/Flex3StyleExplorer.html#`.

Loading stylesheets at runtime

Flex allows loading of stylesheets at runtime using the `StyleManager` class. By using this technique, you can dynamically change your application's appearance at any time and also separate your content from presentation logic. For example, you can embed assets such as images or media files used by your application into a stylesheet and load it at runtime. This technique decreases application loading time, since assets (stylesheets) are not embedded into the main application.

For loading stylesheets at runtime, you need to compile your CSS file(s) into an SWF file, and then use the `StyleManager.loadStyleDeclarations("cssfile.swf")` method to load it. The steps for loading a stylesheet at runtime are given below. We will use the existing project created in the previous exercise, `StylingExample`:

1. Open the `StylingExample` Flex project.
2. Right-click on the `mystyle.css` file in the **Flex Navigator** view and select the **Compile CSS to SWF** option from the pop-up menu as shown in the following screenshot:

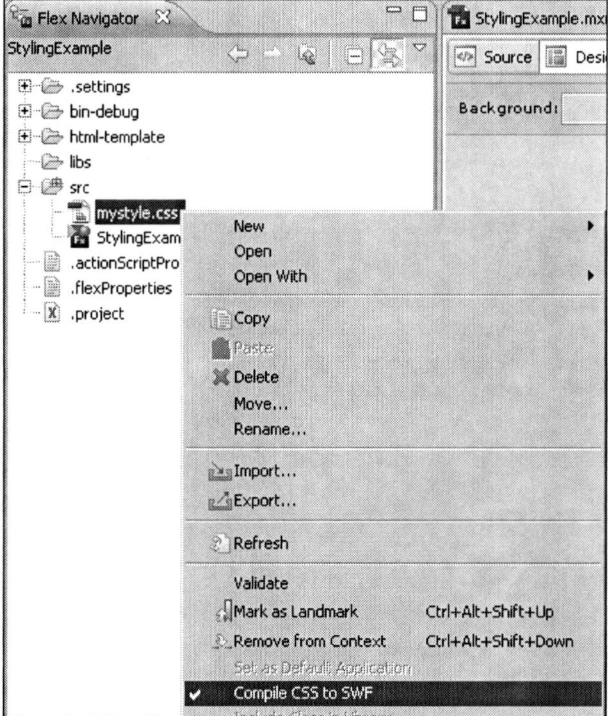

3. The **Compile CSS to SWF** option lets you compile your CSS files into SWF files while building a Flex project. Once this option is checked, you can build your project as you normally do by selecting the **Project | Build Project** menu.
4. Alternatively, you can also use the `mxmlc` command-line compiler to compile CSS into SWF; an example is mxmlc mystyle.css.
5. When Flex Builder builds your project, it also compiles CSS files into SWF files and places them into the `bin-debug` folder along with other binaries.

6. Now open the `StylingExample.mxml` file and remove the `<mx:Style>` tag declaration, and modify it as follows:

```
<?xml version="1.0" encoding="utf-8"?>
<mx:Application xmlns:mx="http://www.adobe.com/2006/mxml">

   <mx:Script>
      <![CDATA[

         private function applyStyleSheet():void {
            StyleManager.loadStyleDeclarations("mystyle.swf");
         }

      ]]>
   </mx:Script>
   <mx:Label text="Hello!" color="red"
    fontFamily="Arial" fontWeight="bold"/>
   <mx:Label text="Bonjour!"/>
   <mx:Label text="Namaste!"/>

   <mx:Button label="Load StyleSheet" click="applyStyleSheet()"/>

</mx:Application>
```

7. In the above code, we have removed the `<mx:Style>` tag and added the `<mx:script>` tag. We have declared a method called `applyStyleSheet()`, which uses the `StyleSheetManager` class to load `mystyle.swf` at runtime. We have used a button to call the `applyStyleSheet()` method.

8. Now run the application, click on the **Load StyleSheet** button, and observe the output. When you run the application, it comes up with the default Flex look and when you click on the **Load StyleSheet** button, Flex's appearance changes dynamically with the styles defined in `mystyle.swf`. This is shown in the following screenshot:

You can also load multiple stylesheets at runtime, which may define the style for individual components in Flex application, as shown in the following code snippet. Please note that we will modify the same example that we have created in the previous exercise, `StylingExample.mxml`.

```
StyleManager.loadStyleDeclarations("defaultLabelStyle.swf");
StyleManager.loadStyleDeclarations("helloLabelStyle.swf");
StyleManager.loadStyleDeclarations("bonjourLabelStyle.swf");
StyleManager.loadStyleDeclarations("myButtonStyle.swf");
```

For the above code to work, create four different CSS files and compile them into SWF files. Now modify the MXML component definition code as shown in the following code snippet:

```
<mx:Label text="Hello!" styleName="helloStyle"/>
<mx:Label text="Bonjour!" styleName="bonjourStyle"/>
<mx:Label text="Namaste!"/>
<mx:Button label="Load StyleSheet" click="applyStyleSheet()"/>
```

We have used the `styleName` attribute of the first two `Label` controls to specify which style to use. The third `Label` and the `Button` control will be applied with default style defined for the `Label` and `Button` selectors. The following are the CSS files; please name them as specified:

`myButtonStyle.css`

```
Button
{
   fontFamily: Arial;
   fontSize: 13;
   fontWeight: bold;
   textRollOverColor: #04C13E;
   themeColor: #00FA4C;
   fillAlphas: 1.0, 1.0;
   fillColors: #BCEECB, #33E66A, #AEF8C5, #83EDA3;
}
```

`bonjourLabelStyle.css`

```
Label.bonjourStyle
{
   color: blue;
   fontFamily: Arial;
   fontSize: 20;
}
```

`helloLabelStyle.css`

```
Label.helloStyle
{
   color: red;
   fontSize: 20;
   fontStyle: italic;
}
```

`defaultLabelStyle.css`

```
Label
{
   color: #FFFF00;
   fontSize: 20;
   fontStyle: italic;
   fontWeight: bold;
   textAlign: center;
}
```

If you are using Flex Builder, make sure that you have selected each CSS file's **Compile CSS to SWF** option. Next, build your project and run it. Click on the **Load StyleSheet** button and observe the output.

Loading multiple stylesheets has an overhead on an application's performance; that is, each time you call the `loadStyleDeclarations()` method, Flash Player reapplies all styles to the display list. This process creates unnecessary overhead on Flash Player and hampers the performance of your application. To avoid this kind of scenario, you can use the `update` flag of the `loadStyleDeclarations()` method, which is the second parameter of this method. You can set the `update` flag to `false` to delay the update process until the last stylesheet is loaded. To do this, you need to handle stylesheet-loading complete event of the `StyleManager.loadStyleDeclarations()` method as shown in the following code snippet:

```
private function applyStyleSheet():void {
   StyleManager.loadStyleDeclarations("defaultLabelStyle.swf", false);
   StyleManager.loadStyleDeclarations("helloLabelStyle.swf", false);
   var evt:IEventDispatcher = StyleManager.loadStyleDeclarations(
                              "bonjourLabelStyle.swf", false);

   evt.addEventListener(StyleEvent.COMPLETE, loadComplete);
}
private function loadComplete(event:Event):void
{
   StyleManager.loadStyleDeclarations("myButtonStyle.swf", true);
}
```

We are loading the first three stylesheets by setting the `update` flag of the `loadStyleDeclarations()` method to `false` and registering the `StyleEvent.COMPLETE` event to listen to the stylesheet-loading success event.

The `loadStyleDeclarations()` method is asynchronous and returns an instance of the `IEventDispatcher` class. You can use this instance to listen to the events dispatched during stylesheet-loading process. For instance, as shown in the above example, we are listening to the `StyleEvent.COMPLETE` event to load and update the last stylesheet by passing the `update` flag as `true`. This way, you are loading all stylesheets but updating only once, which minimizes the overhead of updating the display list every time. You can also use `StyleEvent.PROGRESS` and `StyleEvent.ERROR` to listen to the progress and error events during loading process.

For styling your application, make a note of all styling properties provided by the component by visiting the Flex language reference guide and then set your styling preference. Avoid using unnecessary styling properties that your application may not require. To improve overall application performance, avoid setting styles to their default values. For example, by default, the `Label` component's font size is `10`. So setting the `fontSize` property to `10` in your CSS file may not be useful.

Styling your application using various techniques is a very vast subject. We have covered many topics to start styling with CSS. There are other ways to style, such as using Skins, visual effects, and so on. To read more about this, see `http://livedocs.adobe.com/flex/3/html/help.html?content=skinning_1.html` and `http://livedocs.adobe.com/flex/3/html/help.html?content=createeffects_1.html`.

Summary

In this chapter, we learned about customizing your application's look and feel with various styling techniques, such as using inline styling in MXML tag, using external CSS file into `<mx:Style>`, and loading stylesheets at runtime to dynamically change appearance. We also discussed the technique for compiling a CSS file into an SWF file and loading multiple stylesheets into your application.

In the next chapter, we will briefly discuss packaging and deployment best practices and a typical development setup to work with different Flex projects.

11
Packaging and Deployment

Packaging is the process of enclosing the application binaries for distribution in a production environment. Deployment is the process of moving your packaged application and related resource files into the production environment.

Like any other web application, Flex applications can also be packaged as web applications and deployed on a web server. Flex applications are essentially SWF files (Flash application) which are embedded into HTML files. They can be served from any web server, but the actual application deployment process depends on the web server and the server technology that you are using. For example, if you are using .NET as your server technology, the process of packaging and deploying Flex application on IIS would be different than packaging and deploying it on Tomcat or JRun with Java server technology.

In this chapter, we will discuss a general approach for packaging your application for deployment and the different deployment options that Adobe Flex SDK provides.

Packaging your application

When you build your Flex application using Flex Builder, it compiles your application sources and puts it into the `bin-debug` folder. Basically, the `bin-debug` folder contains your application binaries. Flex Builder creates the following files and folders into your `bin-debug` folder:

`history`	The `history` folder contains supporting files for creating browser-navigation-enabled Flex applications known as **deep linking**. This folder contains the following files: • `history.css` • `history.js` • `historyFrame.html` For more information, see `http://livedocs.adobe.com/flex/3/html/deep_linking_1.html#121714`.
`AC_OETags.js` `playerProductInstall.swf`	These files contain the logic to detect whether the user has installed Flash Player and if it is the correct version. It also prompts for installation if Flash Player is not installed or the correct version was not found. This is known as **Express Install**. For more information, see `http://livedocs.adobe.com/flex/3/html/playerdetection_1.html#166055`.
Wrapper HTML file	Flex Builder creates a wrapper HTML file to embed your SWF application. Usually, the HTML wrapper file name will be same as your main application file name. In this case, it is `ExampleProject.html`.
Application SWF file	This is the compiled SWF application file and it will have the same name as your main application file name.

The packaging directory structure should be planned while you create your project. For example, you must plan on how your application accesses its assets such as images, static text, XML files, and so on. If you have embedded all your application assets into your SWF file, you can deploy and run a standalone SWF file without worrying about the location of application assets. But if your application is loading assets dynamically at runtime, you must include all application assets into your deployment directory at the correct location.

Flex provides an option of embedding assets into your application, thus making them a part of the compiled SWF file. But if you have too many assets with large size, embedding them into your application will increase the size of your SWF application. It would also take a long time to download. To read more about embedding assets, see `http://livedocs.adobe.com/flex/3/html/help.html?content=embed_4.html`.

For example, suppose your application is loading images at runtime using relative path in the `<mx:Image>` tag, as shown in following code snippet:

```
<mx:Image source="/ExampleProject/assets/images/company_logo.png"/>
```

Now, you must deploy the `company_logo.png` image file into the `\assets\images\` folder under your web application root folder, that is, `ExampleProject` in this case. This is a common way of referencing assets into a web application.

Alternatively, you can also use the complete URL of your asset file to load it at run-time, for example `http://www.yourserver.com/ExampleProject/assets/images/company_logo.png`. In this case, assets can be deployed anywhere on the web server and they need not be on the same web server.

Maintaining the correct location of your application assets while deploying is very important to make sure that your application executes correctly.

Packaging an application for deployment also depends on the nature of your project. For example, if your application is integrated with BlazeDS or LCDS on your server for accessing the server business layer, you must ensure that you also deploy BlazeDS or LCDS web application files along with your application. BlazeDS or LCDS provide a ready-to-deploy blank web application archive (`.war`) file that includes all library and configuration files required for deploying BlazeDS or LCDS. The BlazeDS web application archive file (`blazeds.war`) contains the following directory structure:

`WEB-INF`	`classes`	Used for storing all your Java classes with respective package information
	`flex`	This folder contains configuration files for configuring remoting, HTTP, messaging, and proxy services used by your Flex application
	`lib`	This folder contains library files (JAR) required by BlazeDS
	`src`	This folder is a placeholder for your Java source files
	`web.xml`	This is the web application configuration file

You can include the above files along with the Flex application binaries and package it as a J2EE web application WAR or EAR file, and deploy it on any J2EE application server such as Tomcat.

Using Flex Ant Tasks

Ant is an industry-standard build management tool used for building and packaging applications. It provides a very flexible and easy-to-use XML-based scripting language for atomizing the application-building and packaging process. Ant works with a variety of languages for compiling and packaging applications. To know more about Ant, see `http://ant.apache.org/`. Flex 3 provides Ant tasks for compiling Flex application source files. Flex Ant Tasks provide mainly two tasks for compiling Flex application sources—`mxmlc` and `compc`. You can use these tasks to compile your Flex application components, libraries, and modules. In addition to compiling tasks, Flex also provides a task called `html-wrapper` which allows you to customize wrapper generation for your application. Flex Ant Tasks comes with Flex 3 SDK. You can find it under the `<flex_sdk_install>\ant` folder or the `<flex_builder_install>\sdks\3.0.0\ant` folder. The Flex Ant Tasks are inherited from Java Ant Tasks, so this directory contains Java source files and a `lib` folder with a `flexTasks.jar` file.

In order to use Flex Ant Tasks, you need to copy the `flexTasks.jar` file into your `<ant_install>\lib` folder. If you do not have Ant installed, then you can download it from `http://ant.apache.org/bindownload.cgi`. To know how to install and set up the Ant tool, please visit `http://ant.apache.org/manual/install.html`. Once you copy the `flexTasks.jar` into Ant's `lib` folder, you are set to write Ant scripts for building Flex applications. If you are already aware of how to write Ant scripts, then it is an easy job. But if you are not aware of Ant scripting, please read the Ant scripting manual from `http://ant.apache.org/manual/index.html`.

To use Flex Ant Tasks, you need to create an XML file (usually named `build.xml`) under your project root folder. This XML file contains a script for building and packaging the application. We will write one Ant script example which uses the `mxmlc` Flex Ant task to compile a Flex application. We will also use the `html-wrapper` Flex Ant task to build an HTML wrapper for our SWF application. We will also write Ant script for packaging our application into a separate folder.

In order to start using Flex Ant tasks such as `mxmlc` or `html-wrapper`, you need to define `taskdef` and point it to the `flexTasks.jar` file. `taskdef` adds a new set of task definitions to project so that the new tasks can be used in the current project. The following code snippet shows how to define `taskdef`:

```
<taskdef resource="flexTasks.tasks" classpath="C:/Program Files/Adobe/
Flex Builder 3/sdks/3.0.0/ant/flexTasks.jar"/>
```

If you already have `flexTasks.jar` set into **classpath**, you need not include the `classpath` attribute in the `taskdef` element, but we will add it as good practice.

Next, we will create some property definitions to be used in our Ant script. Consider this as declaring static variables in your program.

```
<property name="FLEX_HOME" value="C:/Program Files/Adobe/Flex Builder 
3/sdks/3.0.0"/>
<property name="APP_ROOT" value="ExampleProject"/>
<property name="BUILD_DIR" value="build"/>
```

We have defined the `FLEX_HOME` property which points to the Flex SDK. The `APP_ROOT` property specifies the web application root name. In this case, it is set to `ExampleProject`. The `BUILD_DIR` property specifies the name of the folder used for storing compiled binaries of a Flex application, which in this case is `\build`.

Next, we will create a `build` folder, which will be used for storing compiled Flex application and assets:

```
<mkdir dir="build"/>
```

The above script element creates a new folder if one does not exist already. Next, we will write a target which uses the `mxmlc` Flex Ant task for compiling Flex application as follows:

```
<target name="compile">
<mxmlc file="src/ExampleProject.mxml" output="${BUILD_DIR}/
ExampleProject.swf">
    <load-config filename="${FLEX_HOME}/frameworks/flex-config.xml"/>
    <source-path path-element="${FLEX_HOME}/frameworks"/>
</mxmlc>
</target>
```

The `<target>` definition contains the `name` and `depends` attributes. The `name` attribute specifies the name of the target and the `depends` attribute specifies the name of the target on which it depends for execution. The `compile` target contains the `<mxmlc>` Flex Ant tasks to compile Flex source and it takes two attributes—the `file` attribute specifies the name of the source file, which in this case is `ExampleProject.mxml`; and the `output` attribute specifies the output filename with folder. The `compile` task also defines Flex config file path along with the Flex framework path.

Ant script can be invoked using individual targets or a chain of targets. A target is a collection of instructions that executes the given task. You can create a chain reaction of multiple targets; when the main target is invoked, it will trigger off the other targets using the `depends` attribute in the `<target>` element by specifying the target name on which it depends for execution. For example, the `main` target is dependent on another target called `wrapper`, which is again dependent on a target called `package`, and finally the `package` target is dependent on a target called `compile`. So when you invoke the `main` target, it invokes the `wrapper` target first and waits for it to complete; and as `wrapper` is dependent on `compile`, it invokes the `compile` target first and waits for it to complete, and so on. In short, it is going to execute all the targets one by one starting from `compile` to `wrapper` if you invoke the `main` target.

The main target is set as default in the <project> root element by specifying the default="<target name>" property. The target name specified in the default attribute value will be executed by default if you do not specify any target name while running the Ant tool.

We also have an independent target called clean, which does not depend on any other target and can be invoked directly while running the Ant tool. You will see how to use the Ant tool further in this section.

Complete build.xml source:

```
<?xml version="1.0" encoding="utf-8"?>

<project name="ExampleProject" default="main" basedir=".">

   <taskdef resource="flexTasks.tasks" classpath="C:/Program Files/
Adobe/Flex Builder 3/sdks/3.0.0/ant/flexTasks.jar"/>

   <property name="FLEX_HOME" value="C:/Program Files/Adobe/Flex
Builder 3/sdks/3.0.0"/>
   <property name="APP_ROOT" value="ExampleProject"/>
   <property name="BUILD_DIR" value="build"/>

   <mkdir dir="build"/>

   <target name="main" depends="wrapper"/>

    <target name="compile">
        <mxmlc file="src/ExampleProject.mxml" output="${BUILD_DIR}/
ExampleProject.swf">
            <load-config filename="${FLEX_HOME}/frameworks/flex-
config.xml"/>
            <source-path path-element="${FLEX_HOME}/frameworks"/>
        </mxmlc>
    </target>

    <target name="wrapper" depends="package">
        <html-wrapper
            title="Example Flex Project"
            file="index.html"
            height="100%"
            width="100%"
            bgcolor="white"
            application="MyApp"
            swf="ExampleProject"
            version-major="9"
            version-minor="0"
            version-revision="0"
```

```
            history="true"
            template="express-installation"
            output="${BUILD_DIR}"/>
    </target>

   <target name="package" depends="compile" description="Package the
application">
       <copy todir="${BUILD_DIR}/assets">
         <fileset dir="assets"/>
       </copy>
   </target>

    <target name="clean">
        <delete>
            <fileset dir="${BUILD_DIR}" defaultexcludes="false"/>
            <fileset dir="${BUILD_DIR}/history/"
             defaultexcludes="false"/>
            <fileset dir="${BUILD_DIR}/assets/"
             defaultexcludes="false"/>
        </delete>
    </target>

</project>
```

To run the Ant tool, make sure you have installed the Ant tool and that the Windows environment variable `%PATH%` contains the `<ant_install>\bin` directory. Now open the command prompt and navigate to your project's root folder where you have created the `build.xml` file, type the following command at the prompt, and press the *Enter* key:

```
ant -buildfile build.xml
```

`-buildfile` is an optional parameter. By default, Ant will look for `build.xml` file in the current directory if omitted.

This will start the Ant build script and you should see the following output:

Buildfile: build.xml

compile:

[mxmlc] Loading configuration file C:\Program Files\Adobe\Flex Builder 3\sdks\3.0.0\frameworks\flex-config.xml

[mxmlc] C:\EclipseJ2EE_Europa\eclipse\workspace\ExampleProject\build\ExampleProject.swf (157011 bytes)

package:

wrapper:

main:

BUILD SUCCESSFUL

Total time: 9 seconds

Once the build is successful, you should see a directory called `build` created under your project root folder with the following files:

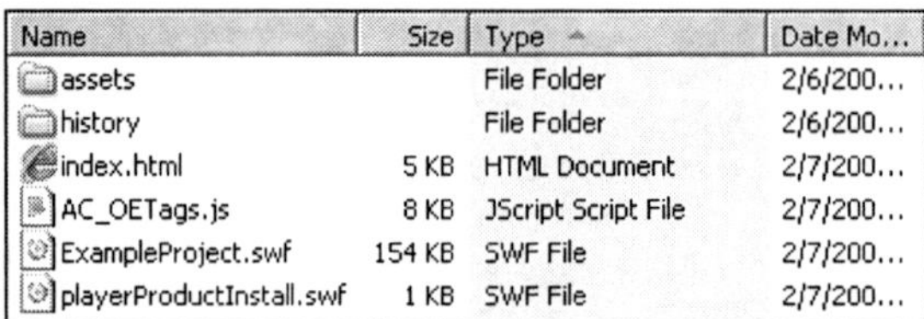

Name	Size	Type	Date Mo...
assets		File Folder	2/6/200...
history		File Folder	2/6/200...
index.html	5 KB	HTML Document	2/7/200...
AC_OETags.js	8 KB	JScript Script File	2/7/200...
ExampleProject.swf	154 KB	SWF File	2/7/200...
playerProductInstall.swf	1 KB	SWF File	2/7/200...

You can also use the following command to invoke individual targets from the build script file:

```
ant -buildfile build.xml clean
```

This command will invoke a target called `clean` from the `build.xml` file.

Deploying your application

By default, Flex Builder sets compiler settings for your development needs, such as warning messages, strict data type checking, and so on. This means that when you compile and build your Flex application, it outputs a debug version of the SWF file that is stored in the `bin-debug` folder. This debug version of SWF file should not be used for the production mode for the simple reason that it contains debug information, and also the overall application size is more than the non-debug version, which may cause performance-related issues.

You can set compiler settings for your deployment needs, such as accessibility, Flash Player version detection, wrapper generation, and browser history management. To modify compiler settings, right-click on your project and choose the **Properties** menu option, and then select the **Flex Compiler** option from the **Properties** window as shown in following screenshot:

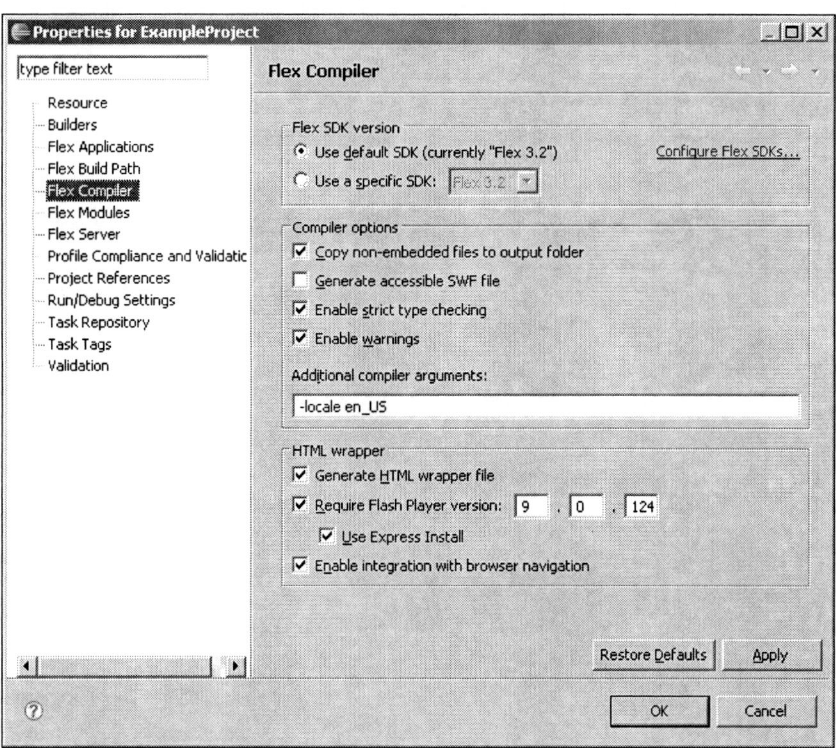

In the compiler settings, you can set many compiler-related options, such as enable accessibility, that are relevant to your production needs. This option lets you create an application that can be accessed by users with disabilities. By default, this option is disabled. To know more about the Flex accessibility, see `http://www.adobe.com/accessibility/products/flex/`.

Once the compiler settings are set, you can use Flex Builder to generate deployment-ready release build by choosing the **Project | Export Release Build...** menu. The **Export Release Build** wizard exports optimized release-quality and non-debug version of your Flex application, and also provides an option to include the source code as part of release build for code-sharing purposes. The following screenshot shows the **Export Release Build** wizard screen:

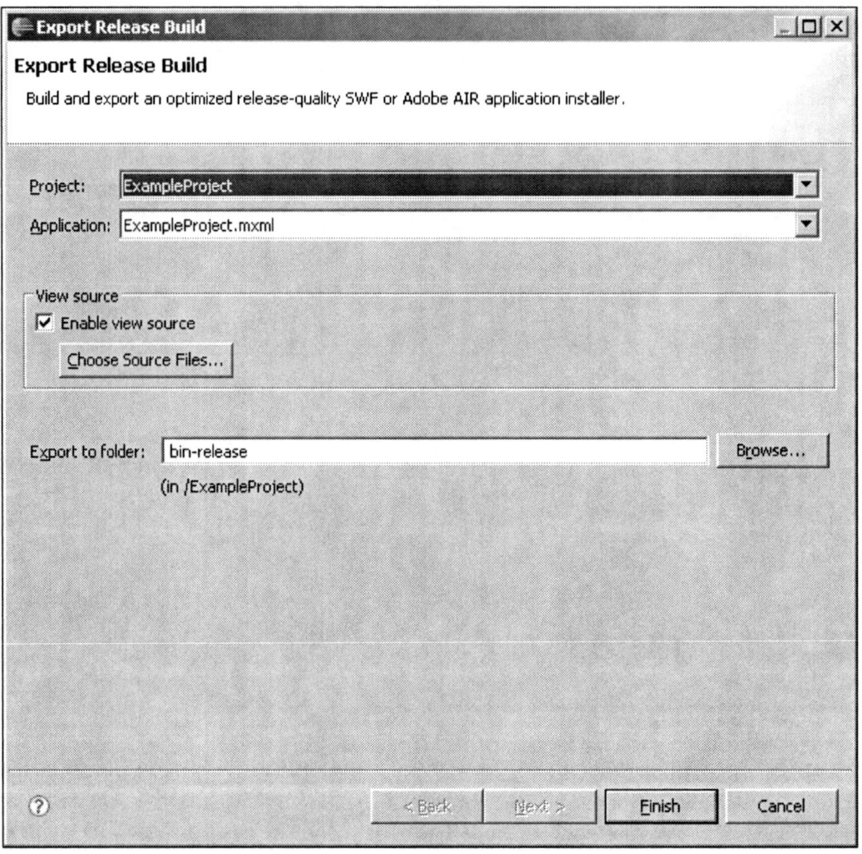

If your project contains multiple application files, you must choose the main application file name from the **Application** drop-down box.

The release build will be created into a new directory specified in the **Export to folder** text box. By default, Flex Builder creates a new folder called `bin-release` into your project's root folder. Alternatively, you can also choose your desired location for storing the release build.

The **Enable view source** option under the **View Source** section allows developers to easily share their source code. You can choose the files that you want to share from the **Choose Source Files...** button. If you choose to enable the **View Source** option, Flex Builder includes a `srcview` folder with selected application source files into the export release build. Now, the export release build automatically adds a new menu item called **View Source** to your application's right-click context menu, as shown in following screenshot:

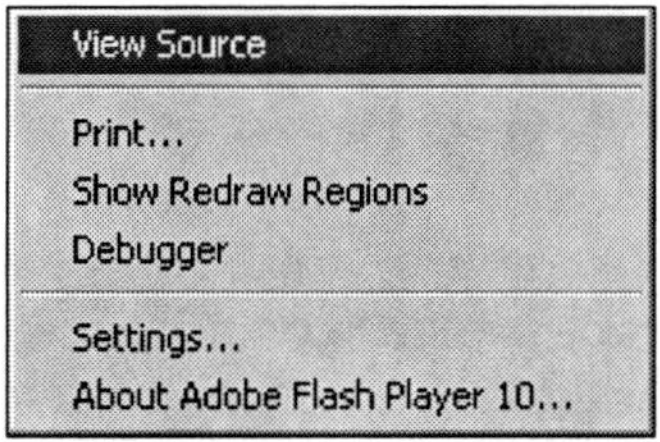

When you run the application, right-click on the application area and choose the **View Source** menu (shown in the above screenshot) to launch the code viewer screen. The code viewer screen opens in a new window as shown in following screenshot:

When you share the source code, Flex Builder automatically builds an HTML-based code viewer and provides an option to download the source code as a ZIP file, as shown in the bottom left corner of the above screenshot.

Flex deployment options

Flex provides the following two deployment options:

- Using a single SWF file deployment
- Using web-tier compilation

Using a single SWF file deployment

This deployment option is commonly used where you first compile your entire application into a single SWF file using Flex compiler, and then deploy it on the web server along with the assets and wrapper used by your application. Typically, deployment of SWF files means copying your Flex application SWF files from your development server to your deployment server. However, depending on your application architecture, you might need to deploy more than just a single SWF file. For example, you might also need to copy any assets or Runtime Shared Libraries (RSLs) that your application uses at runtime. Generally, the assets that you need to include while deploying your application are as follows:

- HTML wrapper
- Deep linking files
- Express Install files
- RSLs
- Modules
- External `.css` files or compiled CSS SWF files
- Application localization resources
- Images, media files such as sound, video files, and other assets that are not embedded into your application
- Data files

The following process shows the typical steps involved in deployment of a Flex application on Tomcat server.

The typical process of deployment involves the following:

1. Build a release-quality SWF using Flex Builder's **Export Release Build** wizard.
2. Copy the content of the `bin-release` folder into Tomcat server's `webapps` folder and rename it to whatever your web application is called (for example, `ExampleApplication`).

3. Copy any runtime assets files (such as images, xml, media files) or any other files into the root of your application folder under the `webapps` directory. Ensure that you maintain a proper directory structure. For example, if your application is referring to an image file as `ExampleApplication/assets/images/logo.png`, you need to copy `logo.png` under the `assets\images\` folder into your web application root folder, `ExampleApplication`.
4. Copy RSLs into the same directory that you specified while compiling your application using the `runtime-shared-libraries` compiler option. To know more about RSLs, see `http://livedocs.adobe.com/flex/3/html/rsl_01.html`.
5. Copy any module SWF files used by your application to load and unload it at runtime. Ensure you maintain the same directory structure that you used in your development setup. To know more about how to build a modular application, see `http://livedocs.adobe.com/flex/3/html/modular_1.html`.
6. Create a custom wrapper for hosting a SWF file. Although Flex Builder generates a standard HTML wrapper for you, in some cases you may need to integrate an SWF application into your web pages such as JSP, PHP, or ASP. You can create custom wrappers to host SWF applications. To read more about creating custom wrappers, see `http://livedocs.adobe.com/flex/3/html/wrapper_01.html`.
7. If your application is integrated with BlazeDS or LCDS, copy the BlazeDS or LCDS web application files into your application root folder and make sure that you configure services of Flex Data Services, such as the Flex Proxy Service, Remoting Service, Message Service, and so on.

Once you deploy your application and navigate to your Tomcat's web root folder (`webapps`), you should see the following files and folders:

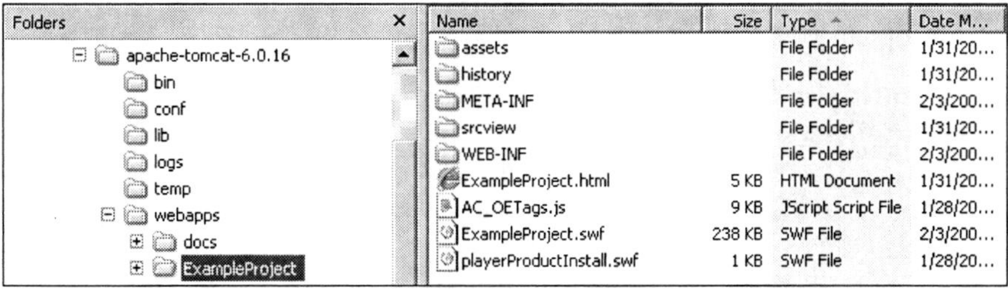

The above screenshot shows the directory structure of a typical Flex application deployed on a Tomcat server. Note that it includes the `assets` folder, which contains static assets used by our application such as images, videos, sound files, or any data files. The `srcview` folder contains shared source files with HTML-based source code viewer. The `WEB-INF` folder contains the BlazeDS web application files.

Using web-tier compilation

This deployment option lets you deploy your MXML and ActionScript files directly on the web server, and lets you compile your application dynamically when the user requests the main application MXML file for the first time. This process is similar to the JSP compilation where you deploy a JSP file on the server and it gets compiled when a user requests it for the first time. This is known as web-tier compilation.

Flex provides web-tier compiler modules for Apache and Microsoft IIS web servers. You do not need a Java 2 Enterprise Edition (J2EE) server to use the web-tier compiler module. The Apache and IIS web-tier compiler modules work with just the Java Runtime (JRE) installed.

Flex also provides the web-tier compiler module for J2EE application servers as a downloadable `.zip` file, which contains a standard web application that can be deployed on most J2EE application servers that support servlets. You can download the web-tier compiler modules from `http://opensource.adobe.com/wiki/display/flexsdk/Downloads`. To know more, see `http://livedocs.adobe.com/flex/3/html/help.html?content=apache_1.html`.

The Flex web-tier compiler module works as follows:

1. The client requests the application MXML file from a browser, for example `http://www.yourserver.com/application.mxml`.
2. The web server with web-tier compiler modules then compiles the MXML file and any ActionScript file that has been referenced in the MXML file into an SWF file by using incremental compiler approach. So any changes in your source code (MXML or ActionScript) would result into recompilation of only those parts of your application that have changed; the subsequent compilation would take less time to complete.
3. The web-tier compiler then returns an HTML wrapper page with a compiled SWF file embedded into it.
4. You can also request for SWF only by appending the `.swf` extension to the application MXML file, for example `http://www.yourserver.com/application.mxml.swf`. In this case, the web server compiles and returns only the SWF file instead of a wrapper HTML. You can still use the `<embed>` tag to embed dynamically compiled SWF file, for example `<embed src="http://www.yourserver.com/application.mxml.swf"....../>`. This option can be used to embed dynamically compiled Flex application into web pages, such as JSP, PHP, or ASP.

Please note that Adobe does not recommend this deployment option for critical production use.

Summary

In this chapter, you learned various ways of packaging your Flex application using Flex Builder and Ant script. We saw some quick examples of writing Ant script using `mxmlc` and `html-wrapper` Flex Ant tasks for building and packaging Flex application.

You also learned how to export a release-quality SWF file using Flex Builder. We discussed different options provided by Flex SDK for deployment, which is deploying a single SWF file and using the web-tier compiler module.

In the next chapter, you will learn another important aspect of designing applications for enterprise—**internationalization**. We will learn how to use internationalization techniques to customize your application for multiple locales.

12
Internationalization and Localization

If you are building a software application that will be used and distributed globally, it is very important that your application supports country- or region-specific languages and settings to ensure that your application is well-received. In short, you need to internationalize and localize your application assets such as text, images, and sometimes behaviour.

We will cover the following points in this chapter:

- Understanding the terms internationalization (i18n) and localization (l10n)
- Localization of Flex applications

Internationalization (i18n) and localization (l10n)

Internationalization is a process of designing and developing software applications such that they can be adapted to various languages and country- or region-specific settings such as date, time, currency formats, and so on, without software modifications. It is also known as **i18n**, which is an acronym for internationalization (i + the number of characters between the i and the n in internationalization + n).

The definition of the term internationalization may vary and some people use other terms, such as **globalization**, which refer to the same process by combining internationalization and localization.

Localization (sometimes shortened as l10n) is a process of customizing your software application to a specific country or region by adding locale-specific language and settings.

Internationalizing your application is a custom process which differs from one application to another. The process of internationalizing one application may not be exactly the same as another, but in general they will follow common guidelines. Internationalization requires designing your application carefully, such that it will be able to handle a variety of languages and regional settings. The process of internationalization includes many general guidelines. In the sections that follow, we will discuss some of the important points to consider as a developer while doing i18n.

Language

You must ensure that your application is capable of rendering and displaying foreign languages based on the locale it is running on. This includes loading resource bundles, dynamically changing strings from your application to show language-specific translated strings, supporting language-specific keyboard input, supporting Unicode encoded characters, and so on. By default, all Flex components are capable of rendering Unicode characters; you do not need any special coding to achieve that.

Assets

You must also ensure that if your application is using any specific assets (such as images containing text, sounds, videos containing subtitles, or color), region-specific files are included to make them compatible with international deployment.

Culture

Your application should be capable of handling locale-specific settings such as date, time and number formats, currency symbols, personal naming preferences, and so on.

Time zones

If your application is dealing with time-specific tasks, you must ensure that you comply with local time zone rules and enable your application to change its behavior accordingly. For example, if your application is sending out emails or making calls, it should consider the working hours of that specific country and change its behavior accordingly.

To design your application for i18n, you can start separating your localizable elements from your source code and ensuring that they can be loaded dynamically and changed as per the locale. Apart from these points, you must also ensure that your application complies with any rules and regulations—such as security norms, copyright laws, and so on—imposed by a specific government.

Please note that the i18n process may not involve actual localization. This is because it defines a process of designing and developing your software application to support future localization without the need of changing the application source code.

Next, we will discuss how to localize your Flex application.

Localization of Flex applications

Localization is the process of including localized assets and resource bundles for supporting multiple locales. A **locale** is a language in combination with a country code to identify the language used in that country; for example in `en_US`, `en` stands for English and `US` stands for United States. Similarly, `en_GB` or `fr_FR` stand for English used in Great Britain and French used in France, respectively. Some countries may also support multiple languages. In such cases, each language has its own code and can be represented by a separate locale. For example, `zh_CN` and `zh_HK` represent Simplified Chinese and Traditional Chinese used in China and Honk Kong. In this case, you need to include different resource bundles for each locale.

A locale of your application is usually determined based on the system's locale on which your application is running. In case of a web application, it is determined by the web browser's locale property. You can access this property using JavaScript and pass it to your Flex application using `FlashVars` to change the strings into that language.

The process of localizing your application starts with creating resource files that defines localized assets and strings used in your application. You can do this by creating a `.properties` file for each locale and loading them into your application. Let's see how to create resource files and define localized strings.

Creating a resource file

Creating a resource file is the same as creating any other file, but with a `.properties` extension. The resource file must have `UTF-8` encoding as it is very important to support Unicode-based languages. Generally, you create key/value pairs in the property file to define a resource key and its localized value. Typically, each line contains one key/value pair. The resource files are generally used to define localized strings used in your application, as shown here:

```
application_title=This is sample title
```

In some cases, you may also need to include localized assets such as images, audio, video files, and so on that can be embedded into the resource file as shown here:

```
application_logo=Embed("images/logo_eng.png")
```

You can use `#` (hash) or `!` (exclamatory mark) symbols to write comments in the resource file, as shown here:

```
# This is a comment
! This is also a comment
```

Let's build one simple Flex application and create resource files to localize it. Follow the steps given here:

1. Create a new Flex Project using Flex Builder and name it `SimpleLocalization`.
2. Copy the following code in the `SimpleLocalization.mxml` file and run the application using Flex Builder:

    ```
    <?xml version="1.0" encoding="utf-8"?>
    <mx:Application xmlns:mx="http://www.adobe.com/2006/mxml">

       <mx:Label text="Hello" fontSize="48"/>

    </mx:Application>
    ```

    This was a simple Flex application which displays the word **Hello** when you run it. Now we will localize this application in such a way that the word **Hello** can be displayed in the French and Chinese languages.
3. Right-click on your project name in the **Flex Navigator** view and select the **New | Folder** menu to create a new folder and name it as `locale`.
4. Once the `locale` folder is created, right-click on it and select **New | Folder** again to create a subfolder called `en_US`. Follow this step to create two more subfolders with the names `fr_FR` and `zh_CN`.

    By convention, resource files are stored in a folder that has locale code as its name, as a subfolder of `locale` under your project root and as a sibling of `src` folder, as shown in the following screenshot:

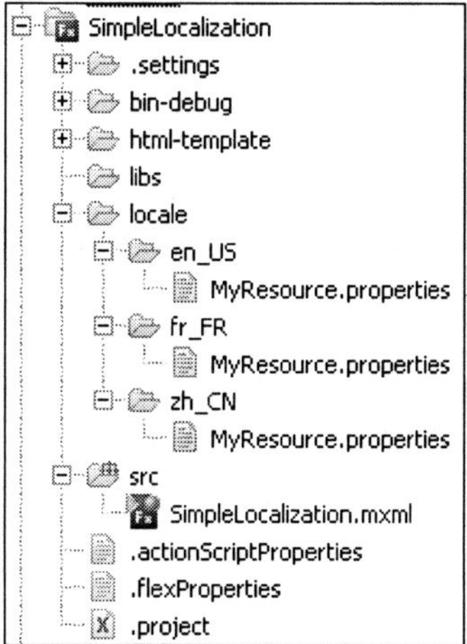

5. Now create a new file under each subfolder and name it `MyResource.properties`. Once you create the properties file, change its encoding by right-clicking on it, selecting **Properties**, and then changing **Text file encoding** to **UTF-8** as shown in the following screenshot. Make sure that you follow this process for each resource file.

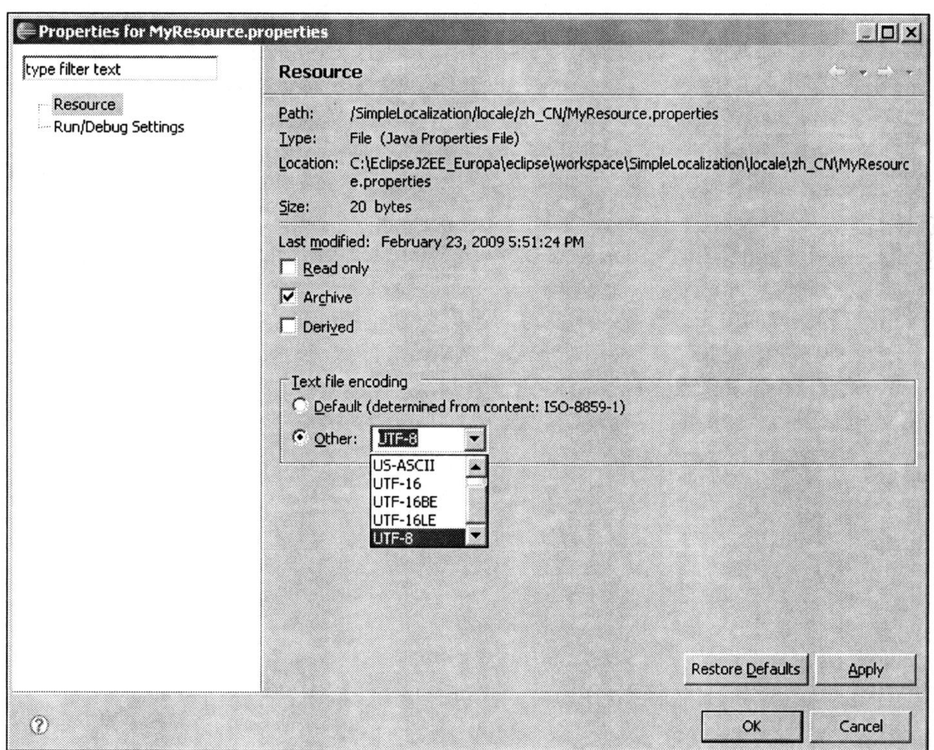

6. Now copy the following key/value into each resource file:
   - Add `greeting_text=Hello` into `MyResource.properties` under the `en_US` folder.
   - Add `greeting_text=Bonjour` into `MyResource.properties` under the `fr_FR` folder.
   - Add `greeting_text=你好` into `MyResource.properties` under the `zh_CN` folder.
7. Once you create your properties file, we are ready to modify our application code. Open the `SimpleLocalization.mxml` file and modify it as shown in the following example:

```
<?xml version="1.0" encoding="utf-8"?>
<mx:Application xmlns:mx="http://www.adobe.com/2006/mxml">

   <mx:Metadata>
      [ResourceBundle("MyResource")]
   </mx:Metadata>

   <mx:Label text="{resourceManager.getString('MyResource',
'greeting_text')}" fontSize="48"/>

</mx:Application>
```

As you can see in the above code, we have defined the `<mx:Metadata>` tag that declares the resource bundle name we are using—`MyResource`. (Do not specify the `.properties` extension.) Next, we have changed the `<mx:Label>` definition and we are now binding its `text` property with the `resourceManager.getString(bundleName, key)` method's returned value. `resourceManager` is an instance of the `ResourceManager` class that is available explicitly to all components that extend the `UIComponent`, `Validator`, and `Formatter` classes. The `resourceManager` property lets you access a singleton instance of the `ResourceManager` class, which loads resource bundles. It also provides various methods to access resource properties, such as `getString(bundleName, key)`, which takes the bundle name and resource key as parameters and returns localized value of that key based on the current locale.

8. Before you compile the application, a few compiler settings need to be updated. Right-click on your project name in the **Flex Navigator** view and select the **Properties** menu. Then, select **Flex Compiler** from the pane on the left-hand side and add `-locale zh_CN -source-path ../locale/{locale}` in the **Additional compiler arguments** text field, as shown in the following screenshot:

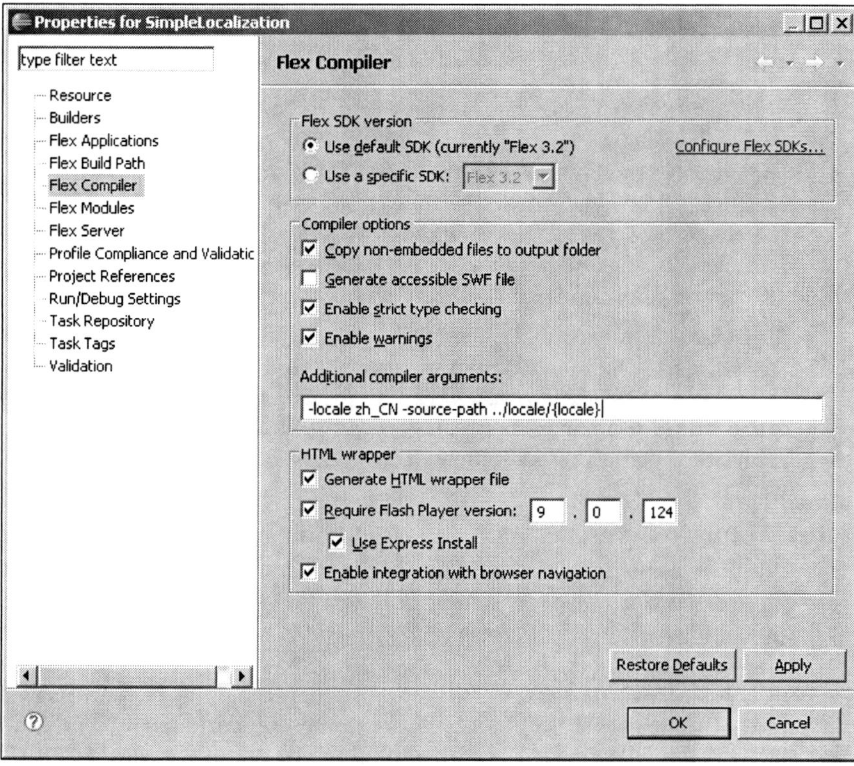

9. The `-locale` parameter specifies the locale that our application will be using, and `-source-path` specifies where to find those additional resource files. `{locale}` is a special variable which will get substituted by the value specified in the `-locale` parameter.

> When you compile your application for a specific locale, the compiler looks for localized framework files. For example, if you are compiling your application for the `fr_FR` locale, you need to have the French version of Flex framework. By default, Flex SDK comes with only the `en_US` version framework, but you can easily create localized framework by using the `copylocale` command-line utility provided by Flex SDK, as shown in following example.
>
> Open command prompt and change the directory to your `<flex_sdk_install_folder>\bin\` folder and type the following command:
>
> `copylocale.exe en_US fr_FR`
>
> `Copylocale.exe` creates a localized framework from the given locale and creates a new folder with the locale name under the `<flex_sdk_install_folder>\ frameworks\locale\` folder. So, the above command will create a `fr_FR` locale framework from the `en_US` framework and store it in the `<flex_sdk_install_folder>\frameworks\locale\fr_FR` folder.
>
> Flex's built-in components, such as `Label`and `Button`, use resources just like your application and components do. These resource files are stored in a separate resource bundle library in the `framework\locale` folder. If a localized framework is missing, then Flex compiler will throw an error while compiling with the `-locale` option.

10. Now compile and run the application, and you should see **Hello** translated into Chinese. Now go ahead and change the `-locale` compiler parameter and set it to `fr_FR`. Now recompile and run the application; you should see **Bonjour**, a French word, instead of **Hello**.

We saw a simple localization example where we compiled an application for a specific locale by using the `-locale` compiler option. You can also add additional locales into the `-locale` parameter to compile your application for multiple locales, for example `-locale en_US fr_FR zh_CN` ... (use a space between each locale). This will compile your application for all specified locales. By default, your application will run in an English locale, but you can dynamically change to other locales by using the `resourceManager.localeChain` property. Modify the `SimpleLocalization.mxml` code as shown here:

```
<?xml version="1.0" encoding="utf-8"?>
<mx:Application xmlns:mx="http://www.adobe.com/2006/mxml">

   <mx:Metadata>
      [ResourceBundle("MyResource")]
   </mx:Metadata>

   <mx:Label text="{resourceManager.getString('MyResource', 'greeting_
```

```
text')}" fontSize="48"/>

    <mx:Script>
        <![CDATA[
            [Bindable]
            private var locales:Array = [{label:"English US",
            data:"en_US"}, {label:"French", data:"fr_FR"},
            {label:"Chinese Simplified", data:"zh_CN"}];

            private function comboChangeHandler():void{
                resourceManager.localeChain =
                [ localeComboBox.selectedItem.data ];
            }
        ]]>
    </mx:Script>

    <mx:ComboBox id="localeComboBox" dataProvider="{locales}"
     change="comboChangeHandler()" labelField="label" width="160"/>
</mx:Application>
```

In the above code, we have added a new bindable `Array` type variable called `locales` and initialized it with default value, that is, English, French, and Chinese languages with their respective locale codes. Next, we have added a `ComboBox` component and bound its `dataProvider` property to the `locales` array. We have used `labelField` to specify which property to be used from data provider to display label in a drop-down box. We have also registered the `ComboBox's change` event and added an event listener method called `comboChangeHandler()`. This method sets the `resourceManager's localeChain` array to `ComboBox's` selected item's locale code. Please note that the `localeChain` property is of the `Array` type, so you need to use `[]` (square braces) to convert `ComboBox's` selected item into an array element.

Now run the application, change the languages using the `ComboBox` control and observe the output. You will see that your application will dynamically change **Hello** text and show it in a selected language.

Sounds cool, huh? But there is a drawback, which is if you are compiling your application for multiple locales using the `-locale` compiler option, your application size increases because the compiler will compile all resources into your application SWF file. This may not be of much difference if you have only a couple of locales. But in a situation where an application needs to support 20 languages, this is definitely a performance issue. This is where resource modules can be useful.

Creating resource modules

Resource modules are separate SWF files that you can compile from resource bundles using the Flex `mxmlc` compiler, much like compiling CSS files into SWF. Resource modules can then be loaded dynamically at runtime as and when your application requires them. This is the best technique when the application needs to support many locales. Since you are not compiling resources as part of your application, it does not have any ill impact on your application's SWF size and performance. Let's start by understanding how to compile resources into SWF files.

Unfortunately, Flex Builder does not have support for compiling resources modules, so you will have to use command-line compilation as shown here:

```
mxmlc -locale=zh_CN
-source-path=locale/{locale}
-include-resource-bundles=SharedResources,collections,containers,contr
ols,core,effects,formatters,LoginForm,skins,styles
-output=bin-debug/Resources_zh_CN.swf
```

Make sure that you have specified the Flex SDK's `bin` directory in your Windows environment variable `PATH`, or else use absolute path for `mxmlc`.

`-locale` specifies the locale of the framework, `-source-path` specifies the path where complier can find additional resource files, and `-include-resource-bundles` specifies the additional resources bundles that need to be included along with your application resources bundle. You can specify multiple resource bundles that are used by your application and component by separating them with `,` (comma). To find out the resource bundles your application is using, use the following compiler option.

You can either add `-resource-bundle-list=bundles.txt` to your Flex Builder's compiler options, or you can use it while compiling your application from a command line.

```
mxmlc -locale -resource-bundle-list=bundles.txt src\<application_file>
```

The `-resource-bundle-list=bundles.txt` option will create a file called `bundles.txt` under your project's root or `bin-debug` folder containing the resource bundle names that your application and its components, including Flex's inbuilt components, are using. You can include this list while compiling your resource module using the `-include-resource-bundles` option. The `-output` option specifies the output file name.

Now that you have compiled all your resource bundles, we can start modifying code to load them dynamically. You can use the `resourceManager.loadResourceModule(resourceModuleURL)` method for loading resource modules dynamically from your Flex application. Since `loadResourceModule()` is an asynchronous call, it returns the `IEventDispatcher` instance that you can use for listening to various events such as `PROGRESS`, `COMPLETE`, and `ERROR`. For example, you may want to change an application's locale once its resource bundle is completely loaded:

```
var resourceModuleURL:String = "Resource_zh_CN.swf";
var eventDispatcher:IEventDispatcher =
resourceManager.loadResourceModule(resourceModuleURL);
eventDispatcher.addEventListener(ResourceEvent.COMPLETE,
completeHandler);
```

Now, you can write the `completeHandler()` method and change the application locale by setting the `resourceManager.localeChain` property as shown in following code snippet:

```
resourceManager.localeChain = [ "zh_CN" ];
```

When you set the `localeChain` property, `resourceManager` automatically dispatches a `change` event that causes the application to update its user interface with new resource string values. You can also set the `update` flag to `true`, which is the second parameter in the `loadResourceModule()` method. This causes the application to update when it completes loading.

Now, before you compile, you need to set the `-locale` compiler option to blank in order to tell the compiler to not compile any resources into application, since we will be loading them at runtime.

Now let's put all these pieces together into a working application example, as follows:

1. Create a new Flex Project and name it `LocalizationExample`.
2. Create a `locale` folder under your project root and create three subfolders as explained earlier: `en_US`, `fr_FR`, and `zh_CN`.
3. Now create the `LoginForm.properties` file under each locale folder and make sure that its encoding is set to `UTF-8`.
4. Now copy the following resource key/value pairs into the respective properties files:

   `LoginForm.properties` under the `locale\en_US` folder:

   ```
   label_title=Sign-In Form
   prompt_username=User Name
   prompt_password=Password
   label_sign_in=Sign-In
   label_cancel=Cancel
   ```

`LoginForm.properties` under the `locale\fr_FR` folder:

```
label_title=Forme de Sign-In
prompt_username=Nom d'utilisateur
prompt_password=Mot de passe
label_sign_in=Sign-In
label_cancel=Annulation
```

`LoginForm.properties` under the `locale\zh_CN` folder:

```
label_title=签到形式
prompt_username=用户名
prompt_password=密码
label_sign_in=签到
label_cancel=取消
```

5. Open `LocalizationExample.mxml` and copy the following code into it:

```
<?xml version="1.0" encoding="utf-8"?>
<mx:Application xmlns:mx="http://www.adobe.com/2006/mxml" creation
Complete="init()">

   <mx:Script>
      <![CDATA[
         import mx.events.ResourceEvent;

         [Bindable]
         private var locales:Array = [{label:"English
         US", data:"en_US"}, {label:"French", data:"fr_FR"},
         {label:"Chinese Simplified", data:"zh_CN"}];

         private function init():void {
            comboChangeHandler();
         }

         private function comboChangeHandler():void {
         var newLocale:String = String(localeComboBox.
         selectedItem.data);
               // Ensure that you are not loading the same
                  resource module more than once.
               if (resourceManager.getLocales().indexOf(newLocale)
                   != -1) {
                   completeHandler(null);
               } else {
                   // Build the file name of the resource module.
      var resourceModuleURL:String = "Resources_"+newLocale+".swf";

      var eventDispatcher:IEventDispatcher = resourceManager.loadRe
      sourceModule(resourceModuleURL);
```

```
eventDispatcher.addEventListener(ResourceEvent.COMPLETE,
completeHandler);
                }
            }

            private function completeHandler(event:ResourceEvent):
            void {
                  resourceManager.localeChain =
                  [ localeComboBox.selectedItem.data ];
            }
      ]]>
   </mx:Script>

   <mx:HBox>
      <mx:Label text="Change Language:"/>
      <mx:ComboBox id="localeComboBox" dataProvider="{locales}"
       change="comboChangeHandler()" labelField="label"
       width="160"/>
   </mx:HBox>

   <mx:Panel title="{resourceManager.getString('LoginForm',
    'label_title')}">
      <mx:Form>
         <mx:FormItem label="{resourceManager.getString('LoginForm'
          ,'prompt_username')}:">
            <mx:TextInput width="160"/>
         </mx:FormItem>
         <mx:FormItem label="{resourceManager.getString('LoginForm'
          ,'prompt_password')}:">
            <mx:TextInput width="160"/>
         </mx:FormItem>
      </mx:Form>
      <mx:Label id="curr" text=""/>
      <mx:ControlBar width="100%">
         <mx:Button id="login" label="{resourceManager.getString(
          'LoginForm','label_sign_in')}"/>
         <mx:Button id="cancel" label="{resourceManager.getString(
          'LoginForm','label_cancel')}"/>
      </mx:ControlBar>
   </mx:Panel>

</mx:Application>
```

6. Open your project properties and go to the **Flex Compiler** pane and change the **Additional compiler arguments** field to `-locale` (blank `-locale` entry). This instructs the compiler not to compile the application for any locale.

7. Now compile all three resource bundles into resource modules using the `mxmlc` command that was explained earlier. Make sure that they are in your `bin-debug` folder and run the application.
8. By default, your application comes up with the English locale and you can change languages dynamically by using the **Change language:** drop-down box.

   French locale:

   Chinese Locale:

Summary

In this chapter, we learned about the typical process of internationalizing your Flex application and how to localize Flex applications by using the `ResourceManager` class. We also learned the technique to create resource bundle modules and load them at runtime in order to dynamically change locales. We also did some detailed coding, to get hands-on experience with the localization concept.

In the next chapter, we will build an end-to-end Flex e-commerce application by using all the major features of Flex learned throughout this book.

13
Creating an E-commerce Application

The best way to test what you have learned so far is to build something using it. In this chapter, we will build a small but complete application using the concepts that we have learned so far. We will use a combination of Flex, ActionScript, and Java technologies and marry them together to build an e-commerce application. The application we are going to build is called **Online Book Store**. This Online Book Store provides an easy way to browse, search, and shop for books online. You have seen many Flex and Java communication examples using `HTTPService`, `RemoteObject`, or `WebService` RPC services. In this tutorial, we will use `HTTPService` to communicate with JSP which generates and returns dynamic XML data from a database table. In the real world, you might not use JSP to write business logic. But to keep things simple, we will use JSP in this chapter.

The general anatomy of the application

The general anatomy of the application is as shown here:

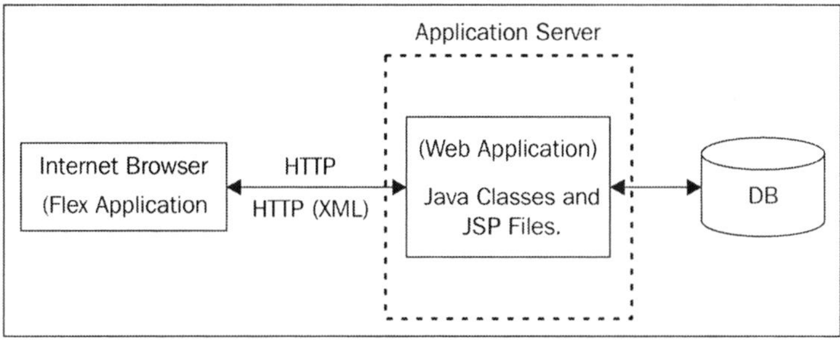

The Online Book Store application screen will look as follows once you build the complete application:

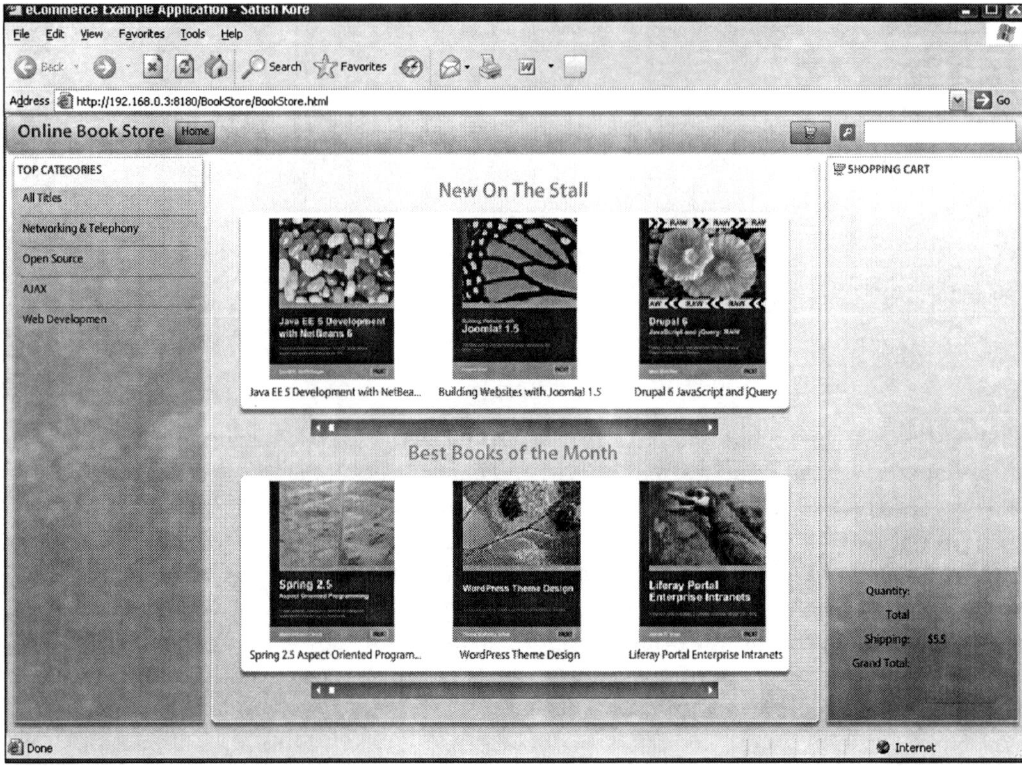

The following is the homepage of the application which lists new books and bestselling books in the middle section, and also provides category navigation menus on the lefthand side. You can also see a **SHOPPING CART** link on the right-hand side, which will list the current books selected by the user as shown here:

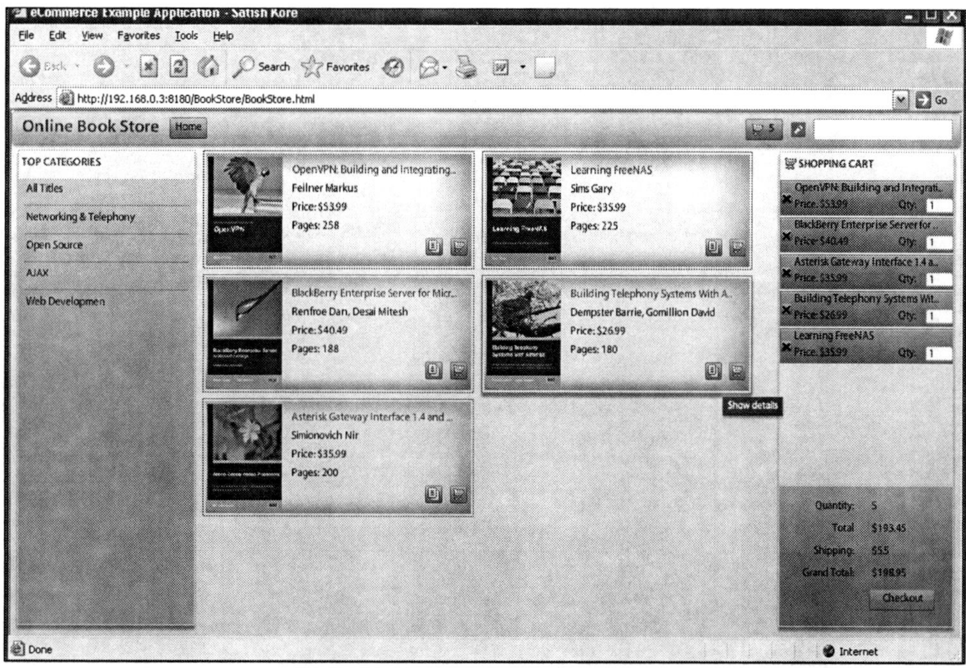

The following is the product listing screen. It lists all the books available in the selected category when a user selects any specific category from the navigation menu. It uses a custom and compact widget as an item renderer to show book details.

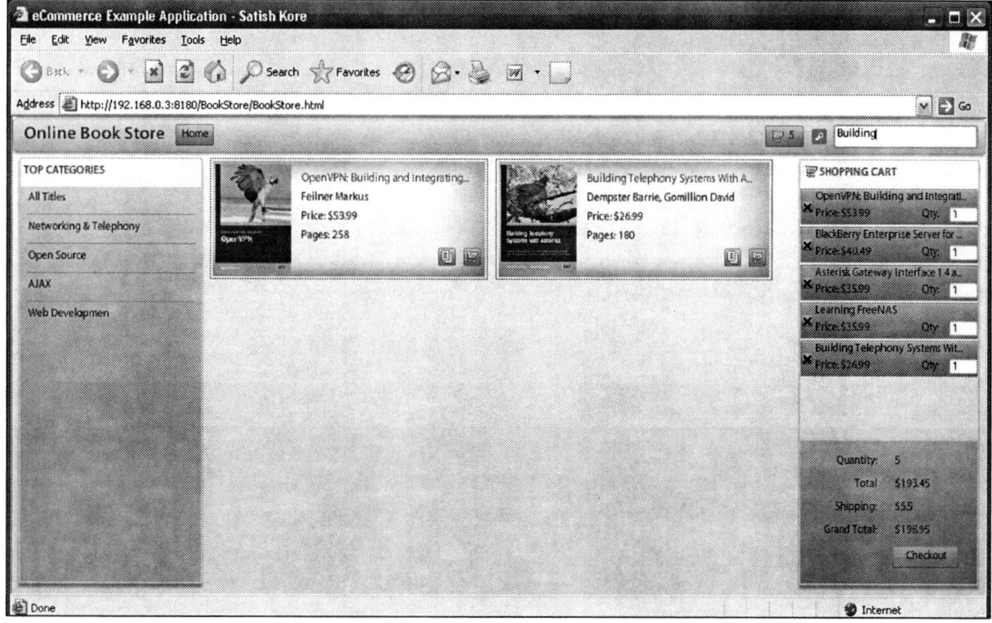

The following is the book search screen where a user can enter a search string in the search box in the top-right corner and press the *Enter* key to search for any matching books:

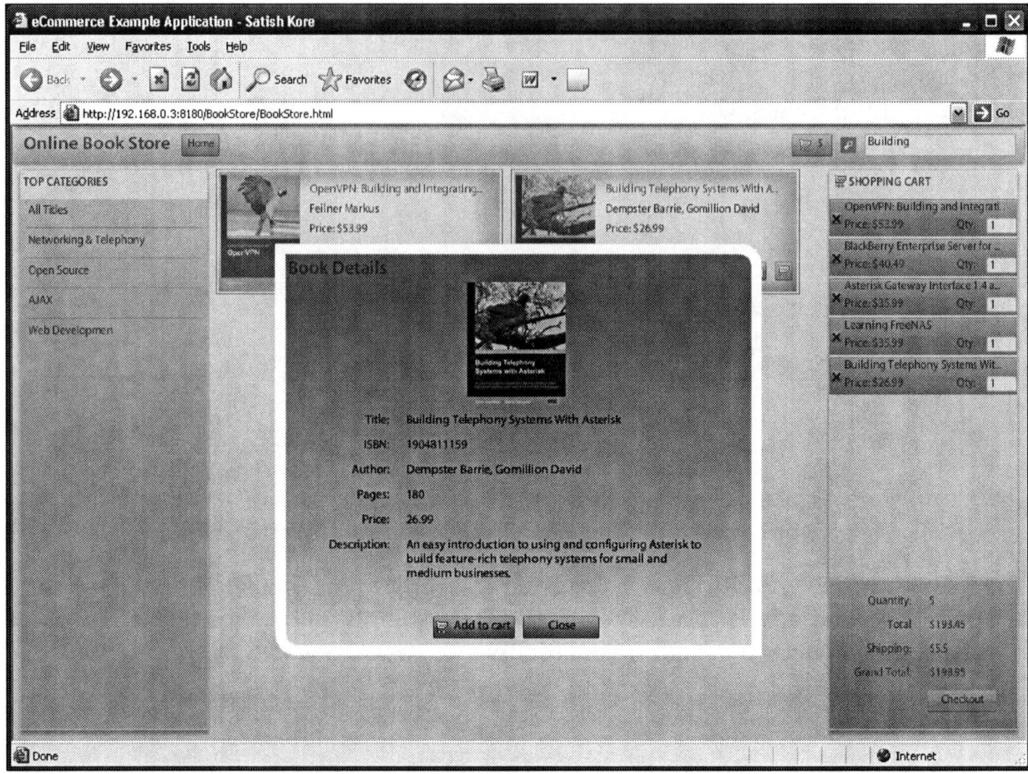

This screen displays the selected book's details in a pop-up window when a user clicks on the **Details** button on the book widget.

Users can also add or remove books from the shopping cart. The shopping cart updates the shopping details dynamically and provides an option to remove a specific book or change its quantity.

Let's start coding

Now let's start building this application using Flex Builder. Again, our goal is to keep things simple and so we will use the `HTTPService` method for retrieving data from the database using simple JSP and Java classes on server.

The Flex code

Let's start by creating the Flex project by going through the folowing steps:

1. Create a new Flex project using Flex Builder and name it `BookStore`. As we are not creating a BlazeDS- or LCDS-based project, we will select **None** in **Application server type**. Click on **Finish** to create the Flex project.
2. Create two new folders under the project's `src` folder, and name them `components` and `events`. The `components` folder will be used for storing custom components and the `events` folder will be used for storing custom events used by our application.
3. Create a new folder under the project's root and name it `assets`. Create two subfolders under `assets`, and name them `css` and `images`. Create one subfolder under `images` and name it `product`. So, you will have the following hierarchy of folders. We will use these folders to store the application's asset files, such as Cascading Style Sheets (CSS) and images.

4. Before we start writing code for the main application, we will create a few custom components. Right-click on the `components` folder, go to **New | MXML Component**, and name the MXML component as `DetailView.mxml`. Now click on **Finish** to create the MXML component and copy the following code in it:

```
<?xml version="1.0" encoding="utf-8"?>
<mx:Panel title="Book Details" xmlns:mx="http://www.adobe.
com/2006/mxml" layout="absolute" width="482" height="396"
fontSize="12" creationComplete="init()">
```

```
<mx:Script>
   <![CDATA[
      import mx.managers.PopUpManager;

      [Bindable]
      public var product:XML;

      [Bindable]
         [Embed(source="../../assets/images/shoppingcart.gif")]
      public var cartImage:Class;

      public var parentComponent:BookDetailItemRenderer;

      private function init():void {
         if(parentComponent == null) {
            cartBtn.visible = false;
            cartBtn.includeInLayout = false;
         }
      }

   ]]>
</mx:Script>

<mx:VBox width="462" height="349" x="10" y="37"
 paddingLeft="5" paddingRight="5" horizontalAlign="center"
 horizontalScrollPolicy="off" verticalGap="2">
   <mx:Image id="img" maxWidth="100" maxHeight="123"
    source="assets/images/product/{product.Image}"/>
   <mx:Form  paddingTop="0" paddingBottom="0"
    paddingLeft="0" paddingRight="0">
      <mx:FormItem label="Title:">
         <mx:Label text="{product.Title}"/>
      </mx:FormItem>
      <mx:FormItem label="ISBN:">
         <mx:Label text="{product.ISBN}"/>
      </mx:FormItem>
      <mx:FormItem label="Author:">
         <mx:Label id="bookAuthor"
          text="{product.Author}" width="300"/>
      </mx:FormItem>
      <mx:FormItem label="Pages:">
         <mx:Label text="{product.PageCount}"/>
      </mx:FormItem>
      <mx:FormItem label="Price:">
         <mx:Label text="{product.Price}"/>
```

```
            </mx:FormItem>
            <mx:FormItem label="Description:">
                <mx:Text text="{product.Description}"
                 width="300" height="45"/>
            </mx:FormItem>
        </mx:Form>
    </mx:VBox>
        <mx:ControlBar width="100%" paddingBottom="15">
            <mx:Button id="cartBtn" icon="{cartImage}"
             label="Add to cart" click="parentComponent.
             addToCardEventDispatcher()"/>
            <mx:Button label="Close" click="PopUpManager.
             removePopUp(this)" width="75"/>
        </mx:ControlBar>
</mx:Panel>
```

The above file is a custom component based on a `Panel`. This `Panel` lays out some `Form` elements to display fields from the XML variable `product` using E4x and data-binding techniques.

5. Create a new custom MXML component based on `HBox` in the `components` folder and name it `BookDetailItemRenderer.mxml`. Copy the following code into it:

```
<?xml version="1.0" encoding="utf-8"?>
<mx:HBox xmlns:mx="http://www.adobe.com/2006/mxml"
   paddingBottom="2" paddingLeft="2" paddingRight="2" paddingTop="2"
   borderStyle="solid"
    borderColor="#6689B4"
    rollOver="rollOverHandler(event)"
    rollOut="rollOutHandler(event)"
    creationCompleteEffect="Glow">

   <mx:Script>
      <![CDATA[
         import mx.core.Application;
         import mx.core.IFlexDisplayObject;
         import mx.managers.PopUpManager;
         import events.AddToCartEvent;
         import mx.controls.Alert;

         [Bindable]
         public var product:XML;

         [Bindable]
         [Embed(source="../../assets/images/shoppingcart.gif")]
```

```
        public var cartImage:Class;

        [Bindable]
        [Embed(source="../../assets/images/details.gif")]
        public var detailsImage:Class;

        public function addToCartEventDispatcher():void {
           var event:AddToCartEvent = new AddToCartEvent(
           AddToCartEvent.ADD_TO_CART, true, true);
           event.book = product;
           dispatchEvent(event);
        }
        private function displayDetails():void {
           var popup:DetailView = new DetailView();
           popup.product = product;
           popup.parentComponent = this;
           PopUpManager.addPopUp(popup, parent.parent, true);
           PopUpManager.centerPopUp(popup);
        }
          private function rollOverHandler(event:MouseEvent):void
        {
              setStyle("dropShadowEnabled", true);
          }

          private function rollOutHandler(event:MouseEvent):void
        {
              setStyle("dropShadowEnabled", false);
          }

   ]]>
</mx:Script>
<mx:HBox width="100%" verticalAlign="middle"
 paddingBottom="2" paddingLeft="2" paddingRight="2"
 paddingTop="2" height="100%"
 backgroundImage="assets/images/back1.png"
 backgroundSize="100%">
   <mx:Image id="bookImage" source="assets/images/product/
    {product.Image}" height="109" width="78"
    maintainAspectRatio="false"/>
   <mx:VBox height="100%" width="100%" verticalGap="2"
    paddingBottom="0" paddingLeft="0" paddingRight="0"
    paddingTop="0" verticalAlign="middle">
      <mx:Label id="bookTitle" text="{product.Title}"
       color="#0C406E" width="180"/>
      <mx:Label id="bookAuthor" text="{product.Author}"
       width="180"/>
```

```
            <mx:Label id="coverPrice"
             text="Price: ${product.Price}"/>
            <mx:Label id="pageCount"
             text="Pages: {product.PageCount}"/>
            <mx:HBox width="100%" backgroundAlpha="0"
             paddingRight="2" horizontalAlign="right"
             verticalAlign="middle">
               <mx:Button icon="{detailsImage}" toolTip="Show
                details" height="18" width="18"
                click="displayDetails();"/>
               <mx:Button icon="{cartImage}" toolTip="Add to cart"
                height="18" width="18"
                click="addToCartEventDispatcher();"/>
            </mx:HBox>
         </mx:VBox>
      </mx:HBox>
   </mx:HBox>
```

This component will be used for displaying a compact preview of the book in the product listing screen, as shown in the following screenshot:

The two buttons at the bottom of the component are **Add to cart** and **Show details**. The **Add to cart** button will dispatch a custom event called `addToCart`, which will be used in a later part of this application. The **Show details** button will open a pop-up window of the `DetailView.mxml` component using `PopUpManager` to show more details of the book.

6. Let's create the custom event used by the above component. Right-click on the `events` folder and create a new ActionScript class. Name it `AddToCartEvent.as` and note that it is derived from `flash.events.Event`. Now copy the following code into it:

```
package events
{
   import flash.events.Event;
   public class AddToCartEvent extends Event
   {
      public static const ADD_TO_CART:String = "addToCart";
      public var book:Object;
```

```
        public function AddToCartEvent(type:String,
        bubbles:Boolean=false, cancelable:Boolean=false)
        {
            super(type, bubbles, cancelable);
        }

    }
}
```

This is a simple event class which defines an event name as a constant and provides a public property called `book` of the type object. The `book` property will be populated when the user clicks on the **Add to cart** button in the product display screen, so that the entire selected book object can be added to the shopping cart.

7. Create a new MXML component based on `VBox` and name it `ProductItemRenderer.mxml`. Copy the following code into it:

```
<?xml version="1.0" encoding="utf-8"?>
<mx:VBox xmlns:mx="http://www.adobe.com/2006/mxml"
   verticalAlign="middle" horizontalAlign="center">
   <mx:Image  source="assets/images/product/{data.Image}"
     toolTip="{data.Description}" width="130" height="154"/>
   <mx:Label text="{data.Title}" width="180"/>
</mx:VBox>
```

This component will be used as an item renderer of `HorizontalList` to display book preview.

8. Create another MXML component and name it `ProductSlider.mxml`. Copy the following code into it:

```
<?xml version="1.0" encoding="utf-8"?>
<mx:VBox xmlns:mx="http://www.adobe.com/2006/mxml"
 creationComplete="prdHS.send()" horizontalAlign="center"
 verticalAlign="top" verticalGap="10" width="100%">
   <mx:Script>
      <![CDATA[
         import mx.managers.PopUpManager;
         import mx.events.ScrollEvent;
         import mx.rpc.events.ResultEvent;
         import mx.rpc.events.FaultEvent;
         import mx.controls.Alert;

          [Bindable]
```

```
        public var productURL:String;

        private function resultHandler(event:ResultEvent):void {
          scroll.maxScrollPosition= event.result.Book.length() -3;
        }
        private function faultHandler(event:FaultEvent):void {
           Alert.show(event.message.toString(), "Error");
        }
        private function scrollListener(event:ScrollEvent):void {
        horizontalList.horizontalScrollPosition = event.position;
          }
        private function displayDetails():void {
           var popup:DetailView = new DetailView();
           popup.product = XML(horizontalList.selectedItem);
           PopUpManager.addPopUp(popup, parent.parent, true);
           PopUpManager.centerPopUp(popup);
        }
     ]]>
   </mx:Script>
   <mx:HTTPService id="prdHS" resultFormat="e4x" url="{productURL}"
    result="resultHandler(event)" fault="faultHandler(event)"/>

    <mx:HorizontalList id="horizontalList" width="540"
           dataProvider="{prdHS.lastResult.Book}"
           itemRenderer="components.ProductItemRenderer"
           horizontalScrollPolicy="off"
           allowMultipleSelection="false"
        liveScrolling="true"
        cornerRadius="4"
        dropShadowEnabled="true"
        borderColor="#FFFFFF"
        borderStyle="solid"
        click="displayDetails()"/>

   <mx:HScrollBar id="scroll" width="400"
           minScrollPosition="0"
           scroll="scrollListener(event)"
           useHandCursor="true" buttonMode="true"/>
</mx:VBox>
```

This is a custom horizontal slider component, which is used for displaying a preview of books using a custom horizontal scroll bar. It uses `HTTPService` to load the XML document from the server and attaches its result to the `dataProvider` of the `HorizontalList` control. This `HorizontalList` control uses the `components.ProductItemRenderer` component as its `itemRenderer`. The component looks as shown in following screenshot:

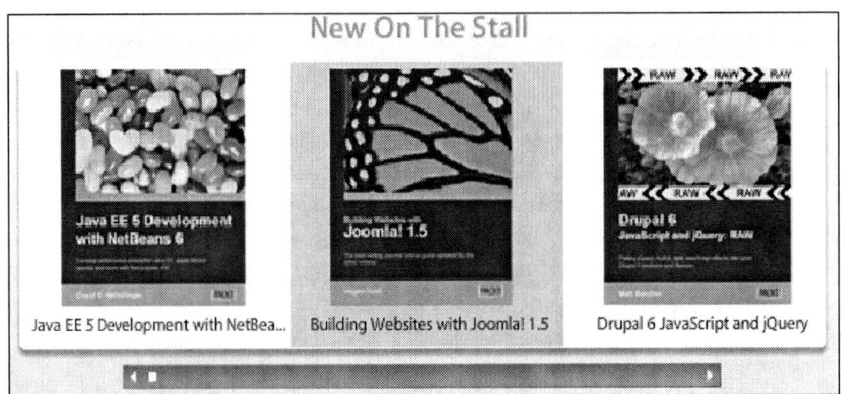

9. Create a new MXML component based on `HBox` in the `components` folder and name it `CartItem.mxml`. This is a simple component which will be used in the shopping cart component to represent the added cart item. Copy the following code into it:

```
<?xml version="1.0" encoding="utf-8"?>
<mx:HBox xmlns:mx="http://www.adobe.com/2006/mxml"
 paddingBottom="0" paddingLeft="0" paddingRight="0" paddingTop="0"
 horizontalGap="0" verticalGap="0"
 backgroundImage="assets/images/cart-item-back.png"
 backgroundSize="100%" borderStyle="solid"
 verticalScrollPolicy="off" horizontalScrollPolicy="off"
 verticalAlign="middle" rollOver="rollOverHandler(event)"
 rollOut="rollOutHandler(event)" borderColor="#6689B4">

   <mx:Script>
      <![CDATA[
         import mx.controls.Alert;

          [Bindable]
         public var product:XML;

          [Bindable]
          [Embed(source="../../assets/images/Close.gif")]
```

```
        public var closeImage:Class;

        private function quantityChanged():void {
          dispatchEvent(new Event("quantityChanged", true, true));
        }
        private function deleteItem():void {
           parent.removeChild(this);
        }
          private function rollOverHandler(event:MouseEvent):void
        {
              setStyle("dropShadowEnabled", true);
          }

          private function rollOutHandler(event:MouseEvent):void
        {
              setStyle("dropShadowEnabled", false);
          }
     ]]>
  </mx:Script>

  <mx:Fade id="fade" alphaTo="0.0" duration="300"
   target="{this}" effectEnd="deleteItem()"/>

  <mx:Button id="deletee" icon="{closeImage}" height="12"
   width="12" click="fade.play();"/>
  <mx:VBox width="100%" verticalGap="0" paddingBottom="0"
   paddingLeft="0" paddingRight="0" paddingTop="0">
     <mx:Label text="{product.Title}" width="165"/>
     <mx:HBox width="100%" verticalGap="0" paddingBottom="0"
      paddingLeft="0" paddingRight="0" paddingTop="0">
        <mx:Label text="Price: ${product.Price}"/>
        <mx:Spacer width="100%"/>
        <mx:Label text="Qty:"/>
        <mx:TextInput id="qty" text="1"
         change="quantityChanged()" height="15" width="30"/>
     </mx:HBox>
  </mx:VBox>
</mx:HBox>
```

The above component uses Flex Effects to create animations such as `<mx:Fade...>`, which gives a nice fading effect while deleting an item from the shopping cart. Flex provides many built-in effects that can be customized and used with components. To read more about Flex Effects, go to `http://livedocs.adobe.com/flex/3/html/help.html?content=createeffects_1.html`.

10. Next, we will create our shopping cart component, which will allow users to add or delete items and display information about current purchases. Create a new MXML component under the `components` folder and name it `ShoppingCart.mxml` based on `VBox` component. Copy the following code into it:

```
<?xml version="1.0" encoding="utf-8"?>
<mx:VBox xmlns:mx="http://www.adobe.com/2006/mxml"
 width="188" height="100%" borderStyle="solid" borderThickness="1"
 borderColor="#D2D9DB" dropShadowEnabled="true"
 shadowDirection="center" paddingTop="5"
 horizontalScrollPolicy="off">
   <mx:Script>
      <![CDATA[
         import mx.controls.Alert;

         public function addItem(product:XML):void {
            var shouldAdd:Boolean = true;
            var children:Array = cartList.getChildren();
            var item:CartItem;

            for each(item in children) {
               if(item.product.Title == product.Title) {
                  item.qty.text = ""+(Number(item.qty.text) + 1);
                  glow.target = item;
                  glow.play();
                  shouldAdd = false;
                  break;
               }
            }
            if(shouldAdd) {
               item = new CartItem();
               item.width = 187;
               item.product = product;
               item.addEventListener("quantityChanged",
                                     updateTotals);
                   cartList.addChild(item);

               glow.target = item;
            glow.play();
            }
         }

         private function updateTotals(event:Event=null):void {
            var children:Array = cartList.getChildren();
            var qty:Number = 0;
            var total:Number = 0;
```

```
            for each(var item:CartItem in children) {
               qty += Number(item.qty.text);
               var temp:Number = Number(item.product.Price)*
                                 Number(item.qty.text);
               total += temp;
            }
            totalTxt.text = currFormatter.format(total);
            quantityTxt.text = ""+qty;
            grandTxt.text = currFormatter.format(total+5.5)
         }
         private function checkout():void {
            Alert.show("Not Implemented.");
         }
      ]]>
   </mx:Script>

   <mx:CurrencyFormatter id="currFormatter" precision="2"
    rounding="up" useThousandsSeparator="," currencySymbol="$"/>

   <mx:Sequence id="glow" effectEnd="updateTotals()">
       <mx:Glow id="glowImage" duration="200"
           alphaFrom="1.0" alphaTo="0.3"
           blurXFrom="0.0" blurXTo="50.0"
           blurYFrom="0.0" blurYTo="50.0"
           color="0x1E529C"/>
        <mx:Pause duration="100"/>
       <mx:Glow id="unglowImage" duration="200"
           alphaFrom="0.3" alphaTo="1.0"
           blurXFrom="50.0" blurXTo="0.0"
           blurYFrom="50.0" blurYTo="0.0"
           color="0x1E529C"/>
    </mx:Sequence>

   <mx:HBox paddingBottom="0" paddingTop="0" paddingLeft="5"
    paddingRight="0" horizontalGap="0">
      <mx:Image source="assets/images/shoppingcart.gif"/>
      <mx:Label text="SHOPPING CART"
       fontFamily="Myriad Pro Semibold" color="#0C406E"/>
   </mx:HBox>
   <mx:Tile id="cartList" width="100%" height="75%"
    borderStyle="none" verticalGap="2"
    horizontalScrollPolicy="off"/>
   <mx:VBox backgroundImage="assets/images/back3.png"
    backgroundSize="100%" verticalAlign="middle" verticalGap="2"
    horizontalAlign="right" paddingRight="5" height="25%"
    width="100%">
```

```
        <mx:Form>
            <mx:FormItem label="Quantity:">
                <mx:Label id="quantityTxt"/>
            </mx:FormItem>
            <mx:FormItem label="Total">
                <mx:Label id="totalTxt"/>
            </mx:FormItem>
            <mx:FormItem label="Shipping:">
                <mx:Label id="shippingTxt" text="$5.5"/>
            </mx:FormItem>
            <mx:FormItem label="Grand Total:">
                <mx:Label id="grandTxt"/>
            </mx:FormItem>
            <mx:FormItem>
                <mx:Button id="checkoutBtn"
                 label="Checkout" enabled="{cartList.getChildren().
                 length>0?true:false}" width="70" click="checkout()"/>
            </mx:FormItem>
        </mx:Form>
    </mx:VBox>
</mx:VBox>
```

This component is a shopping cart container which does some custom validation. For example, it checks if an item has been added previously, and if it exists then it increases the quantity instead of adding the same item again. It also calculates and updates the total and grand total counts, and displays the counts at the bottom.

11. Now, we will create the main product screen which will assemble all these custom components and which provides a central view of our application. Create a new MXML component based on `HBox` under the `components` folder and name it `ProductsScreen.mxml`. Copy the following code into it:

```
<?xml version="1.0" encoding="utf-8"?>
<mx:HBox xmlns:mx="http://www.adobe.com/2006/mxml"
 width="100%" height="100%"
 creationComplete="categoryHS.send({action:'getCatagory'});"
 xmlns:components="components.*">

    <mx:Script>
        <![CDATA[
            import mx.controls.Alert;
            import mx.events.ItemClickEvent;
            import mx.rpc.events.ResultEvent;
            private var products:XML = null;

            private function handleResult(event:ResultEvent):void {
                lb.dataProvider = event.result[0].Catagories.Catagory;
```

```
        }

private function itemClickHandler(event:ItemClickEvent):void {
            displayArea.selectedIndex = 1;
            booksHS.send({catId:lb.selectedIndex+1});
        }
        private function displayBooks(event:ResultEvent):void {
            products = event.result as XML;
            addProductsToView(event.result.Book);
        }
private function addProductsToView(products:XMLList):void {
            if(products.length()<=0) {
               Alert.show("Search did not return any records");
            } else {
               thumbContent.removeAllChildren();
               for each(var product:XML in products) {
                  var thumb:BookDetailItemRenderer =
                  new BookDetailItemRenderer();
                  thumb.width=285;
                  thumb.height=121;
                  thumb.product = product as XML;
                  thumbContent.addChild(thumb);
               }
            }
        }

        public function searchProducts(searchStr:String):void {
            var searchSegements:Array = searchStr.split(" ");
            var searchItems:XML = <books></books>; //Root node

            for each(var segment:String in searchSegements) {
               for each(var item:XML in products.book) {
                  var titles:Array = String(item.title).split(" ");
                  var descriptions:Array = String(item.
                              description).split(" ");

                  if(titles.indexOf(segment) != -1 ||
               descriptions.indexOf(segment) != -1) {
 if(!searchItems.children().contains(item))
                        searchItems.appendChild(item);
                  }
               }
            }
            addProductsToView(searchItems.children());
        }
    ]]>
 </mx:Script>
 <mx:HTTPService id="categoryHS" url="http://localhost:8180/
  BookStore/ProductService.jsp" resultFormat="array"
```

```
    result="handleResult(event);"/>
  <mx:HTTPService id="booksHS" url="http://localhost:8180/
   BookStore/ProductService.jsp" resultFormat="e4x"
   result="displayBooks(event)" fault="Alert.show(''
   +event.message);"/>
  <mx:VBox width="188" height="100%" borderStyle="solid"
   borderThickness="1" borderColor="#D2D9DB"
   dropShadowEnabled="true" shadowDirection="center"
   paddingBottom="0" paddingTop="5">
     <mx:Label text="TOP CATEGORIES"
      fontFamily="Myriad Pro Semibold" color="#0C406E"/>
     <mx:LinkBar id="lb"
      backgroundImage="assets/images/back2.png"
      backgroundSize="100%" direction="vertical"
      width="100%" labelField="CategoryName" height="100%"
        itemClick="itemClickHandler(event)" />
  </mx:VBox>
  <mx:ViewStack id="displayArea" width="100%"
   height="100%" backgroundAlpha="0.0">
     <mx:VBox verticalAlign="middle"
        horizontalAlign="center"
        paddingLeft="10"
        paddingRight="10"
        cornerRadius="4"
        dropShadowEnabled="true"
        borderColor="#FFFFFF"
        borderStyle="solid">
        <mx:Label text="New On The Stall" fontSize="20"
         fontFamily="Myriad Pro Semibold" color="#75A1C9"/>
        <components:ProductSlider productURL="newBooks.xml"/>
        <mx:Label text="Best Books of the Month" fontSize="20"
         fontFamily="Myriad Pro Semibold" color="#75A1C9"/>
        <components:ProductSlider productURL="bestBooks.xml"/>
     </mx:VBox>
     <mx:Tile id="thumbContent" hideEffect="Fade"
      direction="horizontal" width="100%"
      height="100%" backgroundAlpha="0.0"
      horizontalScrollPolicy="off"/>
  </mx:ViewStack>
</mx:HBox>
```

This component creates a navigation menu bar used for displaying book categories on the lefthand side of the screen, and it uses `HTTPService` to call a JSP file to dynamically load these categories from the database. It also loads products based on the category the user has clicked on using another `HTTPService`, which calls a JSP page to load an XML document containing a list of books matching the category from the database.

This component uses Flex's navigator container, `ViewStack`, to create a paged layout between multiple screens. You can switch between these pages/views using the `ViewStack's selectedIndex` property as it is used in the `itemClickHandler()` method in the above code. This is used to show different views/pages on some user action without reloading the entire HTML page.

This component also lays out two `ProductSlider.mxml` custom components and loads two different XML documents into it using its `productURL` property. The component provides a `searchProducts()` method for searching and returning matching products. The product screen looks as shown in the following screenshot:

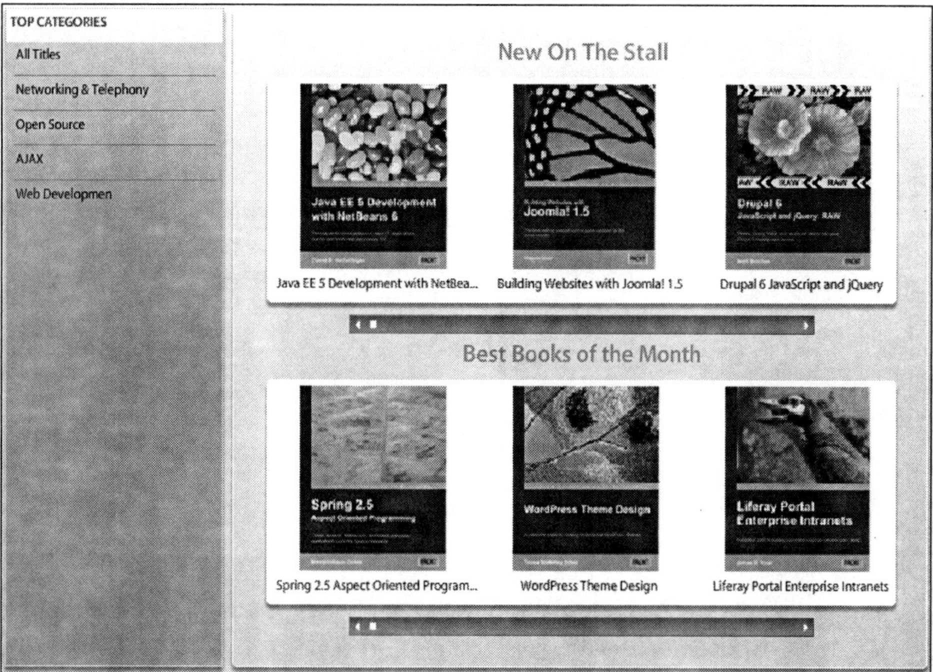

12. Now, we will write our main MXML application code to assemble all these components into a proper layout, as shown in the following code. Copy this code into your main application file, that is, `BookStore.mxml`.

```
<?xml version="1.0" encoding="utf-8"?>
<mx:Application xmlns:mx="http://www.adobe.com/2006/mxml"
 pageTitle="eCommerce Example Application"
 paddingLeft="0" paddingRight="0" paddingTop="0"
 paddingBottom="10"
 xmlns:components="components.*" creationComplete="init()"
 xmlns="http://www.degrafa.com/2008">

   <mx:Style source="../assets/css/MyStyle.css"/>
   <mx:Script>
      <![CDATA[
         import events.AddToCartEvent;

         private function init():void {
            addEventListener(AddToCartEvent.ADD_TO_CART,
                                          addToCartHandler);
         }
         private function addToCartHandler(event:AddToCartEvent):
                                                            void {
            shoppingCart.addItem(event.book as XML);
         }

         private function searchProduct(event:KeyboardEvent):void
{
            if(event.keyCode == 13) {
               productsView.searchProducts(searchTxt.text);
            }
         }
      ]]>
   </mx:Script>

   <mx:ApplicationControlBar width="100%" horizontalAlign="right">
      <mx:Label text="Online Book Store" styleName="logoStyle"/>
      <mx:Button id="homeBtn" label="Home"
       click="productsView.displayArea.selectedIndex=0"/>
      <mx:Spacer width="100%"/>
      <mx:Button id="cartButton"
       label="{shoppingCart.quantityTxt.text}"
       icon="@Embed(source='../assets/images/shoppingcart.gif')"
       useHandCursor="true" buttonMode="true"/>
      <mx:Image source="assets/images/search.gif"/>
      <mx:TextInput id="searchTxt" width="150" keyUp="
                                 searchProduct(event)"/>
   </mx:ApplicationControlBar>
```

```
    <mx:HBox width="990" height="100%" paddingLeft="0"
     paddingRight="0">
        <components:ProductsScreen id="productsView"/>
        <components:ShoppingCart id="shoppingCart"/>
    </mx:HBox>

</mx:Application>
```

The application file declares the `<mx:Style>` tag to use external CSS called `MyStyle.css`. This CSS file defines the general look and feel of all components.

It uses the `ApplicationControlBar` component to create a nice-looking stripe on top of the application screen. It contains a `Label` with the name of the application, the **Home** button to switch the view back to the in the following, an easy access cart button that shows the number of items in the shopping cart, and a search text box that allows users to search for books by typing keywords.

In the `init()` method, which is invoked on the `creationComplete` event of the `Application` tag, we have registered an `addToCart` event and written a event handler function called `addToCartHandler`. This adds a selected product to the `ShoppingCart.mxml` component. When you type keywords in the search text box and press the *ENTER* key, it invokes a wrapper method called `searchProduct`. This method in turn calls the `searchProducts` method of `ProductScreen.mxml`, which will populate the production screen with matching books.

Finally, we will put two of our main components—`ProductsScreen.mxml` and `ShoppingCart.mxml`—together inside the `HBox` control so that they are aligned horizontally. This completes our component creation and assembling task on the Flex side.

13. Now we will write a CSS file that is used by our main application. Create a new CSS file under the **assets/css** folder and name it `MyStyle.css`. Copy the following code into it:

```
/* CSS file */
@font-face {
    src: url(Myriad.swf);
   fontFamily:'Myriad Pro Semibold';
   fontWeight:Semibold;
}

@font-face {
    src: url(Myriad.swf);
    fontFamily:'Myriad Pro';
   fontWeight:Regular;
```

```
}
global
{
   themeColor: #4E84B9;
   fontFamily: "Myriad Pro";
   fontWeight: normal;
   fontSize:11;
   color:#000000;
   disabledColor:#1e1e1e;
   focusThickness:1;
}
Button
{
   cornerRadius: 2;
   paddingLeft: 2;
   paddingRight: 2;
   paddingTop: 2;
   paddingBottom: 2;
   highlightAlphas: 0.39, 0.14;
   fillAlphas: 0.5, 1.0, 0.5, 1.0;
   fillColors: #76A4D2, #4E84B9, #76A4D2, #3E79B0;
   disabledColor:#777777;
   disabledIconColor:#777777;
   textRollOverColor: #ffffff;
   fontWeight: normal;
   borderColor: #76A4D2;
}
ToolTip {
   color:#FFFFFF;
   backgroundColor:#0C406E;
   fontSize:10;
   cornerRadius:0;
}
TextInput {
   borderStyle:solid;
   cornerRadius:2;
   height:20;
}

ApplicationControlBar {
   backgroundImage:Embed(source="../../assets/images/head-back.
                                                          png");
   backgroundSize:"100%";
   borderStyle: solid;
   dropShadowEnabled: true;
```

```
    shadowDistance: 0;
    dropShadowColor: #000000;
}
Application {
backgroundImage:Embed(source="../../assets/images/background.
png");
    backgroundSize:"100%";
    modalTransparencyBlur:0.8;
}
.logoStyle {
    fontFamily: "Myriad Pro Semibold";
    fontSize:18;
    color:#0C406E;

}
LinkBar {
    borderColor: #1378BE;
    rollOverColor: #6689B4;
    selectionColor: #4E84B9;
    separatorColor: #76A4D2;
}

Panel
{
    background-color: "90deg #6689B4 #E0EBF5";
     background-blend:           lighten, normal, multiply;
     border-alpha:               1;
     border-color:               "#FFFFFF #FFFFFF #FFFFFF #FFFFFF";
     border-width:               "10px 10px 10px 10px";
     border-top-right-radius: 24px;
     border-bottom-left-radius: 24px;
     border-bottom-right-radius: 0px;
     border-top-left-radius: 0px;
     borderSkin: ClassReference("com.degrafa.skins.CSSSkin");
     title-style-name: "titleStyle";
     header-height: 50;
}

.titleStyle
{
    font-size: 18;
    color: #0C406E;
    fontFamily: 'Myriad Pro Semibold';
}
ControlBar
```

```
{
   horizontalAlign: center;
   paddingBottom: 0;
   paddingTop: 1;
   verticalAlign: middle;
}
HScrollBar {
     downArrowUpSkin: Embed(source="../../assets/images/
                                          downArrow.png");
     downArrowOverSkin: Embed(source="../../assets/images/
                                          downArrow.png");
     downArrowDownSkin: Embed(source="../../assets/images/
                                          downArrow.png");
     upArrowUpSkin: Embed(source="../../assets/images/
                                          upArrow.png");
     upArrowOverSkin: Embed(source="../../assets/images/
                                          upArrow.png");
     upArrowDownSkin: Embed(source="../../assets/images/
                                          upArrow.png");
     thumbDownSkin:
         Embed(source="../../assets/images/thumb.png",
         scaleGridLeft="7", scaleGridTop="5",
         scaleGridRight="8", scaleGridBottom="7");

     thumbUpSkin:
         Embed(source="../../assets/images/thumb.png",
         scaleGridLeft="7", scaleGridTop="5",
         scaleGridRight="8", scaleGridBottom="7");

     thumbOverSkin:
         Embed(source="../../assets/images/thumb.png",
         scaleGridLeft="7", scaleGridTop="5",
         scaleGridRight="8", scaleGridBottom="7");

   fillColors: #00529b, #ffffff, #0000ff, #ffffff;
   trackColors: #5363b9, #75a1c9;
}

VScrollBar {
     downArrowUpSkin: Embed(source="../../assets/images/
                                          downArrow.png");
     downArrowOverSkin: Embed(source="../../assets/images/
                                          downArrow.png");
     downArrowDownSkin: Embed(source="../../assets/images/
                                          downArrow.png");
     upArrowUpSkin: Embed(source="../../assets/images/
                                          upArrow.png");
```

```
        upArrowOverSkin: Embed(source="../../assets/images/
                                              upArrow.png");
        upArrowDownSkin: Embed(source="../../assets/images/
                                              upArrow.png");
        thumbDownSkin:
            Embed(source="../../assets/images/thumb.png",
            scaleGridLeft="7", scaleGridTop="5",
            scaleGridRight="8", scaleGridBottom="7");

        thumbUpSkin:
            Embed(source="../../assets/images/thumb.png",
            scaleGridLeft="7", scaleGridTop="5",
            scaleGridRight="8", scaleGridBottom="7");

        thumbOverSkin:
            Embed(source="../../assets/images/thumb.png",
            scaleGridLeft="7", scaleGridTop="5",
            scaleGridRight="8", scaleGridBottom="7");

        trackSkin:
            Embed(source="../../assets/images/scrolltrack.png",
            scaleGridLeft="7", scaleGridTop="4",
            scaleGridRight="8", scaleGridBottom="6" );
    }
    Alert {
       paddingTop:20;
    }
```

The above CSS declaration defines the common look and feel of the components, such as `Button`, `LinkBar`, `TextInput`, and so on. It also creates two fonts that will be used throughout our application using the `@font-face` selector name. This creates the font type from the SWF file that defines these fonts. This CSS also defines the style of `HScrollBar` and `VScrollBar` by using custom images for defining each component of the scroll bar, such as scroll track color, down and up arrows, and so on. You may notice that the scrollbars in our application have a different look than the default one.

We have used one third-party open source library framework called **Degrafa** (`http://www.degrafa.org/`) to demonstrate how to use third-party libraries and controls in your project. We have copied the **Degrafa** library SWC file into our project's `libs` folder. All libraries from the `libs` folder will be automatically referenced and included in your application while compiling is done using Flex Builder.

The `Panel` selector in the CSS file uses enhanced styling properties provided by **Degrafa** to change its look from the typical square or rectangle shape with rounded corners to the following:

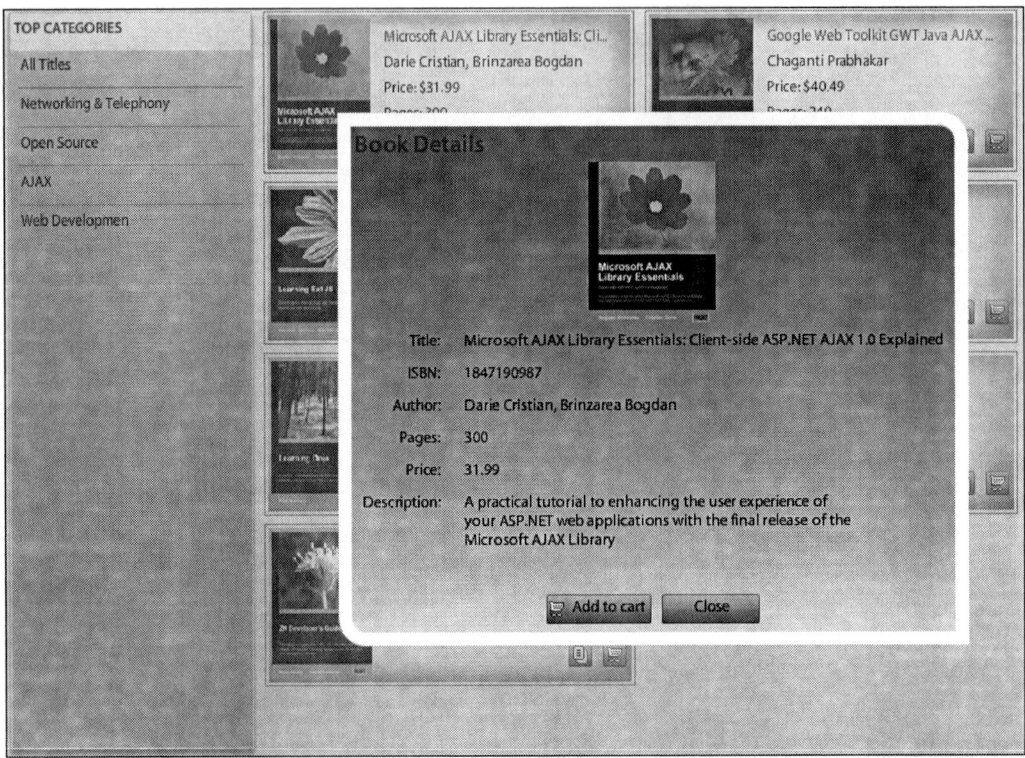

The Java code

We are done with the Flex side of coding. Next, we will create our server-side Java programs.

1. Create a new Java project in your favorite IDE. Next, create a new Java class file under the `com.ecommerce` package and name it `ECommerceDelegate.java`. Copy the following code into it:

```
package com.ecommerce;

import java.io.IOException;
import java.io.StringWriter;
import java.sql.Connection;
import java.sql.DriverManager;
import java.sql.ResultSet;
import java.sql.ResultSetMetaData;
```

```
import java.sql.SQLException;
import java.sql.Statement;
import javax.xml.parsers.DocumentBuilder;
import javax.xml.parsers.DocumentBuilderFactory;
import javax.xml.parsers.ParserConfigurationException;

import org.w3c.dom.Document;
import org.w3c.dom.Element;

import com.sun.org.apache.xml.internal.serialize.OutputFormat;
import com.sun.org.apache.xml.internal.serialize.XMLSerializer;

public class ECommerceDelegate {

   Connection con = null;
   Statement stmt = null;
   String connectionUrl = "jdbc:mysql://localhost:3306/ecommerce";
   String userName = "root";
   String password = "ecommerce";

   public ECommerceDelegate() {
      connect();
   }

   private void connect() {

      try {
         Class.forName("com.mysql.jdbc.Driver");
         con = DriverManager
                .getConnection(connectionUrl, userName, password);
      } catch (Exception e) {
         e.printStackTrace();
      }
   }

   public String getXMLList(String CatID) throws Exception {
      String SQL = "";
      if(CatID.equals("1")) { //All Books
         SQL = "SELECT * FROM ecommerce.product";
      } else {
         SQL = "SELECT * FROM ecommerce.product WHERE
                CATAGORYID="+CatID;
      }
      return toString(toXMLDocument(executeQuery(SQL),
                     "Catalog", "Book"));
   }

   private ResultSet executeQuery(String query) throws Exception {
      stmt = con.createStatement();
      ResultSet rs = stmt.executeQuery(query);
      return rs;
   }
```

```
    public Document toXMLDocument(ResultSet rs, String rootName,
                                  String childRootName)
        throws ParserConfigurationException, SQLException {
        DocumentBuilderFactory factory = DocumentBuilderFactory.
                                         newInstance();
      DocumentBuilder builder = factory.newDocumentBuilder();
      Document doc = builder.newDocument();

      Element results = doc.createElement(rootName);
      doc.appendChild(results);

      ResultSetMetaData rsmd = rs.getMetaData();
      int colCount = rsmd.getColumnCount();

      while (rs.next()) {
         Element row = doc.createElement(childRootName);
         results.appendChild(row);

         for (int i = 1; i <= colCount; i++) {
            String columnName = rsmd.getColumnName(i);
            Object value = rs.getObject(i);
            Element node = doc.createElement(columnName);
            node.appendChild(doc.createTextNode(
            value == null ? "" : value.toString()));
            row.appendChild(node);

         }
      }
      return doc;
   }

   public String toString(Document doc) throws IOException {
      StringWriter writer = new StringWriter();
      OutputFormat format = new OutputFormat();
      format.setIndenting(true);

      XMLSerializer serializer = new XMLSerializer(writer, format);
      serializer.serialize(doc);

      return writer.getBuffer().toString();
   }
   public String getCatagoryList() throws Exception {
      String SQL = "SELECT * FROM ecommerce.categories";
      return toString(toXMLDocument(executeQuery(SQL),
"Catagories", "Catagory"));
   }
}
```

This is our main delegate Java class file which is responsible for making JDBC connection with database, executing queries, and converting result sets into XML. Converting to XML may not be the best-suited method in a real-world scenario, but for the sake of simplicity we will convert the ResultSet into an XML document. Please change the `connectionURL`, `userName`, and `password` properties to the way that you personally want them.

2. Create a new JSP file and name it `ProductService.jsp`. Copy the following code into it:

```
<%@page import="com.ecommerce.ECommerceDelegate"%>
<%
    String catId = request.getParameter("catId");
    String action = request.getParameter("action");
    try {

        ECommerceDelegate delegate = new ECommerceDelegate();

        if(catId != null) {
%>
        <%=delegate.getXMLList(catId)%>
<%
        } else  if(action.equals("getCatagory")) {
%>
        <%=delegate.getCatagoryList()%>
<%
        }
    } catch (Exception e) {
        out.println("A problem occurred while fetching XML");
        e.printStackTrace();
    }
%>
```

This JSP file will be invoked by the Flex application using `HTTPService` in `ProductScreen.mxml`. This JSP file reads the request parameter, and on that basis it invokes the `ECommerceDelegate` class methods and returns the XML result.

3. Now compile both Flex and Java applications, and bundle and deploy it on your application server. Make sure that you maintain proper directory structure, as shown in the following screenshot. Please see that the highlighted files in the following screenshot are in the same location in your web application.

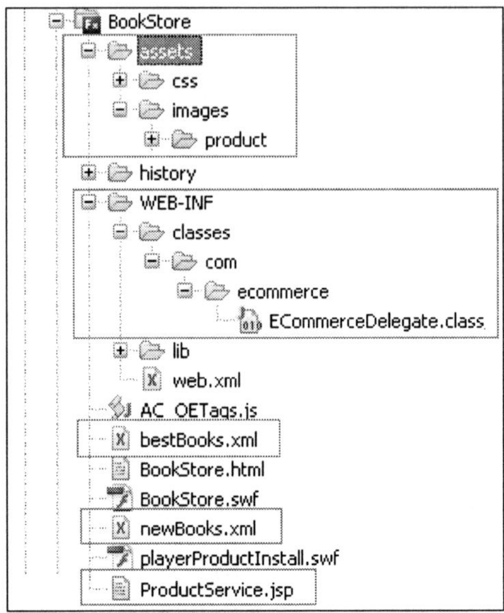

Directories and files

Let's see what each of the directories and files contains by looking at the following table:

`assets`	Contains application assets, such as CSS and images
`images`	Contains general images used by the application
`images/css`	Contains Cascading Style Sheet (CSS) and font SWF files
`images/product`	Contains product-related images, which will be displayed in the application in the product listing screen
`history`	Contains files that are necessary to enable history-management or deep-linking in your Flex application
`WEB-INF/classes`	Contains all your Java class files with their respective package structure
`WEB-IN/lib`	Contains any dependency Java JAR files, such as Database Driver JAR

`web.xml`	Your web descriptor file
`AC_OETags.js`	Contains logic for version-checking and embedding functionality
`bestBooks.xml` `newBooks.xml`	Contains a list of books in the XML form used by the `ProductSlider.mxml` component
`BookStore.html` `BookStore.swf`	Your application wrapper HTML file and SWF file
	An application that initiates Express Install
`ProductService.jsp`	JSP invoked by `ProductScreen.mxml` for displaying product list and categories

> In order to run this application, you will need to create database tables and records. This tutorial uses MySQL 5.0 as the database. Please download SQL queries from Packt's official web site and create database tables before your run this application. You can also download the complete source code from Packt's official web site.

Now we are ready to run this application. Open a new browser window and type the URL of your web application.

While developing larger and complex projects, it is always recommended that you use standard frameworks and follow best practices as they make development process simple and easier. It also helps you to write quality code, and organize your code such that it can be easily adopted by any new programmer at any development phase. As Adobe has also released Flex SDK under the open source license, you will find many open source and community-driven frameworks such as:

- Cairngorm (`http://opensource.adobe.com/wiki/display/cairngorm/Cairngorm`) is one of the popular and lightweight microarchitecture frameworks for building applications using Adobe Flex
- PureMVC (`http://www.puremvc.org/`) is another popular and lightweight framework for creating applications based on the classic Model, View, and Controller
- Mate (`http://mate.asfusion.com/`) is a tag-based, event-driven Flex framework

Apart from frameworks, you can also find out more about best practices and other related articles on Adobe's web site as listed here:

- `http://www.adobe.com/devnet/flex/architecture.html`
- `http://www.adobe.com/devnet/flex/articles/best_practices_pt1.html`

Summary

In this chapter, you learned how to develop a Flex application using MXML, ActionScript and Java classes, and JSP on the server side. You also learned how to communicate with a database and return dynamic XML result to your Flex application. This chapter also introduced the typical application development anatomy using Flex and Java backend, and showed you how to develop a multipage web application. Later in this chapter, we discussed about the common frameworks available in Flex that you can use to develop larger and more complex applications.

Index

Symbols

110n 233

A

ActionScript 25
ActionScript 3.0
  about 67
  events, working with 91
  features 67
  MXML, using with 88
ActionScript 3.0, using with MXML
  <mx:script> tag, using 88, 90
  about 88
  include directive, using 90
ActionScript 3.0 fundamentals
  about 69
  access modifiers 71
  classes 72
  error handling 84
  exceptions 84
  flow control and looping 80
  functions 75
  getter method 79, 80
  interfaces 72, 73
  keywords 87
  methods 75
  packages 71
  reserved words 87
  setter method 79, 80
  variables 69, 70
ActionScript 3.0 language features
  about 67
  dynamic classes 68
  E4X 68
  method closure 68
  new primitive data types 68
  object-oriented programming 69
  regular expressions 69
  runtime exceptions 68
  sealed classes 68
  strict data typing 68
  XML 68
ActionScript components
  about 97
  creating 97
  using 97
addChild() method 100
addEventListener() method 91
addItem() method 129
addToCardHandle method 62
addToCart custom event 61
addToCart event 267
addToCartHandler 267
addToCartHandler() method 138
Adobe
  web sites 277
Adobe Flex SDK 8
AMF 148
anonymous function, ActionScript 3.0 76, 77
Ant
  about 220
  features 220
Ant tool
  about 220
  running 223
  setting up 220

B

BlazeDS
  about 144
  features 144-146

book explorer example
about 131, 139
BookDetailItemRenderer.mxml, creating 134, 135
book layout, creating 135-137
custom event, creating 133
main application, creating 135-137
simple book catalog XML file, creating 132
book property 256
BookStore project. *See* **Flex project**
bottomLabelColor property 99
bubbles property 95
BUILD_DIR property 221

C

Cairngorm 277
Charles Web Debugging Proxy
about 200
features 200
classes, ActionScript 3.0
about 72
inheriting 74
classpath attribute 220
click event 42
client-side logging, using
mm.cfg file, setting up 192, 193
clone function 97
commitProperties() method 98
components, Flex Builder
about 13
Eclipse-based IDE 13
Flash Player 9 or later 13
Flex SDK 13
types 29
constraint-based layout 39-41
container class 100
containers
about 29, 31
backgroundColor properties 35
box containers 35
constraint-based layout 39
features 31
form containers 38
hbox and vbox combination 35
hbox containers 35
layout containers 31, 34
layout manager 31
navigation containers 31
navigator containers 36
nested layout 36
types 31
vbox containers 35
controls 29
createChildren() method 99
creationComplete event 267
about 42, 139
example 42
cross-domain policy file 176
currentColor property 97
currentTarget property 93
custom events
creating 44
dispatchEvent() method 44
custom events, ActionScript 3.0
creating 95, 97

D

data, formatting
about 51
example 51
data binding
<mx:Binding> tag, specifying ways 53
[bindable] metadata tag, using 55-57
about 52
BindingUtils methods, specifying ways 53
complex data structures 53
curly braces syntax, specifying ways 53
example 52
specifying ways 53
data validation
about 45
example 46- 49
triggerinig 50
user entry, restricting 50, 51
Degrafa 271
depends attribute 221
deployment
about 217
options 228
deployment options, Flex
about 228
single SWF file deployment, using 228
web-tier compilation, using 230

directories and files
AC_OETags.js 277
assets 276
bestBooks.xml 277
BookStore.html 277
BookStore.swf 277
history 276
images 276
images/css 276
images/product 276
newBooks.xml 277
playerProductInstall.swf 277
ProductService.jsp 277
WEB-IN/lib 276
WEB-INF/classes 276
web.xml 277
dispatchEvent() method 44, 93
do..while looping, ActionScript 3.0 83
drop-in itemRenderers 64

E

E4X
about 120
example 121
features 120
Namespace class 121
QName class 121
XML, using as dataProvider 126
XML class 121
XMLList class 121
XMLList object 124
XML object 123
XML object, working with 125
XML operators 122
error handling, ActionScript 3.0
about 84
custom error class object, creating 86, 87
try...catch...finally statements 84, 86
event class 95
EventDispatcher class 93
event handlers 41
event propagation, ActionScript 3.0
about 94
bubbling phase 94
capturing phase 94
targeting phase 94
events
using, in MXML 41
events, ActionScript 3.0
ActionScript components, creating 97
ActionScript components, using 97
addEventListener() method, using 91
commitProperties() method 98, 99
createChildren() method 99, 100
currentTarget properties 93
custom events, capturing 95
event, dispatching 93
event handlers, registering 91
event propagation 94
layoutChrome() method 100
measure() method 101
removeEventListener() method, using 92
target properties 93
updateDisplayList() method 101
working with 91
exceptions, ActionScript 3.0 84
External API
about 107
external container, getting information about 109
ExternalInterface class 108
ExternalInterface class, using 108
features 107
JavaScript code, calling from ActionScript 109, 110
JavaScript code, calling from JavaScript 111, 112
supporting browsers 108
external CSS files
about 204
CSS, creating 207
CSS, designing 208, 209
inline style declarations, exporting into 210
label component, styling 205
using, for customizing Flex application 204, 205, 206
ExternalInterface class 108
external itemRenderers 65, 66
external XML documents
loading 129, 130

F

Fiddler 200
Firebug-Firefox browser add-on 200
flash.events.Event class 95
Flash Debug Player
about 191
client-side logging, using 192
downloading 191
Flex Builder Debugger 194
installing 191
network activity, monitoring 199
Flash Player Debugger 191
Flash Player security sandbox
about 175
proxy services, creating 177-180
Flash Player security sandbox, accessing data methods
data access methods 176
Flash Player security sandbox, data access methods
BlazeDS proxy services, using 177
cross-domain policy file 176
Flex
about 25, 141
data, formatting 51
data, validating 45
data binding 52
debugging techniques 191
deployment 217
deployment options 228
features 25
Flash Player Debugger 191
packaging 217
RPC services 149
server-side remote data 149
validator syntax 46
web-tier compiler module 230
working 26
FLEX_HOME property
creating 221
Flex 3 SDK
about 8
configuration files 9
directory structure, installing 8
flex-config.xml files 9
installing 8
Flex 3 SDK directory structure
/ant 8
/asdoc 8
/bin 8
/frameworks 8
/frameworks/libs 9
/frameworks/locale 9
/frameworks/projects 9
/frameworks/rsls 9
/frameworks/themes 9
/lib 9
/runtimes 9
/samples 9
/templates 9
about 8
installing 8
Flex Ant tasks
about 220
FLEX_HOME property, defining 221
using 220-222
Flex application
compiling 26, 27
customizing 201
deploying 224-227
deploying, on Tomcat server 228, 229
Flex compilers, configuring 27
haloBlue theme 204
packaging 217-219
running 28
Flex application, customizing
external CSS files, used 204
inline tyles, used 202
stylesheets, loading at runtime 210
Flex application, packaging
files, creating in bin-debug folder 217, 218
Flex Builder
about 12
an Eclipse plugin 12
as a standalone IDE 12
components 13
installation options 12
installing 12-18
Flex Builder Debugger
about 194
application, debugging 195, 196
breakpoints, setting 195
breakpoint view 198

debug view 196, 197
expression view 198
variables view 197
Flex compilers
about 10
application compiler 11
compc, using 10
component compiler 10
configuring 27
mxmlc, using 11
SWC file, generating 10
Flex data access components
about 149
Flash Player security sandbox 175
methods 149
Flex data access methods
about 149
HTTPService class 150
RemoteObject class 164
WebService class 156
Flex framework validators
<mx:CreditCardValidator> 45
<mx:CurrencyValidator> 45
<mx:DateValidator> 45
<mx:EmailValidator> 45
<mx:NumberValidator> 45
<mx:PhoneNumberValidator> 45
<mx:RegExpValidator> 45
<mx:SocialSecurityValidator> 45
<mx:StringValidator> 45
<mx:ZipCodeValidator> 45
about 45
Flex itemRenderers
about 63, 64
drop-in itemRenderers 64
external itemRenderers 65, 66
inline itemRenderers 64
Flex project
creating 18-22, 250
Flex LiveDocs 23, 24
source code editor 23
UI designer 22, 23
Flex project, creating
about 250, 251
AddToCartEvent.as, creating 255
BookDetailItemRenderer.mxml, creating 253, 254
BookStore.mxml, creating 266
CartItem.mxml, creating 258, 259
CSS file, writing 267-271
DetailView.mxml, creating 251-253
main MXML application code, writing 266
MXML component, based on HBox 253, 258
MXML component, based on panel 251
MXML component, based on VBox 256, 260
ProductItemRenderer.mxml, creating 256, 258
ProductSlider.mxml, creating 256, 258, 265
ProductsScreen.mxml, creating 262-264
ShoppingCart.mxml, creating 260-262
Flex remoting application
BlazeDS, downloading 166
creating 166
project, setting up 166
flow control and looping, ActionScript 3.0
about 80
do..while looping 83
for..in looping 83
for each..in looping 83
for looping 83
if/else statement 81
looping 82
switch statement 81
while looping 82
for..in looping, ActionScript 3.0 83
for each..in looping, ActionScript 3.0 83
for looping, ActionScript 3.0 83
formatter classes
<mx:CurrencyFormatter/> 51
<mx:DateFormatter/> 51
<mx:NumberFormatter/> 51
<mx:PhoneFormatter/> 51
<mx:ZipCodeFormatter/> 51
about 51
form containers 38
frameworks
Cairngorm 277
Mate 277
PureMVC 277
function expression 75
function parameters, ActionScript 3.0
...(rest) parameter 78
about 77

default parameter values 78
rules, ...(rest) parameter 79
functions, ActionScript 3.0
about 75
anonymous functions 76, 77
defining, function expressions used 75
defining, function statements used 75
defining ways 75
function parameters 77
named functions 76
function statement 75

G

getter method, ActionScript 3.0
about 79
defining 79

H

haloBlue theme 204
HTTPService class
about 150
basic syntax 150
events 150, 151
example application 151-155
fault event 153
features 150
HTTPService tag, using in MXML 150
JSON data, working with 186-188
properties 150
REST-style web service 150
resultFormat property values 153
result property 151, 153
send() method 151
using, in ActionScript 155
XML data, working with 182-186

I

i18n
about 233
assets 234
culture 234
language 234
time zones 234, 235
init() method 267
inline itemRenderers 64
inline styles
about 202
example 203
interfaces, ActionScript 3.0
about 73
implementing, in class 73
internationalization. *See* **also i18n 233**
invalidateProperties() method 98
itemClickHandler() method 265

J

Java project
creating 272
ECommerceDelegate.java, creating 272-274
ProductService.jsp, creating 275
JSON data, HTTPService class
working with 186

K

keyboard event
about 42
example 42
keyboard events
keyDown 44
keyUp 44

L

labelFunction property 127
layoutChrome() method 100
layout containers 34, 35
layout manager, containers
about 31
absolute layout 31
horizontal layout 32
layout properties 32-34
root container 32
vertical layout 31
layout property 28
lexical keywords, ActionScript 3.0 87
LiveCycle Data Services
about 141, 142
Community Edition 145
data management services 143
deployment architecture 141, 142
features 142-145

messaging services 143
RPC services 143
LiveCycle Data Services vs BlazeDS
feature comparison table 146, 147
LocalConnection 113
LocalConnection class
about 113
connect() method 114
features 113
incomingBids() method 117
init() method 116
LocalConnection.allowDomain() method 113
LocalConnection.allowInsecureDomain() method 113
LocalConnection.connect() method 117
send() method 114
sendMessage() method 116
using 113
localization 233, 234
localization, of Flex application
about 235
resource file, creating 235-241
resource modules, creating 242-245

M

Mate 277
measure() method
about 101
properties 101
methods, ActionScript 3.0 75
mouse events
about 43
click 43
doubleclick 43
handling, iin MXML 43
mouseDown 43
mouseMove 43
mouseOut 43
mouseOver 43
mouseUp 43
mouseWheel 43
Multimedia eXtensible Markup Language. *See* **MXML**
MXML
about 25, 28
event handler mechanisms, using 42
events, using 41
keyboard event 42
layout property 28
mouse events, handling 43
mouse events example 43
MXML file, anatomy 28
namespaces, using in code 30
namespaces concept 29
mxmlc Flex Ant tasks
using 220
MXML custom components
addToCart custom event 61
BookDetails.mxml component 61
combox component 58
creating 57, 59, 61, 62
MyCustomEvent class 97

N

named function, ActionScript 3.0 76
navigator containers 36, 37
network monitoring 199
network monitoring tools
Charles Web Debugging Proxy 200
Fiddler 200
Firebug-Firefox browser add-on 200
ServiceCapture 199
WireShark 200

O

observer pattern 41
online book store application
book search screen 250
demo screen 248
homepage 249
product listing screen 249
running 277
open source Flex 3 SDK
installing 8

P

packaging
about 217
Flex application, packaging 217
productURL property 265

properties of event class, ActionScript 3.0
bubbles 96
cancelable 96
currentTarget 95
event Phase 96
target 95
type 95
PureMVC 277

R

RemoteObject class
about 164
events 165
Flex remoting application, creating 166-171
properties 165
RemoteObject tag, using in MXML 165
strongly-typed objects, working with 172, 174
using 164
removeEventListener() method 92
reserved words, ActionScript 3.0
about 87
lexical keywords 87
syntactic keywords 87
REST 150
RIAs 25, 141
root containers 29
RPC services 149
RSS data
loading 130

S

searchProducts() method 265
selectedIndex property 265
server-side Java programs 272
server-side technologies
AMF.NET 141
AMFPHP 141
BlazeDS 141
GraniteDS 141
LiveCycle Data Services 141
WebORB 141
ServiceCapture
about 199
features 199, 200
setter method, ActionScript 3.0
about 79
defining 79
stylesheets
loading, at runtime 210-215
SWF files 26
syntactic keywords, ActionScript 3.0 87

T

target
about 221
clean target 222
compile target 221
main target 222
package target 221
wrapper target 221
target property 93
toString method 97
trace() method 193

U

UIComponent class 97
UI component methods
about 98
commitProperties() 98
createChildren() 98
layoutChrome() 98
measure() 98
updateDisplayList() 98
Universal Description and Discovery Information. *See* **UDDI**
updateDisplayList() method
about 101-106
properties 102
URI 30
URLLoader class 129

W

web-tier compiler module
about 230
working 230
weblog. *See* **blog**
WebService class
about 156
events 157

example application 158-162
operation tag 157
operation tag, events 157
operation tag, properties 157
properties 157
SOAP headers, requisites 163
SOAP headers, working with 163
using, in ActionScript 162
WebService tag, using in MXML 157
while looping, ActionScript 3.0 82
WireShark 200

X

XML
about 119
basics 119, 120
using, as dataProvider 126-129
XML data, HTTPService class
working with 182
XMLListCollection class 129
XMLList object
about 124
attribute(attributeName) method 124
attributes() method 124
child() method 124
children() method 124
conatins() method 124
copy() method 124
descendants() method 124
elements() method 124
length() method 124
parent() method 124
valueof() method 124
XML object
about 123, 124
working with 125, 126
XML operators
( ) 122
+ 122
+= 122
. 122
.. 122
< > 122
@ 122
[ ] 122
{ } 122

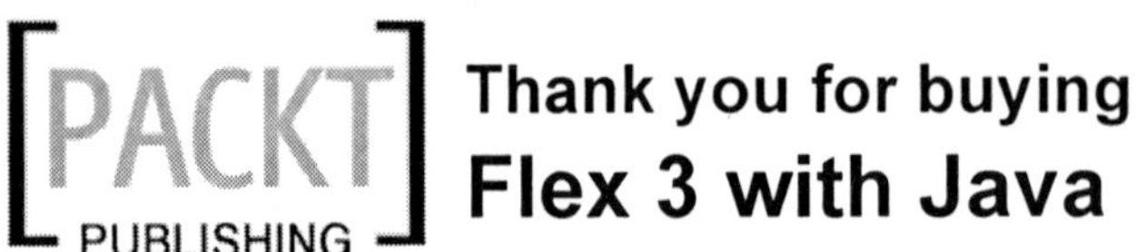

Thank you for buying
Flex 3 with Java

Packt Open Source Project Royalties

When we sell a book written on an Open Source project, we pay a royalty directly to that project. Therefore by purchasing Flex 3 with Java, Packt will have given some of the money received to the Flex project.

In the long term, we see ourselves and you—customers and readers of our books—as part of the Open Source ecosystem, providing sustainable revenue for the projects we publish on. Our aim at Packt is to establish publishing royalties as an essential part of the service and support a business model that sustains Open Source.

If you're working with an Open Source project that you would like us to publish on, and subsequently pay royalties to, please get in touch with us.

Writing for Packt

We welcome all inquiries from people who are interested in authoring. Book proposals should be sent to `author@packtpub.com`. If your book idea is still at an early stage and you would like to discuss it first before writing a formal book proposal, contact us; one of our commissioning editors will get in touch with you.

We're not just looking for published authors; if you have strong technical skills but no writing experience, our experienced editors can help you develop a writing career, or simply get some additional reward for your expertise.

About Packt Publishing

Packt, pronounced 'packed', published its first book "Mastering phpMyAdmin for Effective MySQL Management" in April 2004 and subsequently continued to specialize in publishing highly focused books on specific technologies and solutions.

Our books and publications share the experiences of your fellow IT professionals in adapting and customizing today's systems, applications, and frameworks. Our solution-based books give you the knowledge and power to customize the software and technologies you're using to get the job done. Packt books are more specific and less general than the IT books you have seen in the past. Our unique business model allows us to bring you more focused information, giving you more of what you need to know, and less of what you don't.

Packt is a modern, yet unique publishing company, which focuses on producing quality, cutting-edge books for communities of developers, administrators, and newbies alike. For more information, please visit our website: `www.PacktPub.com`.

PACKT
PUBLISHING

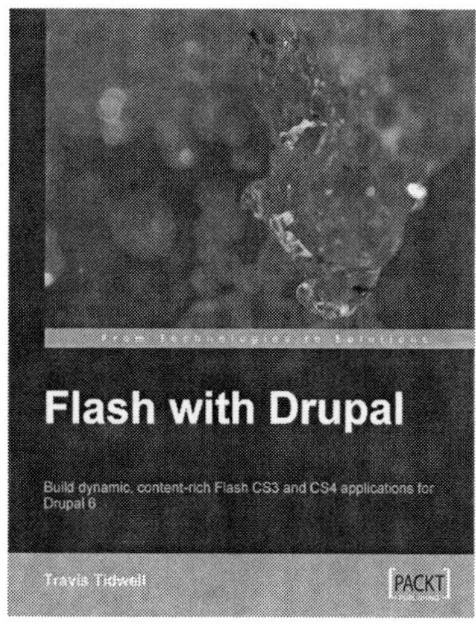
Flash with Drupal
Build dynamic, content-rich Flash CS3 and CS4 applications for Drupal 6
Travis Tidwell
PACKT

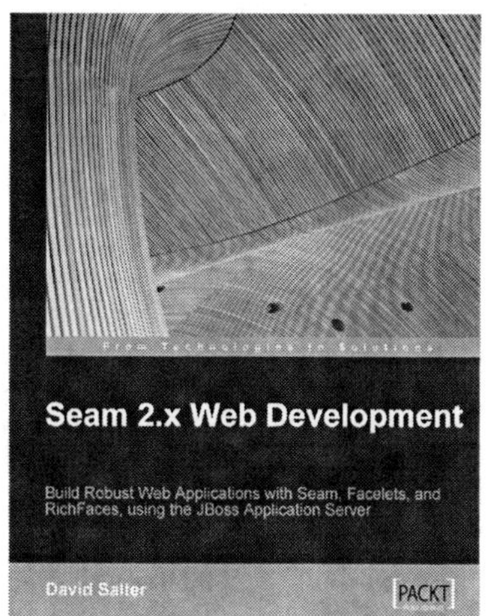
Seam 2.x Web Development
Build Robust Web Applications with Seam, Facelets, and RichFaces, using the JBoss Application Server
David Salter
PACKT

LaVergne, TN USA
22 August 2009
155557LV00003BA/9/P